A Viking Voyage

A Viking Voyage

IN WHICH AN UNLIKELY CREW ATTEMPTS AN EPIC JOURNEY TO THE NEW WORLD

W. HODDING CARTER

Ballantine Books
New York

This story is for Anabel, Eliza, and Helen
so they will know how their dad used his time away

In memory of Bob Miller

Acknowledgments

There is only one person who has made every single aspect of this book possible—my wife Lisa. Others have contributed greatly, but nobody could possibly match her sacrifices, commitment, and incisive guidance. I love her dearly.

In Wisconsin, Gary Comer and the people at Lands' End, especially Mike Smith, Mike Atkins, Beverly Holmes, and Lisa Mullen, got behind this project both financially and emotionally and stayed with it even when all looked hopeless. They could easily have walked away but didn't. I will be forever grateful. Randy Lagman made it possible for us to communicate with the outside world, and David Leiberman ran a superb Web site. And thank you Jeanie Anderson for taking care of the details. While I'm out that way, I also want to thank Dr. Larry Michaelis in Chicago for providing us with our well-stocked medical kit, as well as sound advice.

In the beginning, when it was a mere idea, John Ivey brought in business savvy; Michael Alcamo, along with Jan Calamita, put me on the right side of the law; and Zali Win conjured up a financial miracle. Russell Kaye kept me humble (and laughing) and his photographs have brought it all to life. Marlene Trossman and Abby

Lattes created a winning fund-raising proposal and my grand-mother, Betty Carter, and William Rielly, a friend from Cincinnati, donated enough money to piece the proposal together.

In Maine, Lance Lee, although we had our differences, instilled a certain zeal and appreciation that might not otherwise have been there. He also sent Apprenticeshop apprentices our way when we really needed them. The Maine Maritime Museum of Bath was the perfect host when all we had was a name. The advice and aid from the Paine brothers and Mark Fitzgerald in Camden were invaluable; as a result, we could turn the boat. Susan McBride tracked down information I never would have uncovered, and David Conover became a friend, a steady adviser, and an inspiring cheerleader. As you will see when reading this book, Sam Manning's illustrations far out-perform my writings. I also want to thank Ann Marie Maguire for donating wood from her land and Allison Hepler for helping out in Maine, Greenland, and Canada.

Snorri's builders assembled a masterpiece. Thank you, Bob Miller, Scott Smith, Dave Foster, Phil Dyer, Lee Huston, James Murdock, Mike Browne, David Dick, Than Porter, John Gardner, Deirdre Whitehead, and, of course, leading them all, Rob Stevens—undoubtedly the most creative traditional boatbuilder alive. David Lake and Keith Herridge worked hard on the rigging, and Gerry Galuza, man of iron, thanks for pounding out those rivets. I hate to think how much more rowing would have been required if it had not been for Nat Wilson's splendid sail.

In a category all by herself, I want to thank Marian Rivman for her uncanny skill and loyalty. Marian always did what she said she would do. She also turned up Joan Hanrahan, her friend who helped things run a bit more smoothly during our sea trials in Maine.

In Great Britain, I would like to thank Owain Roberts for his invaluable advice—not only about our rudder but also on how to conduct an expedition. Tich and Di Craddock are the best Viking outfitters around. Their clothing and equipment withstood the tests of time, weather, and waves.

In Norway, the Bjørkedals not only know how to build excellent wooden boats but also serve as gracious hosts. Per Weddegjerde taught us how to sail a *knarr* and did so with patience and a great deal of humor.

In Denmark, the Viking Ship Museum has brought history to

life. I wouldn't have had a boat without its exceptional work, of course. At the museum, Max Vinner helped clear the way, and I will always be appreciative.

In Greenland, we had a slew of hosts, but the standouts were Elias and Karen Larsen, Poul and Jeanne Holm, and Bendo Thorsteinson; please feel free to stay with us whenever you wish. Also, nearby in Iceland, Edda Geirsdottir at the Eimskip shipping company rescued *Snorri* from spending the rest of her days lost at sea on top of some errant container ship.

In Canada, I would be remiss if I did not thank Coast Guard Canada for its fine work not only in escorting us in the Strait of Belle Isle but also, of course, for that little rescue mission performed by the captain and crew of the *Pierre Radisson*. Parks Canada and the Viking Trail Tourism Association in Newfoundland smoothed our transition back into the modern world. Especially appreciated was the work of Chip Bird at Gros Morne National Park; Debbie Anderson, Morgan Anderson, Art Eddison, the Deckers, and all the guide staff at Parks Canada L'Anse aux Meadows Visitors Center; and Randy and Cathy Letto at Viking Trail. The Viking Encampment personnel had obviously read their *Hávamál* and made us feel at home. I also want to thank Gary Pittman at Parks Canada and Randy, Cathy, Fred Russell, and Barb Genge at Viking Trail for continuing to ensure *Snorri* is comfortable in her new home. But most of all I want to thank every resident of L'Anse aux Meadows and the surrounding area. You warmed our hearts and our bodies.

Lastly, I want to thank the people who literally helped transform an idea into a book. Sally Wofford Girand, my agent, encouraged, cajoled, and put her foot down at all the right times. Thanks for standing by me. At Ballantine, Peter Borland and his assistant Emily Grayson's cheering could be heard loud and clear, even into the Arctic Circle. When it came time to edit, Peter excised the bad and encouraged the good, leading me to do my best. Thank you for your guidance, patience, and truly remarkable work.

A Viking Voyage

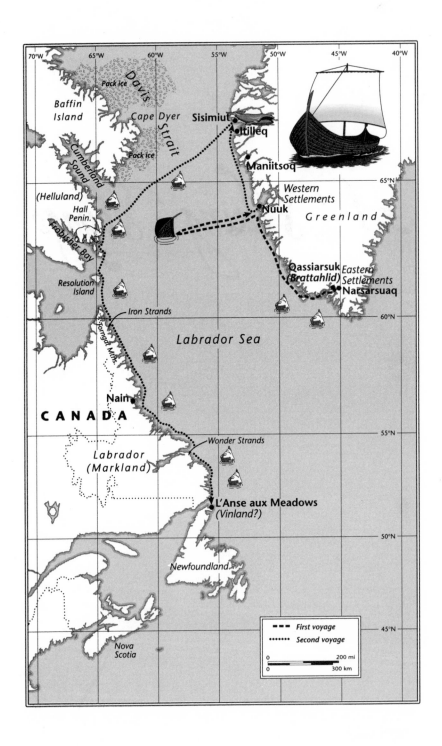

Baffin
Island

Davis

Pack ice

Cape Dyer

Pack ice

Sisimiut

Itilleq

Maniitsoq

Cumberland
Sound

(Helluland)

Hall
Penin.

Frobisher Bay

Strait

Western
Settlements

Nuuk

Greenland

Resolution
Island

Iron Strands

Qassiarsuk
(Brattahlid)

Eastern
Settlements

Narsarsuaq

Torngat Mtns.

Labrador Sea

Nain

C A N A D A

Labrador
(Markland)

Wonder Strands

L'Anse aux Meadows
(Vinland?)

Newfoundland

Nova
Scotia

- - - First voyage
······ Second voyage

0   200 mi
0   300 km

Chapter One

If you are really, truly into Vikings, then you should immediately abandon this book, grab your horned helmet (which no self-respecting Viking actually ever wore, by the way), and go froth at the mouth in some fog-enshrouded ancient rubbish heap like a good little berserker, convinced that you alone have found the much-ballyhooed Vinland.

If instead you enjoy tales of quixotic idiocy, passion, determination, frightening beauty, love, loss, enlightenment, failure, and redemption, then read on. This is your story, and I have lived to tell it.

These things always begin innocently enough. Sometimes with a mere thought.

Why not retrace the Viking voyages to the New World?*

I get ideas like this all the time. Some people sit in rush-hour traffic fantasizing about bashing their fellow drivers with a sizable ham hock. When I find myself delayed, I decide it's high time to ride an elephant across Hannibal's route through the Alps, although I know nothing about elephants or war.

---

* Some stern people may object, but I use the term "Viking" freely, not only to mean raiders of the sea, but all people during the 700s to the 1100s originating from what is now Scandinavia.

I just like retracing the steps that renowned or notorious people once took. I have dogged Lewis and Clark by rubber boat, foot, and horseback from St. Louis to the Pacific, paddled a canoe in Thoreau's wake in the Maine woods, and chased after John Wilkes Booth by minivan in northern Virginia.

In the case of the Vikings, I initially did just enough research to find out that Leif Eriksson sailed to a place he called Vinland—a place somewhere along the eastern edge of North America between Labrador and Florida—in the year 1000. He raised a few sod buildings, wintered at his new quarters, and then returned to Greenland, claiming to have found a great new land for his people. His fellow Greenlanders were suffering from a paucity of wood as well as quality farmland, and a place claiming an abundance of arable land, frostless winters, grapes, and plenty of salmon drummed up more excitement than the latest gated community outside of Atlanta would today.

This was enough for me. The millennial anniversary of Leif's voyage was coming up, and my research showed that no one had yet dared (or bothered) to retrace his exact route. I would fly to Greenland, hitchhike across the country to the different abandoned Viking settlements, and then buy some functioning vessel and motor it along the prescribed route to what is generally accepted as Vinland.

That is what I told my wife (at the time my girlfriend) and friends. I was running a contract post office for the dying town of Thurmond, West Virginia. While I referred to myself as the postmaster, the Postal Service sent me letters addressed "Dear Mr. or Ms. Contract Postal Unit," and although I never tired of hearing how Billy used to spy on naked prostitutes back in the thirties, I craved adventure. So I repeated to everybody who would listen, including those whose hearing was long gone but pretended to understand every word I said, that I was bound and determined to retrace, in my own fashion, Leif Eriksson's voyage to the New World.

Imagine my surprise when I did a bit more research and learned that Greenland has no roads connecting its towns and settlements. Its deep fjords, formidable mountains, and endless ice have made highway infrastructure a very low priority. Travel in summer is solely by boat, airplane, or helicopter. In the winter, which is not when the Vikings would have been sailing, Greenlanders travel by dogsled, snowmobile, or air. If you fall in the ocean up there, even in the summer, the temperature of the water will kill you in five minutes. Sea ice (or pack ice, as I learned to call it) and icebergs are everywhere. Southeastern Baffin Island, my destination after Greenland, has ice-free shores for only a brief period each summer and then only in select areas. Pack ice, when mixed with high winds, can crush the hull of nearly any boat. I don't even need to mention what icebergs, which are glacier fragments, can do to vessels much stronger than a Viking boat—say, a luxury liner, for example.

And, of course, I knew something about the polar bears. They live there. They like fresh meat. No account I read about traveling in a boat in northern waters was complete without a polar bear encounter—and not a single mention of their cuddly cuteness.

Worst of all, I knew nothing about sailing. I had not even read a single Patrick O'Brian novel. I did not know athwartships from "You sank my battleship!" The most memorable sailing accomplishment in my life was flipping my family's Sunfish beneath a moored barge on the Mississippi River, losing both the sail and the mast.

The nightmares did not start then—they would come later—but I did begin to worry. That very worrying, however, was the clincher. It ensured I would do everything I could to retrace Leif's route. The little voice in my head suggesting, "That's insane!" forced me to do it. At similar times I've eaten a fish as it still flopped on my plate; sneaked into Burma to interview Khun Sa, the world's largest producer of heroin; or eaten 135 oysters in fifteen minutes at the Louisiana Oyster Festival. Mostly, though, I have an unyielding need to walk in much bigger shoes than my own. I crave to see just how brave, stoic, undaunted, or even insane our historical figures were. In following Hannibal or Leif Eriksson, I put myself in their situation, get in way over my head, and then attempt to survive.

I do this as a chicken—no chest beating here. I whine, complain, and try to back out as often as I can. Usually I do not enjoy the process, and sometimes I quit. I go off half-cocked, underinformed, and unadvisable. If I am lucky, however, I learn enough to make it to the end.

Chapter Two

The Vikings emigrated en masse (more than ten thousand settlers in fifty years) from Scandinavia to Iceland, starting in 870,
where they excelled at tending sheep, fishing, and quarreling. Although Iceland had a relatively republican legislative body, making
it a highly unusual medieval settlement, all the good land was
claimed within a century. So the Vikings moved farther west when a
man named Erik the Red led the colonization of Greenland in 985.
Twenty-five ships set sail with him, but only fourteen successfully
completed the five-hundred-mile crossing. As time went on, despite the ice permanently covering 85 percent of the island's land
area, Greenland became a happening outpost, with merchants arriving from Scandinavia, Iceland, and England, and Christian clergy
flung there at regular intervals. There were two settlements situ-
ated about three hundred miles apart on the southwestern coast of
Greenland in two of the very few arable spots in Greenland. The
eastern settlement was the more southerly of the two, and it is
where Erik the Red made his farm, Brattahlid.

The Greenland Vikings did not just barely eke out a living.
They thrived for hundreds of years, with the two settlements even-
tually reaching a combined population of roughly six thousand.
They hunted walrus and bear in the far north, and products made

from these goods, especially the cordage fashioned from walrus skin, were highly sought-after items in Europe. Clothing recovered at archeological digs reveals that some Greenland Vikings were dressed in the height of European fashion into the 1400s. However, by the end of that century the Vikings in Greenland had vanished, and their disappearance has remained an anthropological mystery ever since. Was it famine? A worldwide temperature change? Defeat at the hands of the encroaching Inuit? Abduction and death by English pirates who were fishing for cod? Or merely the withering away of a colony that, in the end, was just too far removed from its kind? Whatever the cause, there is something both heroic and tragically appealing about these northern wanderers, and the more I read, the more I wanted to become a westward-traveling Viking.

"One need not be a lord or prince's son to be a saga hero. But one must be a man of unbreakable will. For the unbreakable will . . . triumphs over the blind injustice of all-powerful fate, and makes man its equal," says Gwyn Jones in *The Norse Atlantic Saga*. Ah, the unbreakable will. This man was speaking to my heart, although I am still not sure how lucky it was that I found his book first. Jones is one of the few sane Viking historians out there, but he also has quite a soft spot for the lore. He pushed me even farther into this Viking venture.

It was from Jones that I learned what kind of ship Leif, Erik the Red's son, would have used to reach the North American mainland: the knarr, an oceangoing cargo or merchant ship. "The oceangoers were sailed with immense courage and skill by men without compass or chart but inured to hardship and learned in the sea's ways," wrote Jones. "They sailed by latitude and the sun and the stars, by landmarks and the flight of birds, by the evidence of marine creatures and the color of water, by rough or dead reckoning, by currents, driftwood, and weed, by the feel of a wind, and when need be by guess and by god."

The knarr (pronounced "kah-narr") was a utilitarian vessel. It had no frightening dragons on its bow. It could be loaded with twenty tons of goods and sent off to trade with the world. The knarr was wide, almost impossible to row, and pieced together of wood and iron rivets. This merchant ship rode high in the water, with just a three-foot draft, which allowed it to enter very shallow waters, like right next to a pillaged monastery, for example. While its lapstrake hull, formed of clapboardlike pine planking, was awfully thin considering the icy waters the Vikings plied, the lore holds that it skipped over wave tops like a goat over mountains. The knarr and the warmongering longship were arguably the most advanced moveable constructions of their day.

That sounded pretty good, but I was not yet sucked in. Building one of these sea goats would be too involved for my needs. This was only going to be a six- or eight-week project, after all. Also, such a boat would have no motor or cabin—ludicrous conditions up in the Arctic. Only a fool would try such a thing. I set Gwyn Jones down for a bit and turned to the Icelandic sagas, which I hoped would give me a better idea of where the trip went and how long it might take.

For the most part, two Icelandic sagas, along with recent meticulously studied archeological evidence, tell us all we know about the Vikings in North America.* The two sagas concerning Leif's voyage are *Erik the Red's Saga* and *The Greenlanders Saga*. In truth, they were more confusing to me than revealing. They are the most contemporaneous accounts of Leif's voyage, but both were written more than two hundred years after the events in question. Sagas were skaldic poems, recited to petty kings, earls, and lords by skalds, historian-poets, who lived by their eloquence and wit. The sagas were passed down orally until the Roman alphabet reached Iceland. Skalds changed the sagas to suit their audience, to get to the roasted boar that waited for them at the end of their story, or maybe even to save their own necks. As a result, it is impossible to know fact from fiction.

Erik the Red's Saga paints Leif as a missionary bringing Christianity to the heathen Scandinavian community in Greenland, where Odin, Thor, and Frey still ruled. In this saga, his voyage to Vinland (the name Leif gives his discovery in North America) departs from Norway. However, *The Greenlanders Saga* has Leif leaving from Greenland and following a mostly coastal route to reach Vinland. Given the proselytizing nature of *Erik the Red's Saga* and the fact that most historians give *The Greenlanders Saga* more credence, I opted to favor the latter.

In *The Greenlanders Saga*, a man named Bjarni Herjolfsson sails

---

* These stories would have originated in Iceland, instead of Scandinavia, because the settlers of Greenland had come from Iceland.

from Norway to his father's home in Iceland with a knarr full of merchandise. In the meantime, however, his father has emigrated to Greenland with Erik the Red. (Erik, by the way, originally had to leave Iceland in 982 on account of being outlawed for killing some neighbors, and he happened upon Greenland while ostracized. He came back to Iceland to convince others to move there with him, including Bjarni's father.) Bjarni really wants to see his dad and heads for Greenland despite never having been there. Not a big deal—Greenland was merely beyond the end of the known world. Lo and behold, Bjarni and his men are blown off course for many days and miss Greenland completely, sailing too far west.

People often get blown off course in the sagas. This device seems to be an attempt to explain why Bjarni, Leif, or someone else left their comfortable little lives in the first place. While the sagas might have been initially devised for kings and earls, they were told throughout the populace to people who were content with staying put.

Anyway, sailing in an open boat, Bjarni and his men were doused with ice-cold water until they wished they had never left their carbon-monoxide-filled hovels. When they finally sighted land, it was covered with low hills and forests. Greenland, however, sports jagged mountains along its coast, and brush that reaches no more than six feet high. This place looked too welcoming to be Greenland, and Bjarni did not let his men go ashore. They sailed for two more days and reached more land. Bjarni saw no glaciers and announced this land, too, could not be Greenland. On closer inspection they saw that the land was flat and covered with woods. Bjarni's crew said they wanted to go ashore. "They reckoned they were in need of both wood and water. 'You lack for neither,' said Bjarni, and got some hard words for this from his crew.'" Sailing northeast for three days, they came to a mountainous, glaciated land. Bjarni said the land was no good and again would not let his men put ashore. By this time he must have been wishing for a repeating bow or some other fanciful weapon to keep his men in check. They sailed four more days and reached Greenland, miraculously at the precise cape where his father had relocated earlier in the summer. Later, Bjarni was ridiculed for not having explored any of the lands he happened upon.

About fifteen years after Bjarni's voyage (the year 1000 is what many authorities have pieced together as a date), Leif headed out to Bjarni's lands, but in the opposite order. Leif called the first land Helluland, which means "slab land" or "flat-stone land." He and his men thought it barren and useless. The second land was flat and wooded, and he called it Markland, which means "woodland." The last place they came to was flush with salmon, choice cattle pasture, days and nights of nearly equal length, and wild grapes. Leif named the land Vinland, which is generally interpreted as "wine land," although there is considerable scholarly argument that the name actually meant "grassland." After spending the winter in Vinland and building houses, he and his crew headed back to Greenland. On the return trip, Leif rescued fifteen men from a ship wrecked on a reef, as well as many of their goods. Afterward he was known as Leif the Lucky, but whether this was because he made it to Vinland and back or rescued the men or kept their bounty is not very clear.

Erik the Red's Saga recounted Leif's voyage in one paragraph. *The Greenlanders Saga*, while relatively richer, is still pretty dull and sketchy. Subsequent voyages to Vinland by Leif's brother, as well as those of an Icelander named Thorfinn Karlsefni and a grisly, murderous voyage by Leif's sister, Freyda, make much more exciting reading. These Vikings skirmished with Native Americans and tried to establish permanent settlements in Vinland. In *Erik the Red's Saga*, Karlsefni is the one who names the lands that Leif discovered, and his sailing directions to these lands are somewhat different from those found in *The Greenlanders Saga*. In both sagas, however, it is clear that Leif was the first European to set foot in Vinland.

But where is Vinland—a place of wild grapes and days and nights of equal length? Given the sailing directions in the sagas, it is obviously somewhere in North America. These directions—sail four days, three, then two more and you're there—also include points of sail and wind direction. While they are vague in comparison to modern sailing directions, the inclusion of wind direction and points of sail has made some modern sailors believe there is a viable route to be deciphered and that if the directions from the sagas are followed, Vinland can be found. Some Vikingphiles surmise that a day (*døgr*) can be interpreted as a sailing term, meaning the distance that a boat sailed in twenty-four hours. Through some very odd calculations and interpretations the distance has been fixed at 144 miles. According to this theory, Vinland would be located 1,296 nautical miles from southern Greenland following an indirect coastal route. Other theorists believe that a day simply means a day and that the voyage took nine days. Given that the two sagas' sailing directions do not complement each other, a nonpartisan observer should run screaming from the room whenever the subject is brought up. If you were to gather a dozen Vikingphiles together, hand each of them a broadsword, and say, "Kill the expert who disagrees with your theory on Vinland's location," you would have twelve dead experts—the last remaining wacko would have conducted an incoherent argument with himself and committed some form of ritual suicide.

The search for Vinland's exact location has been an ongoing quest for the past three hundred years. It really caught on in America in the late 1830s when a scholarly study called *Antiquitates Americanae*, published by Professor Carl Rafn of Denmark, sparked widespread interest in the "Viking discovery of America" and in Vinland's location. Rafn's book placed Vinland in Massachusetts and Rhode Island. Suddenly everyone from Virginia to Maine was finding Viking artifacts, although none proved authentic. Books were written by Americans who had figured everything out. The most popular "find" was a tower in Newport, Rhode Island, that looked somewhat like a Viking structure, which the Viking scholar Rafn "verified." It turned out to have been built by a Governor Arnold in the 1600s, but to this day some people still fervently believe the Vikings built it. Writers and artists entered the frenzy to out-Viking each other, even Longfellow. His poem "Skeleton in Armor" is narrated by the purported Viking builder of the Newport tower. The poem seems plain silly to me, especially the final stanza: " 'Thus, seamed with many scars, / Bursting these prison bars, / Up to its native stars / My soul ascended! / There from the flowing bowl / Deep drinks the warrior's soul, / *Skoal!* to the Northland! *Skoal!*'—Thus the tale ended."

Scandinavian Americans have understandably always sought proof that their ancestors got to America first, and their search has produced some extraordinary finds, including the Kensington Stone. In 1898 Olaf Ohman, a Swedish American, unearthed a two-hundred-pound stone while plowing his farm in Kensington, Minnesota. Runic inscriptions decorated its upper half. Translated, it reads, "Eight Goth and twenty-two Norwegians on a voyage of exploration west of Vinland. One day's journey north of this stone we camped close to two rocky inlets. One day we went out fishing and on our return found the dead bodies of ten of our men, red with blood. AVM deliver us from evil. Fourteen days' journey away from this island, ten men are keeping watch over our ships. Year 1362."

The Smithsonian Institution was convinced of the stone's authenticity and displayed it in 1948. Soon afterward, however, the stone was proven a fake—the runic letters used were not even in existence in the fourteenth century—although writers still receive hate mail for calling it such.

In the course of envisioning my own forthcoming adventures, I was given a self-published book called *Norse America*—more than two hundred confusing pages describing and verifying various Norse "facts" and "finds" in North America. According to this book, it's likely the Vikings made it to, among many other locations, such far-flung locales as South Dakota, California, and Tennessee. One of the only states left out of this catalog was my birth state, Mississippi. So, as much as I wanted Vinland to be my hometown of Greenville, it had not made the A-list.

Putting aside the most extreme theories, I eventually went with the most conventional: Helluland is southern Baffin Island, Markland is southern midcoast Labrador, and some kind of settlement was established in northern Newfoundland, which may or may not be Vinland.

This Newfoundland settlement was tracked down by Helge Ingstad, a lawyer by trade and hero to all modern Vikings. A number of factors convinced the amateur Vikingologist that Vinland was in Newfoundland, not the least of which were two maps from 1590 and 1605 that included a peninsula marked "Promontorium Winlandiae," corresponding with northern Newfoundland. In 1960 Helge and his wife, Anne Stine, a formally trained anthropologist, searched Newfoundland by air and sea. After months of fruitless surveys, they came upon L'Anse aux Meadows in northern Newfoundland. There a great plain of green meadows reminded Helge of Bjarni's description of Leif's Vinland: not mountainous, and covered with forests. Helge asked the local people if any ruins existed in the area, and a man named George Decker excitedly replied,

"Yes, follow me!" George led him on a footpath to a marine terrace surrounded by heather, willows, and grasses and cut through by a small river with leaping salmon. On this terrace were many obvious ancient house sites. After eight years of cumbersome archeological digs, led mostly by Anne Stine, the Ingstads had ample proof that this terrace had once been the location of a Viking settlement. Helge believed that the house sites they unearthed were Leifsbudir, "Leif's buildings" or "Leif's booths," the name given to Leif's Vinland houses in *The Greenlanders Saga*, and that L'Anse aux Meadows was Vinland.

Of course, no two Vikingphiles agree completely with Helge's L'Anse aux Meadows/Vinland theory. L'Anse aux Meadows, however, remains the only archeologically proven Viking settlement in North America. While the house sites found there might not be the remains of Leif's winter quarters, they are undoubtedly Viking, as are the iron rivets, spindle whorl, and other recovered items. Nobody seriously disputes this, and so I decided L'Anse aux Meadows would be my Vinland.

The route that took shape would have me leaving Brattahlid, Erik the Red's farm in southwest Greenland, traveling 500 miles up the coast to Sisimiut (the closest bit of Greenland to Baffin Island), directly crossing 220 miles of the Davis Strait to Cape Dyer on Baffin Island, and then following the Baffin and Labrador coastlines down to L'Anse aux Meadows. Most serious studies suggest this route because it follows the sea currents and most of the prevailing wind patterns. Having taken on the ways of my fellow nuts, I decided that crossing to Baffin Island from Sisimiut made the most sense because it was the closest point to Baffin. I "reasoned" that the Vikings would have liked that. Using a piece of thread and my world atlas, I estimated this to be a journey of roughly 1,900 miles. I figured that by riding ferries up the Greenland coast and then buying some beat-up old sailing or fishing boat in Sisimiut, I could complete the trip in six weeks. The whole project would cost between $20,000 and $30,000. I would have to do a little fund-raising, but it would not be a big deal.

Ha!

It was the fall of '94 when I decided on my route. Afterward, I remember, I was sweeping the floor of our remodeled shack along the New River in Thurmond, West Virginia, when Lisa came in from work. That meant a thirty-minute drive, the last half of which wound past a beautiful but toxic waste–filled creek that led to our tiny town. It is a slightly unnerving drive because the road has one lane and big things like boulders and trees frequently find their way into the middle of it. So I should have given her a few minutes to unwind, but a little bit of mania usually accompanies my far-flung travel ideas and I feel constricted, almost claustrophobic, until I can talk about them, make them more real. Lisa should have just held the flat of her hand against my mouth, signaling for me to hold on a minute. But she has a beautiful, fatal flaw: She takes me seriously.

She thought the route sounded great. Neither of us knew a thing about the Arctic or subarctic, so it was kind of like talking about traveling to a habitable planet around Alpha Centauri. Since it was so removed from our existence, the next phase of our conversation was just as easy to slip into.

"I'm not sure if I should travel in a modern way, like I've been planning, or if maybe I should try to build one of these knarrs," I said.

"The first way would be easier. It's the kind of thing you're used to."

"Yeah," I said, glad that she was leaning toward the easier route.

"So maybe you should build the Viking boat. Try doing it the real way. It would be amazing."

I started to argue, suggesting it might be too expensive—that I would probably have to get a sponsor, even. If I did it the easier way, I could probably do it on a small loan or just overtax my credit cards . . .

It was settled. I would do it the hard way.

The next day, when Lisa was back at work, I made a list of potential crew members:

- Lisa, great outdoorswoman, wonderful, becomes deadly seasick at mere mention of waves
- Preston Maybank, retraced Lewis and Clark trail with me, pretends to sail well
- John Abbott, hippie wilderness leader, no sailing experience
- Jan Calamita, good cook, lawyer, negligible outdoor skills, little sailing experience

- Gordon Simmons, anarchist, hates the outdoors, no sailing experience
- Conrad, Lisa's brother, faints at sight of blood, including his own, no sailing experience
- Abby, Lisa's sister, willing to go, no sailing experience
- George Pond, college friend, good swimmer, funny, probably never sailed a day in his life
- Bruce Burgin, photographer, outdoorsman, very organized, no sailing experience but was in navy
- Russell Kaye, photographer, whines in the outdoors, willing, no sailing experience
- Sam Hiser, between jobs, willing, no sailing experience
- Dad, dictator in a boat, a little too old, okay sailor

I immediately signed up three from the list: Russell Kaye, the red-haired, gentle-giant photographer; John Abbott, the skinny wilderness instructor; and Jan Calamita, the city-boy law school classmate of Lisa's. Not a single sailor in the bunch. What these three had in common, though, was a lot of hair—Jan's all over his body and Russell's and John's practically down to their butts.

Russell will commit to just about anything and then spend the remainder of his life wondering, "What was I thinking?" There is not a single person who can whine as well as he—a trait that fills me with happiness while on the trail because I know at least one person is suffering more than I. He had recently become a father and was living in terror in a Brooklyn apartment where he had not paid rent in seven and a half years.

John Abbott is a wiry, befreckled creature bursting with frenetic energy, usually revolving around where he has misplaced something. He is the outdoors-program specialist at the University of Vermont. He is a kindhearted person who can survive any situation. When he said he would love to go, I felt an immediate relief because I knew I would always have somebody I could count on.

Jan Calamita is on the short side and sturdy, with a strong back. He had never really done much in the outdoors besides a canoe trip with me in which his major accomplishment was survival. However, he was sick of his days and nights at a high-powered Manhattan law firm and, more important than anything else, he was willing to go. I signed him up as cook, remembering the heavenly glazed pheasant, braised endive, creamy cumin-scented squash, and countless other dishes he had presented so exquisitely when he and Lisa were in law school.

Preston Maybank, the fellow who retraced the Lewis and Clark trail with me, laughed derisively when I asked him to come along, said, "Hell, no. Do you think I'm insane?" and promptly hung up.

Exhausted but delighted that I had three suckers, um, crew-mates, I turned to other matters, like trying to make a baby. I mean, Lisa and I knew how and all, but it just was not happening at first. This took about five months. During that time I wrote a book proposal about the Viking voyage. I also asked the National Geographic Society to sponsor the project. Their magazine's adventure editor said they had had their fill of replica retracing stories thanks to Tim Severin, the man who sailed a leather boat from Ireland to America to prove the Irish were the first Europeans in North America. I had already read Severin's book. It was an entertaining read, as exciting as Thor Heyerdahl's *Kon-Tiki* (the bible for replica voyagers), but at the time I did not see what it had to do with my idea. St. Brendan supposedly sailed a curragh, one of the leather boats, to some western lands in the 700s. He met dragons and all sorts of fantastical creatures. This was pure myth—nothing like the hard facts found in the Viking sagas.

The Viking project became intertwined with our daily lives. As my family grew, so did the Viking Project. Lisa and I heard the *tump-tump* of a heartbeat during a sonogram in June. John Ivey, a money-managing friend, and I worked up a fund-raising proposal based on a reference I had read to a Viking replica costing a little under $200,000 if it were built in England. The *tump-tump* turned to *tump-tumps*; we were having twins. I formed a corporation. Lisa and I, nagged by our parents and grandparents, got married. John Ivey and I started sending out the fund-raising proposal.* Lisa and I moved out of the rented shack and bought a house closer to her job.

About this time I started corresponding with Lance Lee, a leader in traditional wooden boatbuilding in this country. Lance had founded numerous boatbuilding schools in Maine and was highly knowledgeable about Scandinavian boats. One of his Apprentice-

---

* By this time I was in the habit of asking everybody I came across to go on the voyage with me. In John's case, he simply looked at me, then changed the subject.

shops, as his schools have been called, built a Scandinavian fishing boat that is a direct descendent of a knarr. This was all that I knew about Lance, gleaned from newspaper articles and word of mouth. His old Apprenticeshop was in Rockport, Maine, not far from where my family vacations in the summer, and his newest one was in Rockland, just five miles away. I had always heard that the Apprenticeshop was *the* place to learn about building a wooden boat in America, and I wanted Lance to be in charge of building the knarr.

My correspondence with Lance mostly confused me. He spoke of paradigms, Nordic triangles, and *his* nonprofit foundation's goals. I did not even know what a paradigm was and figured it was like some fancy pyramid until I looked it up. I think Lance was a big fan of Robert Bly. He would write me things like, "In essence we have immersed in timber framing to meld Sea and Land, the themes of 'Expedition/quest' and shelter, the changing bevel and curvilinear with the square corner and preponderantly straight line construction and the utilitarian rather than pedestrian aspects of architecture with the quixotic and yearning for that elusive experience which is one part Unknown, one part danger and one part rite of passage or even 'trial by self-invited fire.' " I would write back that I needed an estimate. He would write or phone back and talk about the paradigm. I would ask for an estimate. He would fly to Norway and Denmark following a conference in a nearby country and I would pay for some of his travel expenses because he thought it would be a great opportunity to pave the road for Scandinavian involvement in the project. I thought it would be a great way to get my estimate.

Although I did not really want to make this a huge international affair, the knarr would be based on Skuldelev Wreck 1, one of five Viking ships raised from the bottom of Roskilde Fjord, Denmark, in the 1960s, and we would have to get the plans from the Viking Ship Museum in Roskilde at some point. While undoubtedly a knarr, Wreck 1 was only 54' long and 16½' in beam, making it probably 20' shorter than Leif's and a good bit narrower. With a smaller boat, at least I wouldn't have to round up as many crew members.

Meanwhile, all I wanted was a simple estimate so I could raise the right amount of money. At that point my entire budget was $3,000; my grandmother had contributed $1,000 to the corporation (named the New Vinland Foundation), and I had loaned it $2,000. I felt backed into a corner. Lance, furiously meeting with Viking authorities and setting up triangular paradigms, was a few sagas ahead of me. When he came back, I flew up to see him in Maine.

I must admit that I had come to fear hearing from him. I felt that I needed him because he was the only person I had heard of who would even contemplate such a project, but the fact that I could not get him to answer a simple question about the estimate was too hard to handle. Going to see Lance constricted my chest and stomach just as if I were raising my hand in a college classroom or asking someone out on a date for the first time. How were we going to work together?

As he showed me photographs, pieces of wool, tarred hemp, and books in Danish, I realized that he wanted this project. It was not so much that he wanted to be my builder; rather, he wanted the entire thing. It was as if a huge billboard flashed across his brow: VIKING PARADIGM OR BUST! Much of his adult work had been leading him to a project just like this. I found this to be endearing, but I sensed it could not work, even if I could overcome all of the confusing communication with him. I just wanted to retrace Leif Eriksson's route as authentically as I could, not save the world.

"What do you think my role is in this project?" he asked after a bit. I stared out the window into the darkness. From this day on, people would be asking similar questions—questions that had easy answers if only I were better at being frank. I should have just said, "To build the damned boat," but instead I searched for the answer he wanted to hear.

"Educator?" I tried.

"Well, I've thought about this and have decided I want to be your gadfly. Have you read *The Gadfly*?"

No, I answered, but said that I had met a lot of gadflies in my life. Admittedly, I was thinking that a gadfly was more like a housefly, but Lance, as if reading my thoughts, informed me that a gadfly was not a pest but more like an adviser. While confusing when talking about my project, he was very open and charming when talking about more personal matters. I began to relax despite the gadfly stuff and talked about my hopes for the project. He very politely dissuaded me from one of my big ideas—that of being my own captain. Lance suggested I might want to look into hiring a captain from Scandinavia, someone who had experience with a Viking replica or a square-rigger. We also talked about my desire to help build the boat. Lance liked this idea; that is what his Apprentice-shop is all about, except the apprentices are usually selected from a pool of volunteers.

He did not give me an estimate that night but said he wanted to talk over the numbers with me and his executive director the next day. In the morning Lance showed me some slides of a spinning wheel in Norway along with a few shots of a sail. A Viking sail was made with wool and the leeward side was covered with grease, he explained. When a too-powerful gust came along, the grease was blown out and the now-porous sail would not be damaged. He had also learned while visiting a sailmaker in Scandinavia that to get the right tension on the spinning wheel for making the sails, "you must get a two-year-old ram that has been pastured and its entrails [which are used] well dried. . . . The ram must be pastured and ex-posed on the high ground of the Faroes." While the Faroes—islands located along the way from Great Britain to Iceland—are quite appealing in a cold, miserable sort of way, I found it dubious that they had the only decent entrails around.

That afternoon I was finally given the estimate. It was $300,000 and would slowly keep going higher and higher. Adding that figure to the budget John and I had calculated for the rest of the project—travel, shipping the boat to Greenland, food, outfitting boat and crew, salaries—raised the entire budget to $500,000.

This was getting insane. I could swim the entire route in a wet suit and have a better chance of pulling it off. Lisa and I were about to have our twins. Obviously, she would no longer be able to go with me, and I did not relish risking my neck with a fledgling family at home. The simple thing would have been to quit right then and there.

But the simple thing did not occur to me.

The intertwining of the Viking Project and my and Lisa's life continued, and it came to resemble a sketchily made sail. Some-times weak threads were used, sometimes strong ones. One day it was done right, the next day poorly. Over time weak sections would develop in the project, as well as in our lives, but we strug-gled along, hoping and planning for both futures.

Our twin girls, Anabel and Eliza, were born in January of 1996, and they were all I thought or cared about. I found myself blubbering while merely holding them in my arms or dancing with them as Lyle Lovett sang "Fat Babies Have No Pride."

The project had a life of its own by this point, however, and quite often trod over our lives, babies or no babies. Lance had tentatively lined up a number of Scandinavian Viking-ship authorities and builders to assist us. They, however, had to know that I was moving forward—that I had money. I, on the other hand, had a lot of rejection letters but no sponsor.

Lance really wanted to do the project only if the Scandinavians were heavily involved, but my foundation had about $300 remaining in its budget. I looked up from the babies long enough to tell him so. As a result, I parted ways with Lance and the Scandinavians.

The sponsorship proposal, despite the clever titles I gave it— usually including hearty Norse names such as Odin, Thor, or Frey—was only being read by the mail room guys. They would grab a glazed doughnut, laugh out loud at the absurdity of sailing an open-decked boat within the Arctic Circle, and then send back a smudged rejection letter or just throw the whole thing in the trash. I longed for the days when Thor Heyerdahl wanted to prove that the South Seas people originated from Peru, went to the Explorers Club, and told the great Arctic explorer Peter Freuchen about his plans to sail a wooden raft four thousand miles across the Pacific. The very next day Heyerdahl was summoned to the home of a "well-dressed young man in patent leather slippers, wearing a silk dressing gown over a blue suit," who immediately offered to back the project.

Where was my silk-dressing-gown-wearing backer?

We tried another tactic. Through friends of friends of friends, we got the home addresses of founders and CEOs of corporations.

Gary Comer, founder of Lands' End, was one of the first people to whom I sent the proposal. He had been an Olympic sailor in his younger days and loved adventure.

Two days later he called me. "I figured that since you sent this to my home address, I could call you at home at night," he said in a pleasant voice. "You did good sending this here." I do not even remember what he said beyond the fact that he thought it was a very good idea and would present it to his board of directors soon. When I got off the phone, Lisa and I danced around in a circle, laughing at the miracle of this single phone call. We lit three hokey New Age candles that someone had given us when the twins were born—one that was for luck, another for money, and the last for love. Although I was not even a sailor yet, superstition was creeping into my life.

I met with the president of Lands' End and a number of other company executives a few weeks later. I was nervous beforehand, repeating like a catechism words and phrases my money friend John had taught me, such as "promotional events," "on-site display space," and "signage." The meetings, although emotionally exhausting, were equally exhilarating, and I eventually relaxed enough to talk about my aspirations for the project. Mike Smith, the president and CEO, told me that if they were to sponsor the project, they wanted to be the only sponsor. They would underwrite the entire adventure. In return, they wanted me to write a number of articles about the project for their catalog. They would not put signage on the boat or sail.

"That is not how we do things," Mike told me. "It is not our way. We prefer to be much less intrusive."

I distinctly remember pinching myself—hard. I did not wake up. Soon afterward Lands' End decided to sponsor the whole thing, even though I no longer had a builder or even a captain.

This is when the nightmares began in earnest. Some well-meaning relative had sent me a newspaper clipping about a 110-foot-tall rogue wave that blasted the bridge of the *Queen Elizabeth* II not very far from where we would be sailing. My nights were tormented by even larger waves, as well as sharks, killer whales, belligerent polar bears, and bellowing walruses. My bluff had been called, and even my subconscious knew it was for real from this point on.

Then we found a new boatbuilder, a guy named Rob Stevens in Hermit Island, Maine. Rob thought the whole thing was nuts, but he borrowed the plans ("lines," as Rob said) for the knarr from Lance. The director of the Viking Ship Museum in Roskilde, Denmark, had given the plans to Lance the previous fall, and Rob had been a student at one of Lance's boatbuilding schools.

It turned out that Rob had wanted to build a Viking ship since fifth grade. He had seen a film in school about Danish scouts building a Viking ship and had wanted to do the same ever since. For the most part, after graduating from Lance's Apprenticeshop, Rob had done repair work. In fact, he had previously been in charge of building only nine boats, none larger than twenty-four feet. However, when I told Lance that I had contacted Rob about the boat, Lance praised him as one of his best graduates.

Rob turned in a $296,000 estimate, and I told him he had the job. Lance's approval of Rob at least made me feel slightly less reckless than, say, getting just one estimate before choosing someone to build the Taj Mahal.

By May of '96 we already had a verbal agreement (our lawyers would never come to agreement on the written contract) about building the boat. We had both read an article in a publication for the Viking Ship Museum that described the building of another knarr, *Saga Siglar*, in Norway. This boat had been built for Ragnar Thorseth, a Norwegian adventurer who eventually sailed his ship around the world. He even sailed it to L'Anse aux Meadows twice. Thorseth, however, skipped the route laid out in *The Greenlanders Saga*. Also, on both trips his ship had a built-in motor and a cramped wooden cabin, accouterments the Vikings had done without.

Thorseth's knarr had been built by a father-and-sons traditional boatbuilding team in less than seven months. Rob promised to have my boat ready by April of '97.

While on vacation in mid-July, Lisa, the twins, and I drove out to meet Rob for the first time and see how things were progressing. To reach Rob's boatyard on Hermit Island, we slogged our way through Route 1 traffic down the Maine coast from Camden to Bath, then headed fourteen miles to the end of one of the fingerlike peninsulas that fan out around Bath and Brunswick, and scrambled over the final one and a half miles on a sandy dirt road that runs the length of Hermit Island, a remote campground that attracts generations of the same families every year. The ocean was on our left and a calm, slow inlet lay to our right. The road seemed to be going nowhere. What sane person would have a boatyard that was this impossible to get to both by land and water?

When we went a few hundred yards past a sign that suggested all cars turn around, we were suddenly stopped short of our destination. A gurgling, churning, backfiring monstrosity completely blocked the way. It was a badly beaten-up black Ford pickup sitting sideways in the middle of the road. A silvery-maned man with scruffy muttonchop sideburns stood in the bed of the truck simultaneously banging on an ancient behemoth of an engine mounted in the truck bed and pouring water into its foaming radiator. The more he poured in, the more spurted out. A lot of the froth landed on his belly, which was of the sort that makes a great resting place for crossed arms or even a pitcher of beer.

Another man approached my window. "It's gonna be a long time," he said, and then spied the campground map sprawled across my lap. "But I figure you're lost anyway." I told him I was looking for Rob Stevens, and with a hint of surprise he admitted that Rob was the one causing all the ruckus. It turned out Rob was using the mounted Model A engine as a winch to drag huge pallets into place to store planking for the knarr.

Rob came over, Lisa and I shook hands with him, and we said a few words. Then he started the engine again. The pallet he was dragging immediately hit a tree. Rob stopped the engine. He and Scott Smith, whom Rob had hired to help with the knarr and to whom I had spoken on the phone but had also never met, wrestled the pallet clear of the tree. The engine quit working. Rob restarted it. It backfired loudly, causing Lisa and me to jump and the twins to wake up screaming. The radiator began frothing worse than before—spewing faster than a spittle bug on speed. The engine began backfiring continuously. They jacked up something that seemed to have nothing to do with the pallet project. A chain popped off something else. Lisa and I attempted to help reset it. A horde of mosquitoes moved in. After half an hour, either the pallet was where Rob wanted it—not much farther from where it started—or Rob had given up for the afternoon. We did not think it an appropriate time to ask.

As Rob showed us around his shop, I tried not to let it bother me that he still had no wood for the boat even though we had reached an agreement eight weeks earlier. When I had asked him about the wood, he would say, "It's on its way," or tell me that it was not needed yet. Nevertheless, it seemed to me that if all the wood was in place, then everything would go more smoothly.

Lisa and I examined the lofting (full-size drawings of the boat's specifications) on the floor, and the twins crawled and drooled on them. The Vikings would have built the boat by eye, but Rob had said he did not think he could manage it. He would build temporary molds to create the right fit for the planking.

As I knew nothing about lofting or even boatbuilding, of course, it appeared to me that Rob knew what he was doing. He could have been building something as seaworthy as the Empire State Building and I would have patted him on his back, exhorting him to keep up the good work. It turns out Rob is an incorrigible procrastinator—a trait that would cause me many sleepless nights in the future. But that day everything was rosy merely because it had to be. I had chosen him as my builder and given him $80,000 to get things going. It was too late to have doubts about him.

"There's something I've been wondering," Rob suddenly asked as Lisa and I continued to stare at the lofting as if it actually meant something to us. "Why aren't you having it built over there—in Scandinavia?" I explained how I had originally wanted to work on the boat myself and that the Apprenticeshop had seemed like the only place I would be able to do that. Once it became clear that the Apprenticeshop was out, I had stuck to building it in America out of sheer orneriness. This made him laugh.

We could not help but like Rob. He seemed wholly unpretentious. He was unkempt, affable, and very patient. His boatyard was cluttered with scraps of things that interested Lisa and me: a wooden canoe, old tools, books. He did not care that our girls, Anabel and Eliza, were spitting up all over the lofting. Even the way he nervously repeated, "Which one is the evil twin? Ha, ha, ha. My wife is gonna kill me for asking that!" was endearing. We liked his pirate's earring. And he obviously loved tinkering with things. We left him after about two hours trying hard to convince ourselves that everything was going to be okay.

The most unsettling thing for me was seeing such effort being made over my project. All the things Rob was doing and had ordered were because of something I had set into motion. Hiring Scott would be followed by taking on two more builders, his best friend, Bob Miller, and Dave Foster, the master builder who had taught Rob at the Apprenticeshop. Later he would hire six more builders, plus pay up to a dozen Apprenticeshop students to work on the weekends. The wall of Rob's shop closest to the harbor would have to be dismantled to remove the fifty-four-foot knarr upon completion. And back in Wisconsin, Lands' End was putting together a team specifically to handle this project. It was daunting. Exciting, yes, but daunting. If only I knew what I was doing, I thought. *If only I were more thorough. If only I had lived back in the days of the Vikings when everything was much simpler . . .*

The heat from the hellish fire nearly made the weak, malnourished young man faint. Yet the cold of the hard-packed snow, slick with new ice and just inches behind him, hardly seemed any better.

"More bellows, slave, or I'll send you reeling!" the coarse blacksmith barked at the weak man. "We have a thousand more rivets to forge. And on Frey's pallet of sin, I swear Thor Thorstein will not be the cause of Karlsefni the Icelander's knarr being delayed!"

Hodding the Plodding, slave from the land of the plundered monks, pressed even harder. His ulcerating sores and gums, thanks to the scurvy that none cared he had, ached with every effort. His feet, with toes blackened from frostbite, cried out in pain.

"Lord Karlsefni wants to see this Vinland that Leif discovered and, by Thor, he will, if I have anything to do with it!" Thorstein bellowed.

How many times must I hear this? Plodding wondered. Karlsefni will just drag me along and make me scoop out the bilge for the entire voyage. The other bilge scooper will probably be Aethelred the Stinky, and I'll have to listen to his ceaseless bragging about his dead cousin, Alfred the Great, King of England. How he held off the Nordmen at Stanford Bridge. Who cares about Alfred? Just because my uncle gave those Nordmen a highly detailed map to the Linberg Monastery doesn't mean that my whole family is traitorous. If only Aethelred the Stinky would not smear goat dung over his entire body. Maybe then I could bear his company. Maybe, after tonight's sacrifice, I can talk Martha the Easy into convincing Karlsefni not to take any goats on the Vinland voyage. What can I trade her?

Plodding patted his body, searching in any pocket for some trinket to trade, but of course his Viking clothing had no pockets. How stupid, he thought.

Just as he realized that his loosened tooth would make the perfect fetish, and thus the perfect bribe, for Martha, Thor swung the back of his meaty paw across Plodding's head. The worthless slave somersaulted through the air like a seal cuffed by a playful ice bear and landed sprawled across the hardened snow. Not a soul cared if he lived or died.

Chapter Three

A pattern developed over the following months, one that would be sustained throughout the Viking project. Information, questions, and burning issues would barrage me. I would duck as much of it as I could, tackling one of a thousand items at a time, while praying that the whole thing would not suddenly collapse.

"You've got to get a captain, a great captain. This won't work otherwise. Rob's telling everybody that you'd have to be crazy to go out on your boat," Russell Kaye gasped to me over the phone. Russell, the photographer crew member, was at Rob's boatyard shooting pictures for a Lands' End catalog. A thousand miles separated us, but I could feel him shaking in his dirty running shoes. "What are you getting us into?"

Another friend called me a few days later. "My tree guys need to know if you want heartwood or sapwood for those planks." It was two months since my first visit to Rob's place and he still had not gotten all the planking for the boat. It was driving me crazy, especially since Rob acted so nonchalant whenever we spoke. So I was trying to get the wood for him.

I did not know the difference between sapwood and heartwood, so I called Rob's shop. Bob Miller answered the phone. Russell, who had spent more time at the boatyard than I, liked Bob a lot because he was a photographer as well as a builder and did not seem quite as crazy as Rob. Bob patiently explained that we needed heartwood because it was stronger.

Russell called the next day, still worrying about Rob. "Nothing belonging to Rob works. His car doesn't have a starter. His pants barely stay up. . . . But I think he can build boats. I gotta go."

I had had a hot prospect for a captain. "I can only commit to something like this if I trust the plans, and so far what I've seen leaves me far from wanting to do this," he told me over the phone one day. I had answers to all his questions about safety. Yes, we would have charts, a lifeboat, a radio, a ship's compass, an EPIRB (emergency position-indicating radio beacon), and even a handheld GPS (global positioning system) device. Whenever we talked, he sounded pissed at me, so eventually I told him he should not go at all.

Meanwhile, Rob and I were planning to go to Norway and Denmark to meet with Viking boat experts in October. Regrettably, my fund-raising proposal was sent to Ragnar Thorseth, the man who had sailed a knarr around the world and sailed to Newfoundland twice. He was not very happy that I wrote, "Other Viking replicas have sailed from Europe (or even Greenland) to North America but none followed the original route."

He wrote in response, "After going through the material, I must decline meeting with Mr. Hodding Carter. The total project stinks of forgery near historic proportions. In its efforts to be original, it has consciously not mentioned that this trip has been made twice at full-scale from Norway the last 10 years. . . . I therefore limit myself to wishing good luck."

Hell, he was lucky I had cut out some of my broader swipes at his voyage in which I pointedly mentioned his motor and cabin. Rob really wanted to meet with Ragnar, so I wrote a conciliatory fax.

Ragnar faxed me a response to my apologetic fax in the middle of the night. The machine woke Lisa and me, and when I returned to bed she was lying stiffly on her back, eyes wide open. I told her he had once again declined to meet us. "I hate this project," she said quietly. "Not only are some of these people horrible, but I'm worried you're not going to live through this journey." I mumbled something about how things that are difficult to accomplish are much more meaningful in the end. Neither of us believed it. Eventually we fell asleep.

It got worse. A few of the museum people in Norway and Denmark also declined to meet Rob and me. The two leaders in the field of Viking naval archeology would not discuss our project with us, and I could only assume that it was because I was no longer working with Lance Lee. They were colleagues of his and probably did not trust the project now that Lance and I had parted ways. It probably had not helped matters that I had refused to give Lance some money that he thought I owed him.

Ole Crumlin-Pedersen, the man responsible for raising five Viking ships out of Roskilde Fjord, including Skuldelev Wreck 1, on which our knarr was to be based, wrote to me, "As you may probably understand the Museum is rather reluctant to take up any responsibility for ships built elsewhere from the design of the original ships, as a good copy requires not only specialized craftsmanship and materials of a quality which is hard to find today, but also an acceptance of a potentially greater risk of disaster at sea due to lack of tradition for sailing this type of ship—and because the Vikings simply accepted a greater rate of losses than we do today! If, after this, you still want to proceed with your plans you can contact Max Vinner [director of the Viking Ship Museum]."

Rob and I went to Scandinavia anyway, although Rob suggested we wear disguises. We had gotten the distinct impression that these people did not like some arrogant Americans meddling around in their heritage. "There's going to be wanted posters of us all over Norway and Denmark," he quipped. At the last minute, however, Max Vinner agreed to meet with us but with the comment that "we can't see we can help you with your knarr project for the time being."

Our first stop was in Bjørkedalen, Norway, to meet with the Bjørkedals, a family who had been building boats for fourteen generations. They had built three copies of the knarr—two for Ragnar Thorseth, because he sank his first in the Mediterranean, and one for the Sunnmøre Museum in Ålesund, Norway.

To our surprise and utmost relief, the Bjørkedals were warm, open, and welcoming. Sigurd, the seventy-six-year-old patriarch, looked a lot like a kind Vladimir Lenin, and Sigurd's son, Jacob, was very friendly. First we had heart-shaped waffles and coffee in their four-hundred-year-old home. Then we talked about our project. They seemed thrilled that we wanted to build a boat like theirs. We were meeting with them more for Rob's sake than mine, but he spoke up only once or twice. He seemed embarrassed; I wished I knew him better so that I could shake him and remind him this was his chance to ask questions.

After the coffee and treats, we toured their boatyard. Its rich odors of freshly cut wood and pine-tar-coated hemp, as well as their kind attitude, melted my embittered heart, and I was once again happy to be pursuing the Vikings.

Next they wanted to show us their lumber mill. I was not too excited but went along anyway. It was a hydropowered mill, run by a gurgling clear stream diverted by a wooden gate. Its simplicity was stunning and its obviousness hit me over the head. I had never even bothered to think about how people without electricity would have sawn huge amounts of lumber. Our modern world insulated me from even considering it. Their mill lit up the lazy recesses of my mind. This was what the project was about: stepping back and learning, not all this bickering over who did what and who deserved to do it.

The following day I sat on a simple wooden bench, and I was thrilled. The bench was aboard *Borgundknarr*—the Sunnmøre Museum's knarr. She was wide (beamy, as a sailor would say) and felt safe. Longboats are nothing in comparison, I thought, rubbing the gunwale, or sheer plank, as Rob was teaching me to call it. Where most disinterested parties saw a practical wooden tub, I found the very essence of grace and beauty.

Per Weddegjerde showed us around the knarr and the Sunnmøre Museum. When I learned that he was the captain of the *Borgundknarr*, I asked him if he wanted to be the captain for our voyage.

"I've always wanted to go to Greenland," he said, and then asked some practical questions. I talked about the boat, how we were trying to keep it as traditional as possible. He kept nodding his head and then stated, "And you will have an engine since it doesn't row very well." I said no. He said, "In that case, I do not want to go. You cannot maneuver this boat well without it and it will take forever to row."

It was my turn to smile and nod.

A woman who had been helping show us around said, "You know, it's always good to have a balance between doing what is good and pure and doing something that is practical. In our country, we all use the water and men have always died on it. We have a respect for it, and today we can't all be Leif the Lucky. It just doesn't happen."

The next day, though, Per mentioned that his wife had given him permission to go on our voyage. Although he would eventually come to America to help us with our boat, Per ended up neither captaining nor crewing the knarr. I believe our not having a motor was simply too impractical for him.

We flew to Denmark next, filled with more than a bit of dread. We knew the meeting at the Viking Ship Museum would not go very well. As a result, we easily decided we preferred the rugged beauty of Norway to Denmark. Denmark seemed tame and a little stale. The people, although we hardly spoke to a soul, seemed too timid for us. Personally, Rob thought the country was generally lacking in substance because he seemed to be the fattest guy around. He was also convinced that some of the negative attitude toward us stemmed from history.

"My ancestors are English. The Danes have always hated us," he would try to explain to me as we stood in yet another marine chandlery, a place that excited him almost as much as our daily visits to ice cream parlors. "Ever since Lord Nelson came and destroyed all the forests merely as a precaution against the Danes helping the French, they have not trusted us."

In Roskilde, at the Viking Ship Museum, Max Vinner was initially barely hospitable. His first words to Rob and me were, "All we can do is show you the Wreck One. Otherwise we're too busy." He then led us on a humdrum tour that taught me things that I had learned two years previously reading books at home. Afterward, though, over coffee, Max loosened up. Maybe the fact that we had not merely left at the tour's conclusion proved something to him. Or maybe he just felt sorry for us. Max and I talked about writing, and Rob and Søren, one of the museum's builders, talked about building for quite a long time. I told Max that I had not sent him a copy of my first book because he might think I was a little crazy. "But everyone who is interested in building a Viking ship and actually sailing it has got to be crazy. We're all a little bit crazy here," he replied. Then he explained that they received an average of two letters or calls a week from people wanting to build and sail a boat based on one of the wrecks. These people invariably want the museum to help them, and it is Max's job to write the rejection letters. He has begun some of them with the words "This letter may save your life."

He then explained their reticence more seriously. "We do not want people to build these boats. Not because we want a monopoly but because we cannot have people building them and then dying. We will be sued and the government will want to shut down all wooden open-boat building and sailing. We were almost sued once for the wreck of a Gokstad ship replica. Their insurance company blamed the sail and we designed the sail. Ever since, we've been careful not to get involved."

By the end of our first day, Max had asked us to work as apprentices on their replica of Wreck 1 in 1998, and I had asked him to join us for the voyage. With a wide grin, he said he would really like that. Max presented us with line drawings of Wreck 1—the same ones that Lance had loaned Rob. Returning to the museum a few more times, we found that these plans were for sale in the gift shop. Everyone had made such a big deal about getting the plans, yet they were for sale to every man, woman, and child who walked through the door.

Our meetings with Max and Søren did not reveal anything new or tell Rob how to build the boat. They just made us feel a little less reviled.

Also, seeing the actual Wreck 1, as well as the other four Viking boats at the museum, helped me appreciate the extensive work that had been done to make it possible for us to build our little boat. Until Wreck 1 was found, the shape and construction of a knarr were mere theory. (Leif's knarr, by the way, was most likely substantially larger than Wreck 1 but otherwise wholly similar.) For Scandinavians and Viking historians, discovering and raising these five boats created as much excitement as would occur in the U.S. if McDonald's went back to frying its french fries in lard. Maybe more.

Local fisherman had always believed that Queen Margrethe I, a beloved Danish monarch during the Middle Ages, had ordered a ship intentionally sunk near Skuldelev in Roskilde Fjord to block enemies from sailing up the best channel that led to the cathedral town of Roskilde. At low tide, the timbers, as well as the stones that had been used to sink the boats, were visible under only three feet of water. Over the centuries, treasure seekers took modest trophies home during extremely low tides, and in 1924, while dredging to make the channel deeper, a keelson, a wooden mount for a mast that rests along the keel, was found.

The Danish National Museum sent someone out to measure the keelson but lost interest in the discovery. However, sporadic official raids were made on the "wreck" over the following decades, and the accumulated pieces convinced the National Museum that the boat was not from Queen Margrethe's time but instead dated from the ninth or tenth century. Finally, in 1957, the museum organized a thorough underwater excavation. Although underwater archeology was a new field, they began to uncover framing and planking. These pieces were so soft, however, that as the archeologists exposed too much too quickly, pieces of the boat were carried away by the current. They learned to uncover less timber at a time. By the end of the first summer's excavation, they also learned there was another Viking boat. During the following two summers they discovered all five of the ships.

Diving for the artifacts was too frustrating, and so the archeologists created a sunken island around the wrecks, pumping out the water and using sheet piling for a circular dam. When the ships' remnants were exposed to the air for too long they would shrink and sometimes twist out of shape. To prevent this, they were packed into airtight plastic bags and then trucked to a lab north of Copenhagen, where they were kept in water while being studied. Afterward the pieces were treated with polyethylene glycol, a curing agent that protects the wood and prevents shrinkage. Eventually the treated pieces were used to reconstruct the original ships, now housed in the museum.

While I persevered with learning about the excavation, Rob was thrilled to learn how the "forefoot was rabbetted" by looking at Wreck 3. Wreck 1 was missing its rabbetted forefoot sections. I did not know what the hell this meant, but apparently it was worth traveling four thousand miles to find out. Rob later explained to me that *rabbetting* meant cutting a groove in wood so that another piece could be attached and that the forefoot was the area where the keel attached to the stems, the two curved ends of the boat. Sort of important. Rob also figured out the rigging (the lines that support the mast and work the sail) by studying a glass-encased detailed model of Wreck 1.

I gazed politely at each reconstructed boat for ten minutes or so, but they were mere husks of the original ships. Maybe I had no imagination, but half-recovered ships did not thrill me endlessly, except for how their information could be used. Rob, however, stood transfixed, mindlessly stroking his bushy sideburns, and then inching up to the display until he was as close as legally permitted, peering through squinted eyes for at least an hour at a time.

"Learn anything?" I'd ask as we headed out a turnstile or plopped into a chair to watch another stilted museum film on finding, preserving, or studying Viking boats.

"Not much," he would respond, and my stomach would tighten into a burning knot. *What are we doing here, then?* I wanted to scream.

In truth, our trip to Norway and Denmark was important. It made Rob more comfortable. He had been led to believe that the ancient Viking and modern Scandinavian boatbuilders were gods; their boats were absolutes. When he looked closely at the Oseberg and Gokstad ships back in Oslo and what was left of the Skuldelev boats in Roskilde, he said to himself, "No, there are problems with the planking. They made mistakes. I can do this." He didn't tell me this at the time, but it gave him the confidence to pull off one of the most audacious boatbuilding projects in America.

Rob got to work when we returned. All along, without telling me or maybe even himself, he had planned on beginning in October and launching on April 23 because that was how long it had taken the Bjørkedals to build their first knarr. In his own way, Rob Stevens had as much chutzpah as I did.

I spent the next few months taking care of our girls, rounding up crew members and a captain, and sporadically checking on the boat.

I still had my three friends: Russell, the project's photographer; John, the wilderness instructor; and Jan, the lawyer/cook, who was making a concerted effort to learn about pack ice and icebergs in the subarctic. However, this was not giving me much relief. What I really needed was someone who would help put me at ease. I asked

Rob if he wanted to go. If he was willing to sail on the boat that he built, then at least I could assume the boat would be seaworthy.

"Sure, I'd like to do that, but I get awfully seasick," he responded. If I had known just how "awfully" he had meant, I probably would have suggested he reconsider. I doubt there is a person who gets more seasick in the entire world than Rob Stevens. After he said yes, I told him my reason for asking him. "Yeah, but you don't know about my suicidal tendencies."

I did have one ace in the hole, however. Back in the summer, I had made a short trip to Greenland to do a little research and had met a man named Elias Larsen down by the docks in one of the coastal towns. Elias was a Greenlander, although his name, like those of most Greenlanders, was Scandinavian as a result of the island's having been occupied by the Danes for hundreds of years. Elias and I had hung out for only a day or two, but he had a mischievous twinkle in his eye and had fished the Greenland coast for much of his adult life. I could not resist asking him to join my crew. A friend of some people I was traveling with had recommended Elias highly.

"Yes, I will go with you, Hodding Carter. I have sailed these waters my entire life," Elias said. He had also once captained a small fishing boat from Denmark to Greenland, so I knew he was used to rougher offshore waters.

It was much later that I realized he had used the word *sailed* in a generic way, to mean travel by boat. Elias was not a sailor, but in the end it did not matter. He was a fast learner, inured to hardship, strong, and funny.

So, including me, I had five crew members without any sailing experience to speak of. A captain and about four to six more people were needed. Every woman I asked to go, by the way, either could not go or did not want to. I would gladly have had an all-female crew, although I am not too sure how happy Lisa would have been about that.

Word was spreading about my project, and soon more than enough people were sending me unsolicited queries and calling me at home. Most of them were crazies, but one guy joined the voyage by making just such a call. Andy Marshall had been a navigator in the Coast Guard. We talked on the phone a number of times. A friend of a friend recommended him, and he was full of the adventurous spirit that I wanted on board. In addition, he had sailed a fair bit, although most of it was day sailing. For some reason, the thing I liked most about Andy was that he had forgotten his own phone number when he left a message on my answering machine. He was, I realized, a kindred spirit.

So now I finally had someone who knew how to sail and could navigate. I was even beginning to feel slightly at ease . . . until I would call up Rob at the boatyard.

"Well, I think we've about got it figured out. We've finished the fourth strake," he would say with a nervous laugh. He said this to me so many times that he eventually caught himself. His lisp, barely noticeable when we first met, seemed to be getting worse. "I guess I've said that a lot, huh?" Strakes are the rows of planking for the hull of a lapstrake boat, where the planks of wood are lapped over each other like on a clapboard house. Our boat had twelve strakes on each side. So, with only four done, they had a long way to go.

Rob was the fastest of all his builders at putting a plank on the boat, and it took him eight hours at best. Since each strake was made up of two to four planks, with seventy-two planks altogether, attaching the strakes alone would take a lot of hours if things were going smoothly, and, as Rob himself said endlessly, this was a learn-as-you-go project. First the keel had been laid and the stems attached. The first plank was steamed to make it flexible and then was fitted to the keel and stern over the temporary mold. This process took a day or two, depending on who was fitting the plank, and sometimes longer. Then the next plank had to be attached farther forward. The point where the planks overlapped at their ends was called a scarph. The scarphs were driving Rob and his crew crazy because the planks would not fit together properly, no matter how many times they did the math before shaping the boards. Rob, however, eventually figured out the culprit. It was the temporary molds that were causing the problems—the very things that were supposed to make building the boat easier. A Viking boatbuilder would have known the curves of a knarr and beveled the planks to the shape he wanted. When he was ready to attach the plank, he would set heavy rocks against the inner surface of the plank and props against the outer surface to get the right shape.

By using the un-Viking-like molds, Rob and his crew kept trying to make the scarphs work mathematically and logically, not with their eyes. Eventually Rob realized this and began exhorting his fellow builders, "Use your eye, don't worry about measuring," repeating it like a mantra until launch day.

"If I were to do this all over again, I would not use the molds," he told me. Then he began asking me what kind of insurance I had in case of fire. I'm still not sure why.

The easiest job on the building project was riveting the planks together. It took two people. One would drive the handmade iron rivet through a plank. The other worker, on the inside of the boat, would slip a rove (like a nut on a screw) down the shaft of the rivet and push it flush against the plank. He then would cut off the end of the rivet, leaving just enough to flatten over the rove with a ball-peen hammer to hold the rivet in place. At the same time, the worker on the outside of the boat would hold a heavy hammer, say a five-pounder, against the rivet head to keep a tight fit as the other worker tapped with the ball-peen hammer. Rob estimated that each rivet took four minutes when things went right or, in other words, usually about eight minutes of worker time. There would eventually be roughly twenty-five hundred rivets in the planking, taking more than two months' worth of work time.

And this for the simplest, most brain-dead job on the project.

Because of the time factor and my not having the resolve to chop down an entire forest for one boat, including at least one tree with a circumference exceeding twelve feet, we decided to compromise in a few areas besides using temporary molds. The planks were not hand-hewn and instead had been milled at a lumberyard. The Vikings split their planks out of whole trees because they did not have saws. These planks, although just as thin, were stronger than ours since they followed the natural grain of the wood. Another compromise was that the stems—the ends of the boat—were not carved out of a single enormous tree trunk, as the Vikings would have done. Instead, a number of pieces of wood were used and glued together.

Even with these shortcuts, the building was painstaking and slow.

I continued to have dreams about rogue tidal waves, but now my nightmares included details such as sailing an ugly boat with metal knees (support framing) and rickety timbers. Rob would invariably be present acting nonchalant. "This is looking good, Rob,"

I would say. "Keep it up." Then, when he was not looking, I would puke in the corner.

Every time I went to see the boat in person, Marian Rivman, the publicist Lands' End had hired for my project and a friend of a friend, would send along a video crew, news team, or reporter. Marian was just doing her job, but I did not want everything I did to be an event. That was not how I had ever imagined things, and it was a source of endless embarrassment. I would be standing there, amazed at the sight of Rob and one of his workers rushing by with an ungainly plank that had just popped out of a steam box, and some guy would stick a microphone in my face, asking how I had come up with this idea. One particular night before visiting the boat, I was more restless than usual and could not sleep. Harry Smith from CBS was going to interview Rob and me. Marian had said that I needed to be able to answer all the questions about why I was doing this and plug Lands' End at the same time. I woke Lisa up with all my worrying, and she asked me to tell her why I was going. I rambled, "I think it's many things, from the thrill to living out my imagination to only knowing how to write about something only if I've experienced it to learning something new to . . ." She suggested I narrow it down. During the interview, though, I just made bad jokes. I felt as though Harry had decided that I was still a child. He asked me if I thought the whole thing was crazy. I stuttered and then just waited for the interview to end. I was furious but not sure why. What did Harry Smith matter? Did he really think I was crazy? Did he think that I would actually answer, "Yes, I think the whole thing is crazy"? Actually, I normally would have said yes, but I had been specifically coached not to say this. What did it matter if I did not sound as though I had all the answers? Not much, really, except that Lands' End had put in a lot of money to "make my dream come true," as it was being reported, and the project could not sound like a lark. The publicist and the Lands' End marketing representative assigned to me had devised a serious-sounding title for the project, Viking Voyage 1000, and I was supposed to live up to my logo. Also, at some point in the very near future the crew I was gathering would be trusting their lives to the voyage.

That night, as I lay in my bed at the Viking Motor Inn outside

Bath, Maine, I could not help but laugh at the scene Rob had caused by telling Harry Smith that he called the boat *The Kevorkian*. Nothing I had mumbled on camera really mattered after that. In another classic example of Rob's timing, he had come shuffling over just as my interview ended and joked about Bob Miller, who was working on a frame. "Yeah, I've gotta watch Bob. He likes to make a heavy boat. I just have to remember to go over and remind him now and then or else . . . ha, ha, ha, *ha!*"

Bob, however, was about the only person who reassured me that things would turn out okay. He would look up at me and smile, usually at a critical moment. Bob had been an instructor at the Apprenticeshop and, compared to Rob, he seemed dependable, or at least sane. Whereas Rob was a loose cannon, Bob seemed grounded. While he liked to joke, he did not scare me and Russell the same way Rob did.

The next day I posed for photographs. I bent over planking or inspected framing, as if I knew what I was doing. It felt awful. Serious skilled work was being accomplished all around me—Rob had six builders hired by this point—and there I was, pretending. During a break, I talked to Deidre Whitehead, a new employee. She was heating handmade iron rivets and roves until they turned blue and then dipping them in a near-boiling mixture of pine tar, linseed oil, and turpentine. It was the same mixture, albeit with the ingredients in a different ratio, that Deidre, others, and even I had slathered onto the growing boat every week. The pine tar smelled divine.* Reeking of ancient fires and long days spent in the outdoors, its odor was more possessive than the earthy aroma of a hay-strewn barn. A single whiff made knees buckle with longing—to go to sea, sing a chantey, curl up with a loved one, or attempt whatever you might desire.

Deidre explained to me that she had to get the rivets and roves hot enough or else the tar mixture simply stuck to the outside of the metal rather than being absorbed by it. She heated the metal bits over a propane stove, transferred them to a Fry Daddy basket, dipped them in the bubbling tar mixture, and then set them over an empty drywall bucket to dry. She was doing this outside Rob's shop,

---

* The tar is extracted from pine by heating or partially burning the wood. When the finished product is mixed with the linseed oil and turpentine, it helps make wood and other materials in a boat water resistant.

where the thermometer registered fifteen degrees. "If the tar isn't hot enough, it cools the metal too fast and it doesn't absorb the tar. I tried to do this when it was ten below and it just didn't work. . . . It really makes you appreciate the practice of pouring hot tar from the battlements. You would die from the smell alone." Obviously, not everyone felt the same way I did about the scent of the tar.

I asked Deidre if it was okay to write about what she had been saying. "Yeah, sure," she responded. "But can I ask you something? Who are you?"

I laughed and said, "That's my boat." Immediately I was embarrassed for having said it. Someone had said it to me the day before, and I guess I was trying it out. Russell overheard.

"Don't mind him," he said, clicking away. "He's become a megalomaniac."

One nice thing that occurred during this visit was that I found three more crew members. John Gardner, a graduate of the Apprenticeshop, had started working for Rob over the winter and, according to Rob, really wanted to go on the voyage. John was not very demonstrative, however. I watched him around the boatyard. A short, strong, good-looking guy, he seemed very confident working on the boat. His trim black hair was perfectly in place, and although his clothes had stains from work, they were tidy. We talked very briefly and all he really said was, "It sounds like it's going to be a good trip." I don't know if it was out of desperation, intimidation by his silence, or a belief that he might be needed for boat repair if Rob was incapacitated from seasickness, but I found myself telling him he was a crew member.

Another guy I chose to join the crew was Homer Williams. I immediately liked Homer for his name alone and for the fact that he was only eighteen. He had been recommended to me yet again by a friend of a friend, and although he was from a small town in Michigan, I was able to meet up with him in Maine because he was about to crew a yacht delivery to Florida. We met for about an hour at a ferry landing outside of Portland. His long, scraggly brown hair was kept in check by a ponytail. Another longhair. At first he seemed laconic, and I worried, *Uh-oh, stoner*, but his eyes lit up when we talked about sailing. He had owned his first boat when he was seven and had been sailing ever since. It was an instinctive thing for him, like chugging a Bud is for other kids his age—not that Homer was not good at that too. Despite his youth, Homer would prove himself to be one of our most competent crew members, and I was never sorry that I impulsively invited him after such a brief meeting.

My last recruit was Doug Cabot, a drummer from Boston. A friend of Andy, the navigator, Doug was dying to go on the trip. Right there was a strike against him. By this point, anybody who was really interested in going seemed crazy to me. After the CBS piece aired, they were advancing from every biosphere project in the world to get to me. However, I consented to a meeting with Doug at Rob's boatyard, where Doug arrived one morning in his ancient VW Bug. He hopped out of his car in what I thought were too-hip clothes, although I can't even recall what they were. The next two things I noticed about him were his long sideburns and his intense gaze. I think the first thing he said to me was, "I really, really want to go." I was instantly convinced that he really, really was a wacko.

However, as we walked around the boat talking about the project and quietly watching the men at work, he seemed pleasant enough. He told me that one of his strengths was his ability to get along with other people. By this time I had chosen nine of the twelve-man crew, and I just wanted to get it over with. I talked to Andy about him later and he spoke very highly of Doug, which was to be expected, since they had been best friends since high school. I asked Doug to go, hoping that if all else failed, he could at least drum out a decent rowing rhythm.

With that settled, I finally turned my full attention to finding a captain. Admittedly I had put this decision off for the longest time because I did not really want one. What was the point of putting this whole thing together and then handing it over after all the preparations, saying, "Here. It's yours. I'll just go along"?

As I very well knew, the point was survival. So, despite my secret desires, I had to find a captain, and fast. Desperate, I called the Hurricane Island Outward Bound School in Rockland, Maine. Hurricane Island puts its students in pulling boats—open wooden craft powered by sail and/or oars. I thought one of their instructors would fit in perfectly on the knarr. I was transferred to a kind woman named Jane St. Claire. I told her about the project, and, perhaps hearing the anguish in my voice, she actually gave it some thought. "I think I know the guy for you. He does, um, things like this. Last year he captained a whaling boat up in Alaska. His name is Terry Moore."

Soon afterward, Terry and I spoke. He sounded reserved but interested. I explained what I was doing. There were a lot of silences in our conversation. *Good*, I thought, *he is considering things*. I was right, and we soon met at a deli in Bath on one of my visits to Maine.

Terry is tall—6'4"—and ascetically skinny but quite strong. That was the first thing I noticed. I'm 6'1" and am not used to feeling short. He was a Peace Corps volunteer in Micronesia. He has sailed since childhood and crossed the Atlantic twice. He has waning red hair and a lot of freckles, and he does not particularly like cold weather.

I wanted to like Terry immediately, and in many ways it was easy. He was quite frank and very sincere in learning about the project. Like an earlier prospect for captain, he had a lot of reservations, but he was also excited. This made me like him even more.

He told me he did not want a chase boat, something a lot of people had been urging. "If we think we're going to need a chase boat, then we should not be out there in the first place," he explained. We talked about equipment for two hours, everything from cookstoves to anchors. He told me many things I did not know and some that I did. He insisted that we would need modern navigational equipment, not radar or depth finders but more basic items like a compass, charts, and a handheld GPS device for backup. In my fund-raising proposal I had written: "I will not use a sextant or a compass and certainly not a modern satellite global positioning system. I want to be as true to the Viking spirit as possible." He had read this and seen some of the publicist's press releases, and he was concerned that I did not know what I was getting us into. I tried to make it clear that I had learned a bit since writing the proposal, that I was willing to make a few concessions to modernity, and that the proposal had been more of a tool to rally people's interest and support. I never intended it to serve as an exact guideline for the voyage.

His willingness to share responsibility and have us solve problems as a group won me over. "I feel uncomfortable calling myself captain because of what most people think that means. I think of myself as a facilitator . . . but also a good leader." I had been afraid of getting stuck with a control freak, since there are so many out there on the water, but Terry seemed pretty loose in this regard. I did worry that he might be too cautious. This was certainly not a formulaic Outward Bound program. Would he be able to dive right in and get going?

Meanwhile, Terry was worried there was not enough time to pull off the voyage in the coming summer and that we were way behind schedule in getting equipment. I could tell he was worried about the crew. Most of them did not have the skills that he thought would be necessary, except for maybe Rob and John Gardner. In case of problems with the boat, their skills would obviously prove invaluable. "I'm interested in seeing the choices you made," Terry said, regarding the crew. "I think I can tell you have a good sense of people, but it'll be interesting to see what kind of sailors they are, since that isn't something you know much about."

At the end of the meeting, we stood outside in eighteen-degree weather in our shirtsleeves, shivering. "How should we leave things?" he asked.

"Well, I'd like to leave things saying I'd like you to be the captain. So what do you think?"

He paused slightly. "I think that sounds good." When other boys were doodling preposterous race cars equipped with cannons and invisible force fields, Terry had been absentmindedly scrawling out square-rigged ships braving the seven seas. This was his chance.

I felt like hugging him but restrained myself.

By the time Terry came on board, an entire Viking village had grown around me. Lands' End was creating a Web site that the crew and I would attempt to supply with journal entries and pictures from the Viking boat. Rob had as many as twenty people working on the boat at a time. Gerry Galuza, the blacksmith who had been making rivets for us, and his assistant pounded out more than three thousand iron rivets altogether. Nat Wilson, a traditional sailmaker who has made sails for the USS *Constitution* and other replicas, began the sail for the knarr. I wrote my first article for the Lands' End catalog. The crew, now all assembled on paper except for one open slot, wanted to know what was going on—to be informed about the boat's progress, and help out if possible. Meanwhile, Terry was going to choose the twelfth crew member, someone to make him feel more comfortable.

In March, a little more than a month before the boat would be launched, Terry, Andy, and I met in Alexandria, Virginia. Andy, as had been evident from our previous conversations, was really looking for an adventure in this project. He was, I could not help but noticing, yet another longhair. He had played a guitar on the streets in Spain to make money and been a cabbie in Boston. His approach to the voyage and life was about as opposite as one could get from Terry's, which was cautious and sober.

Each of us was supposed to arrive at the meeting with a list of things he thought needed to be done. Andy had not brought a list but had a lot of questions and ideas in his head. I had a list about a page long. Terry handed over three and a half pages. We spent an entire day discussing the items on his list—what was needed and why. As the day progressed, Andy and Terry would disagree over the necessity of many items that Andy found too modern, and at one point Andy blurted out his real feelings: "I think we should just go up there like the Vikings and forget about all of this modern equipment!" Although Terry remained composed, I could feel him wince internally. "There is nothing I would like better," he said, "if, like Vikings, we had been sailing these boats our entire lives. But we haven't."

I convinced myself that the balance between these two personalities would be perfect—one being supremely cautious, the other worrisomely carefree.

Everything regarding this project was an attempt to achieve balance or an attempt to recover from a loss of balance, I was learning—not only with my crew but also with my family. Lisa was feeling abandoned and more and more concerned about my well-being. On top of this, we were going to have another baby at the end of August. It was not the best timing, of course, but since it had taken four or five months to get pregnant the first time, we had thought it would take as long the second. We were wrong. Only if we were very lucky would I be home in time for the baby's birth. Things had been chaotic before, combining the fledgling family with the fledgling Viking project, but in retrospect that had merely been the peaceful lull before the all-out berserker attack.

At the end of March I flew home to West Virginia to an empty house. Lisa, the girls, and our two dogs had headed for Maine two days earlier. I had long since quit my job as postmaster over a dispute concerning my dogs' presence in the post office, and we were moving up to Phippsburg, a town just ten minutes from Rob's boatyard. We would live there for two months to put the project in order and perform sea trials after the boat was launched. The boat was supposed to be ready in three weeks. As I packed my bags, Marian the publicist called and among other things told me, "Hodding, this is going to be bigger than you ever imagined. I'm going to make you a star!" I told her all I really wanted was to be with my family.

I caught up with them in New York. Lisa was understandably harried but happy to see me. We began driving to Maine the next day but got caught in a heavy snowstorm, with high winds and blinding snow. We barely made it to a Super 8 Motel in Sturbridge, Massachusetts, before the state police closed the highway. We suffered through a sleepless night of fidgety children and dogs and then slogged our way north on partially cleared roads. Since the snow had continued through the night, the storm was heralded as the worst ever in April. We arrived at our rental home near dusk, exhausted but relieved. The house, surrounded by evergreens and enormous boulders, faced the mouth of the Kennebec. It was stunning but also a potential deathtrap for the twins. We furiously unpacked and set up barriers around the woodstove and the open, second-story landing. Our dogs, Huck and Willa, ran off. We wanted to give them a chance to burn off the last few days but worried they might get lost. I drove slowly down the unfamiliar dirt road, calling to them every few minutes. I could not find them.

We went out to a quick dinner with the publicist. Marian had rented a nearby house to be on hand for the launching and the subsequent sailing trials. We went over the things I should try to talk about in interviews scheduled for the next day. When we returned home, Huck and Willa still had not come back. We were too exhausted to look for them anymore that night and hoped that someone would call, since Lisa had put new tags on them. We fell asleep by ten o'clock.

In the middle of the night someone called. I nearly tumbled down the stairs to reach the phone but did not make it in time. As I crawled back in bed Lisa mumbled about dreaming someone had called earlier about our dogs being on his porch. She fell quickly back asleep. I could not, however, since I was now wide awake worrying about the dogs and the Viking project. How was Rob going to finish the boat in time?

In the morning there was a message on the answering machine. Lisa had not been dreaming. "This is Richard Lemont at Baxters Head," he said, and gave his number. "Your dog has been causing problems at my dad's. He's on the porch and I want to know what you want me to do with him." We sighed in relief. At least one of the dogs had been found. Lisa called but only got a machine. She left an apologetic message asking for directions. No one called back.

We went to the boatyard to look over the vessel. I called the Lemonts again. No answer. Lisa called again at noon and left another apologetic message. No one replied. While we were having lunch back home, a woman called on behalf of the local animal control office. She told me there had been a report that our dogs had caused problems at John Lemont's farm and killed a cat. The farmer had shot and killed both of our dogs. I was to meet her at four-thirty.

Lisa began to wail, and we hugged for a long while. We had rescued Huck from an animal shelter when we first started living together four years earlier. He was a goofy, lovable dog. The mayor of Thurmond, West Virginia, had named him honorary sheriff, even giving him a framed notice to that effect. Willa had simply adored Huck; she had been in love with him ever since the day we found Willa abandoned alongside the river that flowed through Thurmond.

I knew I should go thrash this man, but I could not act. I felt impotent. What if he shot me too? What should I do? Marian told me I had to keep a low profile, that causing a scene would hinder the project. We met the woman from animal control at the end of our dirt road that afternoon. As I carried the dogs' stiff bodies into our van, I could not help looking at them and then I could not stop crying. They had been our friends and constant companions.

The shooting became a very public event because of the Viking project. No one seemed to understand it. A local fifth-grade class adopted us, sending a heartbreaking letter lamenting our dogs' deaths. Neighbors brought us food and flowers. Letters poured in from around the state. "We are not like this," nearly all of them said. We even received a call of sympathy from Governor Angus King, a kind man and adventure buff who had been following our project in the papers.

We continued on. I did interviews and bought equipment for the voyage. I was buying things like flares, a kerosene stove, life jackets, screwdrivers, cutlery, sponges, flashlights, and manual bilge pumps. A real Viking boat would have had two slaves whose only jobs were to bail the boat with a wooden bailer, but, as can be seen, I was making concessions right and left. Meanwhile, and from this point forth, Lisa was doing the important work. She was holding our family together. She had quit her job and set everything aside for my Viking Project.

But Huck and Willa were dead. We could not escape it. From an autopsy, it turned out that Lemont had shot the dogs from behind. They had not been leaping at him or anything else, as he had complained. They also had not killed his cat. He had shot it himself after Huck and Willa had roughed it up, as they should not have done. The animal control officer quit her job over the case because she felt the town constable was covering things up. The local paper mocked the handling of the case, but the truth was that Maine has screwed-up, contradictory laws on shooting dogs. The DA, however, did eventually get Lemont to plead no contest to one count of cruelty to animals. He was convicted of this misdemeanor and had to pay a relatively small fine.

Chapter Four

Rob had ten full-time employees working furiously to finish the
boat by the twenty-third of April, launch day, and was making last-
minute decisions that should have been made weeks if not months
earlier. His hair was grayer, and he never seemed to sleep. He spent
no time with his wife. Occasionally I would find him sleeping in his
car in the middle of the day, although his house was right next to
the boat shop. Others swore Rob could and did sleep while standing or with his eyes open. His level of commitment to this project
had reached epic proportions, the stuff of myths. "Why, I saw Rob
Stevens fitting a scarph at three in the morning, dangling from the
ceiling with one hand, while pine-tarring the hull with his feet. . . ."

The boat was coming together, though. What only a few weeks
earlier had resembled a salvaged wreck now looked like a viable
Viking vessel. Signs were posted at the boatyard asking people not
to talk to the builders, but the flurry of activity alone caused most
visitors to hold their tongues. Yet people still came down in the
hundreds to watch this Viking boat be built. The scene reminded
me of *Mike Mulligan and the Steam Shovel*, a book I adored as a kid.
Much like Rob and his builders, Mike and his steam shovel, Mary
Ann, were outdated and outgunned by modern machinery—unless
people watched them. Then the pair worked furiously. On their last

project, more and more people came to watch, urged on by a little boy who wanted to see Mike and his steam shovel succeed in digging a basement and foundation in one day. Steam and dirt filled the air. No one could see much near the end of the day, but before the sun set, they had finished the job.

I think all his visitors did the same for Rob. As the deadline approached and more and more people came down to watch, Rob gained the strength and stamina of five men. As I watched from a corner of the shop, steaming planks that had to be quickly fitted into place whizzed by. Sawdust was kicked into the air. Someone would shout out in mock pain and then cuss. It was a swirl of action and fun spurred on by reverent onlookers.

It was good to see so many people admiring the boatbuilders' work. Skills had been taught to them that were in danger of being lost forever. The more people came to watch, the more likely it was that these skills might endure—and the more likely it was that the boat might be finished on time. I, however, always felt in the way whenever I visited the site. Bob Miller, Rob's friend from the Apprenticeshop, invariably took time to make me feel welcome, and so would Scott Smith, who had been working on the boat since the beginning. But I could not shake the feeling that I was adopting a baby from parents who no longer wanted to let go.

Four days before the launch, the builders were fitting in the last lodging knee—a wooden support for the hull and crossbeam. There were still many small things to be done and even a few big ones, but it looked as though they were going to finish. This was the end. From a boom box in the middle of the shop B. B. King cried out, "The thrill is gone," and a chill ran up my spine. Rob would spout off about how sick he was of the boat, but you could see it was not the case. It was apparent to everyone but him.

This was one of the moments I had been working toward for over two years, but the thrill was certainly gone, shot out of me with our dogs' last breaths, with gut-wrenching decisions made by Lisa and me at late hours—decisions about what to do with the dogs' remains, about whether or not we could take an afternoon off to be together, about all the everyday issues that felt as though they were beneath a magnifying glass for the world to inspect—with repressed anticipation over our expected child, and with the complexities of overseeing a half-million-dollar project. I tried my best to hide this from Terry, Rob, everybody. It did not seem right to be morose surrounded by so much work and effort.

Rob launched the boat on the twenty-sixth of April, only a few days behind schedule. Nearly a thousand people showed up despite the launch not being a publicized event. It took two days to roll her about two hundred yards to the low tide mark. We had debated asking for a hundred volunteers and shouldering it down with rollers, but in the end Rob opted for heavy machinery. He used his Model A engine as a winch and, with the help of a few friends, even kept it running. For a traditional wooden-boat builder, he has an unexpected love of power tools.

Among the many well-wishers, a few kooks appeared too. Nancy Knarr from Virginia drove up to Maine and insisted that she should be a crew member because of her last name. She bossed people around and made sure she took part in the launch. She was far more possessive of the boat and project than I. Terry and I mostly sidestepped her request to become a crew member, but in the end she understood we did not want her. A few weeks later she wrote an urgent letter to Lands' End, pressing them not to let us make the voyage. In her humble opinion, we were a disaster waiting to happen.

Launch day, though, could not be ruined by one person's behavior. It was like a huge family picnic. Our twin girls, Anabel and Eliza, poured dirt on each other's head. Dogs wandered in and out of everything. Children played tag. Hundreds of conversations bubbled to life. Homemade sandwiches were passed around. There was lots of back-slapping and hugging. It was a spontaneous celebration, and it lifted Lisa's and my spirits. The celebration had really begun the night before at the boat shop, where Rob had thrown a party for the builders. Bob Miller stole the show, lampooning both Rob and me. He dragged Rob out and dressed him in ridiculous Arctic travel gear, including a metal bucket for a helmet and a soup pot full of lichen because I had written that we would be eating lichen, just as the Vikings had. After much laughter at Rob's expense, who looked even sorrier than Don Quixote, Bob said with his face shining red and his eyes welling with emotion, "I just have to say this has been the best boatbuilding project I have ever worked on."

Finally, on launch day, the tide began to rise around the boat. A

RUSSELL KAYE

Birth of a knarr

helicopter circled above. The crowd grew noisier. A few of us clambered on board. Others came over to ask if they could get on too—friends, boatbuilders' wives, family, and total strangers. By the time she was actually floating, with only a few spigotlike leaks between the laps, which were quickly patched with cotton, more than sixty people were crowded on board.

Lisa bashed an unscored bottle of champagne against the stem, and the crowd roared appropriately as glass and bubbles scattered across the bow. We hugged and kissed. A reporter screamed out for the boat's name. I answered, *"Snorri,"* even though I was under orders from Marian, the project's publicist, not to. We were having a naming ceremony in a month that Lands' End executives would attend. The name was suddenly supposed to be a secret, although I had been telling people for months that I intended to name her after Snorri, who, according to *The Greenlanders Saga*, was the first European child born in North America, daughter of a Viking woman named Gudrid.

We decided to row out to the middle of the harbor with everyone still on board. Terry called out instructions, and *Snorri* glided across the surface like a carefree water bug. I rowed next to a man named Dean Plager. He had contacted Terry and me months earlier, asking to be a crew member after seeing the CBS story about us. We had a full crew by then, but Dean decided to come up for the launch anyway.

It seemed that rowing *Snorri* would be no problem. Of course, she did not have a mast or the twelve tons of ballast that would bring her down to the optimal waterline for sailing, but she still glided across the water very smoothly.

To my surprise and chagrin, a few more weeks would pass before we could prove that *Snorri* could sail.

Meanwhile, Terry, who was spreading cautionary words to all who would listen, scared the hell out of Russell. "I hope everyone understands that this voyage is not a well-organized and trained event—that everything is being done by the seat of our pants," Terry would say, and then I would reassure Russell that Terry was too used to Outward Bound, where everything was done the same way year after year. One night Terry and I had Russell try on an immersion suit—the superthick neoprene suits that allow a person to survive Arctic waters for days—to prove to him that there were things he could do to save himself in an emergency at sea. The immersion suit would allow him to live up to four days in forty-degree water. Our efforts had an opposite effect on Russell, however, and he seemed to be even more on the verge of backing out.

Other problems piled up. Rob had not finished the mast. The rigging, according to Rob and Terry, had not been served, seized, or whipped properly.* Meanwhile, Terry said things to Marian that made her believe that he did not think we would be sailing in

---

* To keep the end of a line from fraying requires a proper whipping (no, not that kind of whipping), which consists of making a very tight wrapping with twine or marline around a line, finishing it off with a small number of stitches to keep the wrapping tight. You then cut the rope next to the whipping and it does not fray. A seizing is performed with marline and is used to create an eye (or loop) in a line. Serving is the wrapping of marline around rigging to prevent chafe and make the line stronger. There are numerous ways to perform these tasks, but to learn the right way read Hervey Garret Smith's *The Arts of the Sailor*.

Greenland that summer. She then decided to tell Lands' End this without telling me first. That took a few weeks to straighten out.

While Rob fiddled with the mast and whatever else was holding us up, Terry, Dean Plager, still hanging around after the launch, and I washed ballast rocks and began loading them by the bucketful into *Snorri*. On average, the rocks I had ordered were each about the size of a football and were caked with dirt. Terry said we needed to clean off the rocks before loading them, otherwise dirt and muck would gum up the bilge and limber holes (gaps between the frame and planks that allow water to run freely through the boat). It was an awful task, especially since we needed more than twelve tons of the rocks as ballast. The frigid ocean water that we used burned our hands. We carried the rocks in drywall buckets because we had to wind through a maze of lobster pots, dry-docked boats, and trucks to get from the rock pile to where *Snorri* was docked. Each bucket of rocks weighed roughly sixty-six pounds, and we eventually carried a total of 364 loads through the maze.

We were able to load only twelve buckets of clean rocks the first afternoon.

We were still washing rocks when the rest of the crew showed up on May 1. While the mast was stepped, or mounted in place, on the day they arrived, we still had eleven tons of ballast to wash and load, and *Snorri* needed to be rigged properly. All along Rob had said he did not want to be responsible for rigging the boat—that Terry should have to do it—but since he was the only one who knew anything practical about *Snorri*, he ended up being responsible for it. I felt that each day that passed without sailing was my punishment for not bringing someone over from Scandinavia to rig the boat. Per Weddegjerde, the captain from the museum in Norway, was coming over soon, but *Snorri* would be rigged by then, for better or worse.

The crew slept on *Snorri* for the first time on May second. That is, everybody but Russell, Rob, and Elias, the Greenlander

Palm-and-Needle Whipping

crew member. Russell had suddenly disappeared. Elias would not be arriving for another week or so, and Rob . . . well, Rob was another story. Although he had previously committed to going, now he was not sure he wanted to be a part of things and only came on board for an initial meeting. So there were nine of us on board the first night, including Trevor Harris, a friend of Terry's from Outward Bound whom Terry had recently asked to join us as our twelfth crew member.

I had asked Terry and my friend John Abbott, the wiry, long-haired wilderness instructor, to develop some team-building exercises. They had both been Outward Bound instructors, and I felt Abbott would put everyone at ease. He was a good listener with a self-mocking sense of humor. Abbott, after reading a bit on the Vikings, decided we needed to hold a *thing*. A Viking *thing* (pronounced "teeng") was a gathering of free men and women to settle disputes, make legislative decisions, and consult on any matters pertaining to the community. *Things* originated as simple gatherings but grew to great governing importance throughout Scandinavia. In Iceland, the Althing, a legislative body made up of thirty-six men, ruled the nation starting in 930, making it the only republic in the medieval world. One Icelandic law that originated from the Althing might explain why our knarr had no figurehead on the bow: "Men should not have a ship with a figurehead at sea, but if they had, they must remove the head before coming in sight of land, and not sail to land with gaping heads and yawning jaws, so that the spirits of the land grow frightened of them."

Terry asked everyone to say why they wanted to go on the trip and what their concerns were about the trip.

We stood or sat in a circle in the dark. A few of us wore headlamps, but Terry complained about getting light shined in his eyes. At first it sounded like he was whining, but his explanation highlighted my ignorance. He said that the lights should have a red lens on them so that no one's night vision was hampered; "It's just a pet peeve of mine."

Everyone was feeling congenial, and although some of the guys felt a little uncomfortable with speaking in a group, especially about their worries or feelings, others seized the opportunity. Before everyone spoke, Abbott and Terry explained that we would attempt

RUSSELL KAYE

1st year crew
1st row (closest row), left to right: Rob Stevens, Trevor Harris,
Elias Larsen, John Gardner, Homer Williams
2nd row (middle), left to right: Hodding Carter, Andy Marshall,
Jan Calamita, Doug Cabot, Terry Moore, Dean Plager
3rd row (back): John Abbott

to hold a *thing* every day so that everyone could express himself and not hold anything in, especially grudges. Also, the *thing*s would help keep our decisions democratic.

So, who was this crew? Who would entrust their lives to a project leader who knew nothing about sailing and a captain who had never even set foot on the type of vessel we were about to sail in some of the most treacherous waters in the world?

They had all sent me résumés, but the vast majority were unmarried and without steady jobs. They were all college graduates except our youngest crew member, who was just out of high school, and a few of them held graduate degrees.

I think the common thread among all of us, except maybe Trevor, Terry's friend, was that they simply yearned for adventure. As a crew, they were willing to take on whatever task was handed them, and they did not need or want to know every little detail before committing.

Homer Williams was only eighteen, but his fluffy beard and long hair made him look something like an ageless mountain man. He had been sailing his own boat for eleven years and had loved his recent sailing experience to Florida: "I was introduced to thirty-foot seas accompanied by sixty-plus-mile-an-hour southwest winds. I weathered this trip with gusto and I am hungry for more!" he had written me. It had probably been the picture of himself in a faux Viking helmet, grinning like a demonic Cheshire cat, that had convinced me. Homer's only flaw was his impatience, although at times even that would prove to be fairly amusing.

"It just sounds like a lot of fun," Homer said during our *thing*. He seemed to think Terry's suggestion that we say why we were going was odd. Who would not want to go? He did have one concern, however: "I'm a little worried about being a part of a group, working together. I haven't done that very much. Don't play head games with me. If you don't like something I'm doing, then say so. Tap me on the shoulder. Just be blunt with me."

Andy, the navigator, who had already butted heads with Terry back in Alexandria, made it immediately evident that his and Terry's styles were very different. He talked about wanting to go purely for the adventure. His résumé had been full of facts and dates, including his years as quartermaster for the U.S. Coast Guard cutter *Spar*, but he clearly enjoyed the more intangible aspects of life. He liked being the impractical rebel to Terry's level-headed, orderly type. "I don't feel very comfortable with the word *team*—it seems too corporate—but I am interested in our unifying," he said. I wondered what was making them clash so early, but I did my best to ignore it. I wanted them both to be on the voyage.

After I talked about my reasons for doing the trip and my growing interest in the Vikings, John Abbott explained that I had asked him years before. I knew he was a good skier and climber and a relaxed outdoorsman. According to his résumé, he had also been "a dedicated adventurer since childhood. Legend has it he ate a whole plate of lima beans without so much as wincing or complaining, at the tender age of six."

Abbott played class clown at times, but that night he explained that part of the reason he wanted to go was work-related. "I'm in the risk management business," he said, as he stumbled backward over his own pack. "This was something that I simply could not pass up. It can only increase my skills. I have some questions and concerns that I still want answers to, but Hodding has done a good job of reassuring me." Abbott joked about wanting to play like a violent Viking, but it was clear to nearly everybody that he was a dyed-in-the-fleece tree hugger.

Terry cleared his throat and announced, "This trip, to me, isn't about being a Viking. I don't really care about that. It's more, for me, about traveling to a far place of the world and seeing what it has to offer." He brought up many of his concerns, including safety and about us all learning how to sail the boat well enough to make the voyage a practical possibility.

The résumé of Doug, the drummer, was entitled "The Man Who Would Be Viking" and had been padded with outdoor skills that I would later learn were something of a fabrication. But then again, I had hardly even looked at the résumés beyond a cursory glance. After my initial fear of Doug's intensity had worn off, I could tell he would put his heart and back into anything that was required of him. That night he said he was scared about going. "But that is one of the reasons I want to go," he explained. "I want to try and approach that fear."

Despite being a city boy, Jan Calamita, our lawyer/cook, has a sturdiness that is very handy away from civilization. He had recently written me a long letter arguing why he should be a crew member, although his position had been safe since he first signaled his willingness to suffer beside me. "I confess I know little of Viking history; my fifth-grade report was on the Cree Indians," he wrote. "You might think that my recent time in Iceland would have served to further my Norse education, but alas . . . Icelanders are more interested in bad-mouthing the Norwegians and making fun of the Inuit than talking serious Norse history. Still, the trip was not a complete loss. I have developed a strong taste for dried fish and hot dogs dressed with deep-fried onion chips and mayonnaise. . . . The truth is, Hodding, that I am of the firm belief that the conscious failure to seize the opportunities of life is about as close to sinning against yourself as you can get." The night of the *thing*, Jan admitted he did not have much sailing experience, and that caused him much worry. "But I am already feeling more at ease."

John Gardner's résumé, just like John in person, had been brief and to the point. After college he had worked in billing systems, whatever that means, and as a branch manager for a health-care benefits company in Illinois. This had driven him a little crazy, and when the company transferred him to California, he took off for Hawaii instead. He became a bartender and surf bum. Gardner is a very handsome guy who looks directly into people's eyes. Both women and men get crushes on him. He and Rob were still in their boatbuilder mode and did not have much to say that night. Gardner only said, "I started building the boat last winter with Rob, and I want to continue on." Nothing more. He really did not like the *thing*. It was too touchy-feely for him.

Rob said he was going because he had some concerns about the safety of the boat and he wanted to see how she sailed. I was a little concerned with how separate Rob and Gardner were acting, but I hoped time would take care of that.

Trevor Harris, the short, blond instructor who Terry knew from Outward Bound, seemed very much at ease working and talking with an unacquainted group. It was quickly apparent why Terry had asked him to come on the voyage: He was confident and levelheaded, and our safety was his biggest concern. He had already organized the crew house, making sure that everyone worked together at the various chores. His industriousness could only be helpful in the coming months, but at the same time, he did not seem to fit in. Some of the guys were already complaining that he was bossing them around too much and that he did not appear to have any interest in why we were undertaking the voyage.

There was something forced about our first *thing*, but at least it seemed to let everyone know whom and what we were dealing with.

About half of us, including me, had horrible dreams that night. In one, I was trapped in a room and could not get out no matter what I tried to do.

We had to get the boat sailing. I had wanted us to be sailing by April 27 or 28, and May 3 had arrived without even leaving the harbor. We worked hard together, loading ballast, hardening rigging, building kitchen boxes, and constructing extra platforms to store gear out of the bilge.

During this time, conversations I had with others revealed that my own position in the project was changing. I was only minimally aware of it because of all the things I had to do just to balance many competing interest: the boatbuilders, the crew, Terry, Lands' End, the shipping companies that would take *Snorri* from Boston to Greenland, Marian, the media, and my family.

Driving to the airport one day, Jan told me he was wiped out.

"Yeah, the rocks were tiring," I replied.

"Oh, no. They weren't so bad. I spent the whole day worrying about our safety. I was scared senseless. But spending time with Terry made me feel much better. He's very reassuring and competent. He has a lot of common sense."

I got the implication.

Another day, in the car again, this time to buy jet fuel for our stove because it would burn more cleanly than regular kerosene, Terry's friend Trevor said to me, apropos of nothing, "So what do you see as your role in this whole thing?" I nearly ran off the road. What was my role? What was my *role*? This was my project. My role was what it had always been. How could he not see that? I was dumbfounded. In retrospect, this was one of the better questions I was ever asked concerning the voyage. I had told a number of people that I did not want to be called the "expedition leader," and sometimes I tried to establish myself as just another crew member. This was ridiculous, of course, because judging how I responded to Trevor, it was clear that I felt a great ownership of the entire project, not just of its implementation. This unresolved issue would cause endless worries for me and problems for the entire project.

Then one day, as a group of boatbuilders and I were working on

Snorri, Rob asked for someone to lower the yard. The yard, a wooden pole attached along the top edge of the sail, probably weighs a third of a ton. Lowering the yard requires uncleating the halyard from a belaying pin and then gradually letting the line slip through your fingers. Since I was the closest person to the halyard and knew what it was, I grabbed it.

"Hodding!" Rob yelled, surrounded by his employees and friends. "It's not that I don't trust you, but I don't. Deidre, come over here and let this halyard down, would you?" Everyone laughed and I obliged, smiling but smoldering.

By the time Per Weddegjerde arrived on May 8, I was feeling worn down, but at least the boat was ready to sail. His arrival seemed like a godsend. In our first conversation, driving home from the airport while snacking on some barbecued ribs, he cleared up why *Snorri* was not down to her waterline. He said his knarr and *Saga Siglar* each weighed six tons without ballast, not the twelve tons Rob thought *Snorri* weighed. The total displacement (overall weight) should be twenty-five tons. In other words, we were about six or seven tons short on ballast. "And remember, Hodding, trim is the most important thing—the balancing of the ballast. If you do not have the right trim, it cannot sail directly."

His words struck true in more ways than one, and his arrival helped me regain some of my own balance. He took some of the edge off Terry and Rob. I think he made them feel that not every single thing rested on their shoulders—which it never had, but given their opinion of me, they had believed it to be so. Or maybe it was simply that he knew more than the rest of us but had nothing to prove—a stark contrast to everyone else. Per took one walk around the boat and immediately told Rob and me four things that needed changing: move the ballast farther aft, shorten the beitiáss, reposition the cleats on the beitiáss, and rig blocks to tighten down the beitiáss when sailing windward. (The beitiáss is a wooden spar used to hold the leading edge of the sail forward when sailing into the wind. Being slobs, we called it the Betty Ass.)

Per asked when we would sail. I started to answer, and Terry broke in.

"I think it would not be smart to go out until we practice our maneuvers—learn all the moves, reef the sail, et cetera, all at the mooring. The crew knows nothing about this boat. I know that you're itching to go out, but . . ."

"No, no," Per said, "that is smart," although it was clear from his expression that he did not really think so. He did, however, think that *Snorri* was well built. "I hate to say this, but I think this is better than ours. Rob has done a good job—very good. He has done much good with the finish work." While I did not doubt Per's sincerity, I did wonder if maybe the Gammel Dansk, a Danish bitter he had brought with him, was getting to him. "You must have a bit in the morning before sailing. Then after sailing. Before going to bed. And almost anytime."

Later, after we had loaded more ballast, we rowed to *Snorri*'s mooring and raised her sail for the first time. The halyard, made of manila but later switched to Dacron because it was chafing too much, runs from the yard through a sheave near the top of the mast and then down at a small angle to the port quarter. It then runs through two blocks for leverage. I hardly knew what any of these words meant, but I could certainly see that it took two people to raise the sail. One person reaches as high as he can and "sweats" the halyard, pulling down as much line as he can. The other person "tails"—pulls on the line around a belaying pin after it is sweated. At first we simply tried pulling it straight down, but Terry demonstrated that it was much more useful to perform a controlled backward fall. This method required half the energy of pulling straight down and raised the sail just as quickly in the long run.

We could not even raise the sail beyond twelve feet the first go-round because the various lines were too entangled.

We lowered the sail. This takes one person on the halyard who simply eases the line around the belaying pin at an appropriate speed. Appropriate would depend on the conditions, Terry explained. About four or five other crew members gather the sail in on the foredeck, trying to keep it out of the water. It is a good time for getting out any aggressions that might be building because you can whack someone with an elbow by "accident" in the confusion of a thousand square feet of flopping canvas.

We untangled the lines, raised the sail again, and successfully brought it to about six feet below the top of the forty-three-foot-tall spruce mast. We knew that was the perfect height because Per told us so. Terry had started out giving most of the orders, but when our initial attempt to raise the yard had failed, Per had pretty much taken over—in a nice way.

We set up starboard and port tacks while still moored. Each tack requires one person on a sheet and one on a brace on the after-deck and three people on the foredeck to set the tack and the beitiáss. (If this seems confusing, just realize it took a lot of people simply to get the sail in the correct position and that we too were confused.)

I tried my best to learn all these new terms. Take *tack*, for instance. Okay, so a tack was a line that led from the forward edge of the sail and was fed through the beitiáss and then wrapped around a belaying pin on the forwardmost crossbeam. So what was all this stuff about a starboard tack being when the wind blew on the starboard side of the boat? I had looked at sailing books and diagrams of the knarr to gain some sense of these terms ahead of time, but it all bashed about in my head, sometimes confusing me, sometimes clarifying things. Sailors and the people who build sailboats love having their own terminology, even though it often seems pointless. Rob would ask me to hand him the bitter end of, say, the tack. Since there was only one end to the tack (if the tack was what I thought it was), then why bother using the term *bitter end*, which means the end opposite from the knot or bend? I could not very well hand him an end that had been seized near the corner of the sail. At moments like that I had to resist whacking him or Andy Marshall over the head with whatever they had asked for. Andy, who knew his marlinespike seamanship from his Coast Guard days and all the terms that went with it, including the term *marlinespike seamanship*, enjoyed correcting us novices when we called a line a rope. You are not allowed to call anything a rope, unless it is the bolt rope, a rope that is stitched around the perimeter of a sail. However, if the line, I mean rope, does not have a set purpose beyond tripping you up when you run to grab the tack—no, no, I mean the brace—then it can also be called a rope. Aagghh!

Now's a good time for a drawing of the boat:

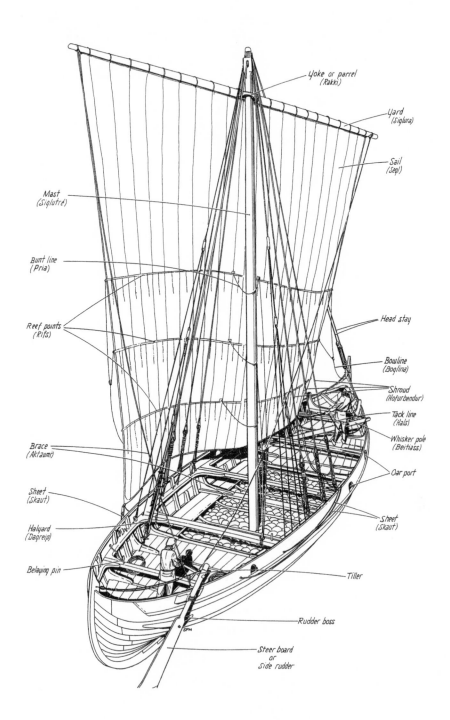

Yoke or parrel
(Rakki)

Yard
(Siglura)

Sail
(Segl)

Mast
(Siglutré)

Bunt line
(Pria)

Reef points
(Rifs)

Head stay

Bowline
(Boglina)

Shroud
(Hofurbendur)

Tack line
(Hals)

Whisker pole
(Beitiass)

Brace
(Aktaumr)

Oar port

Sheet
(Skaut)

Sheet
(Skaut)

Halyard
(Dagreip)

Belaying pin

Tiller

Rudder boss

Steer board
or
Side rudder

Considering my own confusion, it was a good thing that Terry insisted we practice before attempting the real thing, although Per probably could have gotten us through safely.

We sailed the next day, May 9. It was an overcast, wintry day, perfectly matching what many of our subarctic sailing days would be. We rowed out of the narrow inlet behind Hermit Island. It was no longer easy to row *Snorri*—nothing like the unballasted launch day. It took roughly an hour to get a mile from the harbor.

At first everyone except Terry seemed to be delighted with how *Snorri* was sailing. Some of us were giddy, even.

"I like how stable she is," Homer said, sidling up to me. Then he lowered his voice. "But I guess I should wait and say that later. I'm not gonna say it now."

"The boat, she is not sneaking so much into the wind. The tiller is okay. She is sailing fine," Per told me, and then he pulled me over to the mast step, where the mast stands above the keel. "Hear that sound, Hodding. It is very good. Our boat makes the same." It sounded like an unstoppable leak had opened up from the pressure of the forty-three-foot-tall mast. I tried to smile.

Terry stood by the tiller, correcting the helmsman's steering and fiddling with the sheets and braces. Gardner paced around the boat, hidden behind his sunglasses, unsmiling. He was coiling ropes and tossing scraps of wood into the ocean. He was definitely going to be our Captain Tidy. Trevor fixed things, making, for example, a permanent rig for the beitiáss blocks. Andy, our navigator, walked around sounding like a sailor. Doug also walked around the boat, pointing at a line or object and repeating its name to himself. The four of them seemed so restless.

Homer, the youngest crew member, grunted and strained at the merest mention of a task, eager to prove himself useful. Rob spent most of his time lying on the deck, staring at the sail. He was trying not to feel seasick, although there was barely any roll to the sea.

Like Per, the excitement of the moment made me think things were working better than they were. Given all the strange things that had been happening to me lately and some of the discomfort between Rob and me or even Terry and me, I was not feeling as ecstatic as I had once thought I would. But it did feel mighty good to finally be on the water.

Even this feeling, though, would not last long. Once as far out as Terry thought safe, we began tacking back to the harbor. This was the real test. Any old boat can sail downwind. I had even done it in a canoe. Successfully sailing into the wind, however, would set *Snorri* apart from other square-rigged vessels. It might even help explain why the Viking boats dominated the European seas . . . or perhaps not.

At first I was sure that *Snorri* was easily making sixty degrees off the wind, just as all the written material claimed a knarr could do.* I looked at the wind's direction and compared it to the direction the boat was heading. In my head I chuckled at Terry for having been so skeptical. "We'll see," he had said on many occasions. "I have my doubts."

Terry had the last rueful laugh. As the hours passed and we jibed back and forth, we could not make it back to Hermit Island. Part of the problem was that when you jibe you fall off the wind to begin another tack and automatically lose more ground than if you tack—cross through the wind—because you are momentarily headed downwind. We were jibing instead of tacking because it was easier. Also, I had not been taking leeway (the boat's sideways drift) into account when guessing *Snorri*'s point of sail, and we were probably sailing more like seventy-five to eighty degrees off the wind. Even worse, there was something horribly wrong with *Snorri*'s steering abilities. *Snorri* tended to veer toward port. On a starboard tack, we could barely turn the boat. Since the rudder hangs off the starboard quarter and is susceptible to many opposing forces, it was not a huge surprise (to Terry, Rob, and Per) that we were experiencing difficulties on that tack, but since we would be sailing all the way down to Boston at the end of the month to load *Snorri* on a container ship, we had to get all the kinks out immediately.

We tried rowing back to the harbor but could not keep from going backward in a fifteen-knot headwind. We dropped and raised the hundred-pound anchor a few times. The heavy anchor chain rubbed away surprisingly substantial amounts of the sheer plank

---

* Imagine the wind as a line headed straight for you. *Snorri*, I believed, was able to move forward sixty degrees off that wind line. An average modern sailboat will make forty to forty-five degrees off the wind, and an ultramodern racer might be able to sail somewhere in the high twenties. If a sailboat were to try to go directly into the wind (zero degrees), it would stop moving forward.

Rowing

when the entire crew hauled the anchor back on board. Eventually, we resorted to alternately pushing and towing *Snorri* back to the harbor with our inflatable dinghy and its fifteen-horsepower engine. We would not be using the engine on the voyage, but I was glad we had it around for the sea trials.

In my ignorance, I had always assumed that the trials would be more for the crew's sake than for *Snorri's*. The other replicas of Skuldelev Wreck 1 had done okay, and while they had reported some rudder difficulties, we had the lines (designs) for *Saga Siglar's* working rudder. Therefore, I reasoned, our rudder would work. I should have been more skeptical. Wreck 1's rudder had not been found when the boat was dug out of Roskilde Fjord. None of the wrecks actually had their rudders with them, in fact. However, a rudder had been found in Vorså, Denmark, and it was considered to be the best example of a Viking side rudder. The catch with this rudder—there's always a catch, I was learning—was that it was found without a boat and it was not properly preserved. The design of *Saga Siglar's* rudder was based upon this Vorså rudder, but I was beginning to think they might as well have based it on one of my doodlings from childhood. It really did not seem like the right rudder for our boat.

Rob spoke with a naval architect up in Camden who seemed confident that our problems arose from the shape of our side rudder. (This type of rudder is also called a steerboard and is believed to be the derivation of the word *starboard*.) The next day we hauled the rudder out and Rob tried to correct its shape by shaving off what looked like minute amounts of wood. Per, though, remained convinced that the rudder's shape was okay and that we simply did not have the right trim. Trim is the way a boat floats in the water from bow to stern. If you move some rocks forward to lower your bow, then you have adjusted your trim, for example. I looked through *Sailing into the Past*, a Viking Ship Museum publication, and it too stressed the importance of having the right trim. Lastly, a Viking ship expert in Norway named Jon Godal, whom all of us had now heard of, had told Per that getting the right trim was a nearly mystical experience.

Although Terry was highly skeptical, in the following days we shifted ballast and our auxiliary anchor, according to Per's suggestions.

Bad weather kept us harborbound for a few more days, and we tended to some of the countless tasks that *Snorri* required. Some of the guys put chafe gear—leather and brass plates—where the anchor chain had torn into *Snorri*. Others of us planed down floorboards that had swollen too tightly into place.

When I asked John Gardner if I could borrow his hand plane to work on some of the boards, he hesitated for a few seconds and looked unintentionally pained. "Um. . . ," he answered, "yeah . . . here's one." I think he only relented because it was my boat. Big mistake.

Doug and I started scraping off the ends of the boards. I noticed that a lot of our shavings were going into the bilge. Since we had spent days cleaning ballast rocks so the bilge would not get mucky, I decided to plane over the side. *Just be careful,* I told myself. I planed one board. Perfect fit. I grabbed another, taking a quick break to massage my forearms, which were a little tired from moving the anchor chain around.

Scrape. Scrape. *This is the life,* I thought with a sigh, *working with my hands.* Scrape. Scrape. *Things really aren't so bad.* Scrape. Scrape. *We'll get the hang of it.* Scrape. Scrape. Whoosh. Out of my palm, inexorably slipping past my vainly grasping fingers, the plane plopped into the harbor.

I looked around. Doug had already started another project. No one had seen. I peered over the side, but since the dock was built along a steep drop-off and huge kelp rose like a forest from the murky bottom, I could see nothing. I switched to pine tarring, saying nothing. Moved some ballast. Just another day on the project. While doing these chores, I surreptitiously took a bearing onshore to mark where the plane had entered.

My stomach was twisting into knots.

I decided I would dive for it but knew I would be down in the chilly water far too long to do it on my own. I needed a wet suit at the very least. As I walked by the boat shop I heard Gardner call out, asking for his plane. I pretended not to hear. For some reason my whole self-esteem depended on everyone not knowing just how incompetent I was. With the boat not working right, my crew not having much faith in me, and countless other pressures, I felt this could be the last straw.

I had been meaning to get some dive gear for the boat just in case this kind of thing happened. I drove home to get Lisa and the girls. Gardner called the house, asking for his plane. I stumbled over my words, saying something about not being too sure where it was but that I would get it to him later. I hung up midsentence.

We tracked down a dive shop about a half hour away. As the girls tore apart a half-dozen displays, Lisa and I madly searched the store for a proper-sized hood, boots, mask, and gloves. It was probably the quickest sale the shop had ever made. I did not want to make a rushed purchase on a dive suit, so I wore my mother-in-law's neon green wet suit, which threatened to castrate me with every step.

We took our time getting back to the boatyard because I wanted everyone to be gone. I had asked a man named Abbott Fletcher to give us a slide show that night about his own sailing trip to Greenland, hoping it might remind the crew just how miserable they would soon be. They were all leaving the yard early to get cleaned up before heading over to our house.

When we got back to *Snorri*, John was just leaving, and I hid in the car until he walked out of sight. I dressed in the car and then rushed down to the water looking like a frightening cross between a funky chicken and a neon swamp thing. As I scurried past the yard I heard Doug and Andy call out (damn them for working late!) and I felt them gape in astonishment. I pressed on. I strode into the water. Even with all that crap on, the cold was harsh. The tide tried to rip me out of the inlet. I had been a college swimmer. I would not be defeated. I clung to some friendly kelp. I dove down but quickly aborted the attempt.

I had forgotten I had to hold my breath. I climbed out of the water to readjust.

Andy, Doug, Lisa, and my sister Margaret, who had just shown up, stood on the shore laughing. Lisa had divulged everything. I would show them. In my mind I heroically dove straight in, while in actuality I slowly inched below the surface. Ah, a beautiful yellowish starfish. Improbably huge mussels. The kelp, no longer friendly, beckoned like menacing realtors for Davy Jones' locker. I stirred up too much mud. Came up. Went down. Up. Down. Twenty minutes passed. I paced off the position on the dock once again. Repeated the dives. Came up with some plastic. Margaret threw me a line, and it gave me enough confidence to dive deeper. I was finally able to follow the hypothetical angle of the plane's descent. I fanned a piece of kelp that stood between me and the bottom, and there was Gardner's plane. I burst to the water's surface the triumphant hero. Everyone had left.

That night, before Abbott Fletcher's slide show but after I had slathered the plane in oil, I told Gardner the truth. He laughed good-naturedly and said he had guessed something like that had happened. I also had guessed correctly: Woodworkers like Gardner spend hours, if not days, rustling through old tool shops, paying $150 for a plane whose modern equivalent might cost $12.50. The plane had been difficult to come by and was a prized possession.

Abbott Fletcher's slide show was like a scared-straight jail visit for the crew that evening. Up until then some of them had sounded as if they were going on a cruise ship, but his cautionary words helped dispel that notion. His first slide showed an ocean choked with ice. "There's our old friend pack ice," he said. Nearly half his slides depicted the frozen salt water that prohibits navigation along the coasts of northern Labrador and southeastern Baffin Island for much of the summer. "We prepared for the cold, but it was of no use," he said. "And unlike you, we had a cabin with a heater." He held up leather hiking boots and proclaimed them useless. The same for his high-tech Gore-Tex gloves. "No good. Get mittens, and even then you're going to be cold." At the beginning of the show the guys had not been very attentive, but by the end all were respectfully asking questions as to what they should wear.

As I walked him to his car and thanked him for the presentation, he offered one last piece of advice: "Besides preparing for the cold, the one thing you and your crew must do is enter a different frame of time. You must let it slow down."

This would be our toughest challenge.

Chapter Five

Marian, the publicist, threw a party for the crew and drew things she called "mind maps"—overlapping circles that attempted to draw all the "forces" together. She said we were now all engaged in Camp Viking. Per grew disgusted and said that in Norway there would not be all this public relations stuff. They would just build the boat and then sail it. The crew seemed to be taking Marian with a sense of humor, even as she told them all that they would be big stars, but Terry worried that her stroking was going to their heads— that they would not see all the work, just the glory.

One of my Lands' End articles had been published, and even more people began contacting me. My favorite letter read: "Dear Hod, I have just finished your book *Westward Whoa*. Had I not then read of your plans to replicate the voyage of Leif Ericson, I would probably have gone on about my business and that would have been the end of that. . . . You were born to be an Explorer in a World that has no territory left to explore, and so you are driven to follow in the footsteps of those who have gone before you in an attempt to prove to yourself and the World that had you been born a few hundred years earlier you could have performed this feat as well as your ancestors who actually accomplished it." I liked this part, although it seemed to give me more credit than I deserved. It continued, however: "That's all well and good but if you approach this expedition with the same lack of preparation that you did the previous one, you will not live to write about it. You seem to have an inkling about the difficulty of what you propose, but only an inkling."

The day after this letter arrived we went sailing in a stiff breeze. We cleared the outlying islands and then began our now ritualistic attempt at tacking and jibing back to the harbor. On the port tack, we fared well and even made some headway against the wind. Then, on the starboard tack, we waited as long as possible to jibe and nearly ran into Little Wood Island when *Snorri* would not fall off the wind.* We tried loosening the sheets and hauling in the prias-lines attached to the middle of the sail that help change its shape. We even had everyone on board running forward together to change the trim, like a high side in whitewater rafting, but she would not turn. Finally, in a hastily executed move, we dropped the sail while Trevor hopped into the dinghy and pushed *Snorri* away from the island.

So we had a $300,000 boat that would not turn. Even I had an inkling that this was very, very bad. I think this is when I began drinking for the first time in five years.

For days Terry had been unable to relax, for obvious reasons. I had not seen him smile once. Admittedly, part of me was glad to see him suffering along with me, but another part worried about this loss of humor. Earlier in the morning, during a *thing*, Andy cautioned that we should not lose our sense of humor. Terry had been talking about how upset he was with Marian for the previous night's party. He did not want anyone taking her too seriously.

With *Snorri* unwilling to fall off the wind, Terry had good reason to be worried.

When Per suggested we move more ballast just minutes after we escaped running aground at Little Wood Island, I half expected Terry to laugh in derision. He did not, but neither did he assist in the latest rock dance. He crawled beneath the floor planks to look

* For you landlubbers, by this I mean we could not do what you might think would be the easiest thing possible: turn away from the direction that the wind is coming from.

at the withy holding the rudder in place.* It had been loosening up, and we had to tighten it periodically. "Look at this water running in here," he said grimly. All he could see, wherever he looked, were more and more problems.

Moving the ballast did not help, and we were unable to make it back to Rob's harbor. We settled for a mooring at a local resort.

That night Per, Terry, and I gathered at my house to discuss the problems. "It was a very . . . um, frustrating day," Per began.

I suggested the rudder might need to be moved farther back. I knew that when I paddled a canoe, turning was easier the farther back I was. Per agreed with me but said the rudder was where it was. He suggested we use a rear rudder, but I was not ready for that. Terry looked at us hesitantly. "I shouldn't say it . . . ," he said.

"We all must say what we are thinking," Per said.

"I can't help wondering if the hull might be out of line," Terry said, embarrassed.

"Yes," Per added immediately. "I was wondering that too. But I could not say it. Rob, he built the boat."

A problem with hull shape had never occurred to me. In the end, it did not really matter. Whether the hull was plumb or not, we had to be able to turn the boat when we wanted to.

We formed a plan of action. I would contact Max Vinner at the Viking Ship Museum. Per would call Jacob Bjørkedal, the Norwegian boatbuilder who had built Per's boat, and Terry would try to deal with Rob and the naval architect. The only bad part of this plan was that Rob did not overly enjoy Terry's company at this time. All along he thought Terry should have shown more interest in the building of the boat and been more proactive with the rigging. Rob also simply did not like any figure of authority. Either way, they would have to work it out.

Terry outlined for me the problems we were experiencing. Under oars or even when pushed by another boat, the rudder needed to be turned toward starboard to maintain a straight course. On the port tack, the rudder functioned adequately. The boat would head

---

* The withy begins on the outside of the rudder, held in place by a stopper knot or a wooden toggle. It feeds through the rudder, past a supporting piece of wood called a boss, then through the hull, where it is tied off to a crossbeam. In Viking times, the withy was made of woven willow or pine roots, or perhaps walrus skin, but we were using a hemp rope.

into the wind or fall off but was a little slow to respond. On the starboard tack, the rudder almost did not function at all. When it did work, the rudder had to be put hard over to change course. Once, while close-hauled on a starboard tack, the boat would not fall off the wind at all. I faxed a long letter to Max quoting from Terry this description of our problems. He wrote back in pen, and I could not read his faxed writing. I then called him, but he was at a book party for one of the museum books he had just written.

In truth, though, I was not sure Max could be of much help. The Viking Ship Museum had determined that the Vorså rudder was the best example of a steerboard. That is why Ragnar Thorseth had used its design with some modifications for *Saga Siglar*.

Terry, Rob, and I combed through *Sailing into the Past* for clues as to what we should do, since there is a lengthy section on the Vorså and *Saga Siglar* rudders. We did not find any. In fact, the answer was right there in the book, but at the time we did not know what our problem was—just the results of the problem—so we skimmed right past it. The only way we could or would ever come up with the answer would be through trial and error. And we would have plenty of that.

Meanwhile, Per had his conversation with Jacob Bjørkedal. The next day Terry, Per, and I went to talk with Rob. He was bent over the rudder, looking as if he were trying to become one with it. Even though we stood just a few feet from him, he did not glance up. Terry said to Per, "What did your friend say?"

"Well, Jacob, he thinks . . . ," Per began, and Rob's head popped up immediately. We were of some use after all. Jacob had taken Per's position that it was still a matter of getting the right trim and balance to the boat. He thought we needed to tighten the back stays to rake the mast aft a bit so that the power center of the sail and the boat were the same. This completely lost me, of course, but both Rob and Terry nodded in agreement. Evidently our sailboat needed to have its power coming from the center of the boat to help it turn better. Terry, however, was still convinced it was the rudder.

He and Rob talked with Mark Fitzgerald, a naval architect from a firm in Camden. David Conover, a filmmaker who was making a documentary on our project, had asked someone at the architectural firm if they had any suggestions. Mark came down to the boatyard and drew up plans for a rudder he thought would work.

David faxed the drawing and scribbled next to it that Cleopatra's barge had had a rudder like it. It was a ghastly modern-shaped rudder with a nominal decorative tail to make it look like a Viking rudder. It's volume was nearly twice that of the old rudder, but its main departure from the Viking design was its foil curves. It was shaped like an airplane wing and was a design clearly of this century. It made Per scoff. Terry asked Rob to build a temporary, full-size plywood mock-up anyway.

Rob still believed that he could get the original rudder to work if he just had time to do enough tests to shape it correctly. He did not want to waste his time building the modernized rudder. "Terry thinks any rudder would be better than the one we have now—even no rudder at all," Rob complained. "So I'll make this mock-up out of plywood but . . . I don't agree with him." He kept ranting about not having enough time, and I yearned to remind him of all those months he could have been building. I kept quiet, knowing in hindsight that I should have allowed more time for the sea trials.

Rob made the plywood rudder, and Per laughed uproariously at it. He said he would never put such a thing on his boat. Per had to go back to Norway before we used the plywood rudder, but he implored me to not try to sail far with it. He also seemed to think the naval architect's newly designed rudder was an insult to his ancestors. "That new rudder. I do not like it," he said, squinching up his face as if a foul odor passed through the room. All in all, though, he approved of *Snorri* and especially of Rob's workmanship. "We have a saying back home: 'Do it the American way.' It means do it fast and not so good. But now I must go home and correct that saying. Rob works very carefully, I think, not fast. I must tell my friend Jacob."

As the rudder was being debated, the crew worked on other projects, such as shaping and installing compass fiddles (wooden brackets to hold the compass in place on the crossbeam), fastening running lights on the mast, and building a wooden hook for the man-overboard ring and strobe. They were working hard and appeared to me to be committed to getting things done right.

The day before we tried out *Snorri*'s plywood mock-up, however, Terry pulled me aside. We sat on overturned drywall buckets in knee-high wood shavings behind Rob's shop. He looked miserable.

"We need to talk," he began. I got the full lump in my stomach. I hate when someone says that to me. He looked me in the eye.

"My comfort level is low, way low. I did not think I was entering an Outward Bound situation where I would be responsible for motivating other people. I guess I assumed, which might have been my fault, that everyone would be willing to do whatever it took to make this happen. Some of the guys just aren't doing that."

I was a little incredulous. As he spoke, all the guys were around the corner busting their butts for no pay. I had promised them a meager living stipend, but that was it. I could not really fathom what he was talking about, so I pointed out all that everyone was doing.

He admitted that they were working hard and eventually said that he was just having a problem with Andy. It had begun back in Alexandria, when the three of us had met to plan the voyage, and it had only gotten worse.

"But, even beyond all that, my comfort level is still about at the bottom. And I don't see how it's going to get high enough before we go to Greenland."

I did my best to lift his spirits, but I was depressed and dismayed by his position. The guys were working hard. The problem was that he had not chosen them and they were not people he would have chosen. He thought they should all be skilled sailors. Throughout history, however, ordinary crew positions have been filled with the unskilled, wanderers, and others jumping at a chance to learn. When the actor Sterling Hayden, a very talented square-rigged sailor, captained the *Florence Robinson* from Gloucester, Mass., to Tahiti in 1939, he had eleven crewmen and he was the only sailor. As Hayden explained in his autobiography *Wanderer*, ". . . the sea is a skillful teacher."

It made sense, though, that Terry would be feeling worried and even a little desperate. We were deliberately placing ourselves in a dangerous situation, and he was feeling hemmed in. Terry does not like schedules or being tied down to doing something on or by a specific date, especially in a vehicle that relies solely on the whims of nature. With CBS, *Headline News*, the *New York Times*, the *Boston Globe*, the AP, and many others reporting our story, it felt as though the whole world were watching. Everyone wanted to know exactly when and where we would be going—in Maine and Greenland.

I told the guys how Terry was feeling.

"I thought we might have to have this conversation, but I was hoping we wouldn't," Doug said.

"Just tell me what to do," Homer said. "You've got to tell me and I'll do it."

Andy nodded but said, "This may be a bad time to bring this up, but I've got a family commitment this weekend and I need to have a day or two off."

I realized I needed to put my foot down. "I'd like you to be here. You have to make up your mind which is more important: the time away or this project. . . . Don't forget this is not just a trial period for the boat. It's also a trial period for the crew. I believe I said this before, but no one's position is set in stone."

I was sort of shocked to hear these words come out of my own mouth and would have gladly changed places with Andy.

Later I called Per and asked him if he thought a friend of his that he had once mentioned would still be willing to captain *Snorri*. I had become hardened with all that had happened over the past few months, and it seemed I might not be able to rely on Terry. I needed a backup.

The next day, however, Terry was in a great mood. He appeared much lighter in spirit, and from that point on, I tried to be his tension-release valve.

It did not hurt anybody's mood that the plywood rudder was doing the job. It turned the boat effortlessly. I had also told Terry about my conversation with the crew—what remained of the crew, that is. John Abbott and Jan had both gone home to work and Elias still had not arrived from Greenland.

Then Rob built a new permanent rudder based on the plywood model, and it worked just as well as the plywood one. I could not help feeling that I had allowed us to sell out—to give in too quickly to "bigger is better" and "newer is better." I also worried, along with Rob, that the new rudder was too big—that it might cause us some other problem that the smaller one had not. We had only a little time before sending the boat off to Greenland, however. *Snorri* had to be seaworthy at that moment.

I excused myself from some of the sea trials at this point because I had to spend time planning for our stay in Boston, where we would tie up next to the USS *Constitution* if I could get the U.S. Park Service's permission. I was also doing interviews, negotiating with the container ship company that was now saying it would not load our boat on in Boston, explaining to crane operators that lifting *Snorri* out of the water in Boston would need to be a delicate operation, cajoling insurance companies because Lands' End wanted to protect themselves against lawsuits and insure the boat during its shipping to Greenland, and scheduling meetings with officials from the Canadian government, since I had decided to donate *Snorri* to Parks Canada so they could display it at their visitor center at L'Anse aux Meadows, Newfoundland. During this time, I recalled with some chagrin what Rob had often said to me when I asked him if he was really going to go on the trip: "We'll see. I'm planning on it. But by then I may be so sick of this boat that I load up all my gear and go canoeing for the summer." At the time I had thought, *Yeah, right, you big poser.* That was back when I was more or less an observer in comparison. Now that I had stepped into his shoes and taken over the project for good, I finally understood what he had been talking about. I was sick of the boat and the project. Most of all, I was sick of myself. One night Lisa cried in bed as I lay awake at 3 A.M., "This was supposed to be fun. Instead we're always serious. We have no time to laugh. You're so stressed." We hugged, but it made no difference.

I realized that things are fun when you just pack up and do them—as I had always done in the past. Light out like Huck Finn. Follow Annie Dillard's sound advice in *Pilgrim at Tinker Creek*: "There is always an enormous temptation in all of life to diddle around making itsy-bitsy friends and meals and journeys for itsy-bitsy years on end. It is so self-conscious, so apparently moral, simply to step aside from the gaps where the creeks and winds pour down, saying, I never merited this grace, quite rightly, and then to sulk along the rest of your days on the edge of rage. I won't have it. The world is wilder than that in all directions, more dangerous and bitter, more extravagant and bright. We are making hay when we should be making whoopee; we are raising tomatoes when we should be raising Cain, or Lazarus."

Yeah, yeah, yeah . . . have a good time, Annie. Be reckless. You do not have a sponsor. You do not do so many interviews you forget what line you have already handed out. You do not spin around in circles ever watchful of mutiny or even the Blood Eagle, a mythical but sensational Viking torture in which your back is sliced open and your lungs are pulled through two slits to flap around like useless wings as blood sprays your flailing body.

Chapter Six

We finally held the Lands' End–sponsored naming ceremony at the Maine Maritime Museum in Bath, officially announcing *Snorri*'s name. Mike Smith, president of Lands' End, came out and spoke. Maine's governor, Angus King, was there, as well as a representative from the province of Newfoundland and Labrador. All had encouraging words. The most trying aspect for Terry, the crew, and me was how to handle a naming ceremony. What was a naming ceremony? We had already launched the boat. We couldn't pretend that Lisa hadn't bashed a bottle of champagne against her bow. I thought it would be good to do something in a Viking manner. A friend told me that the champagne-over-the-bow thing stemmed from Viking times. Back then, he said, they just sacrificed a virgin slave across the bow and it was blood that trickled down the artfully lapped planks. Being a newly converted Viking apologist, this seemed a doubtful bit of lore. Since the Vikings first raided the Northumbrian island of Lindisfarne in 793, killing women, children, and priests as well as looting the church, they had been painted by the Christian world as evil. The Vikings certainly were pirates. One of their chief occupations was raiding to acquire slaves to trade throughout Europe. But, they were also victims of modernization. Their enemies—the Celts, the Anglo-Saxons, the Saxons, the Franks, the Frisians—had learned to write in Latin on paper while the Vikings continued to etch in stone and wood. As a result, the Christians sent letters from one court to another about the ferocious Vikings, creating a one-sided history. They have been reviled ever since. Twentieth-century historians, though, have used archeology and a more open-minded study of the facts to create a fuller Viking picture, but the result is still merely an impression. Was the Blood Eagle real? Did they really sacrifice virgins across the bow of a new boat? We do not know. Did Charlemagne brutalize and terrorize surrounding heathens, including the Vikings? Yes. Did the Vikings establish trade routes spanning four continents, from North America to Constantinople? Yes.

Would we sacrifice a virgin across the bow for the Lands' End party, especially since no one on the crew fit the bill? It seemed highly doubtful. Eventually John Gardner suggested we all stand onstage and simply raise a glass of champagne in salute to *Snorri*, and that is what we did. Many family members and friends came, plus hundreds of schoolkids. We set up educational stations on the museum's lawn, each manned by two crew members so that children could participate. At one station the kids attempted to use our eighteen-foot ash oars. At another they tried on an immersion suit and laughed as their classmates were engulfed in bright red neoprene meant for someone weighing up to three hundred pounds. Doug, who besides being a drummer was adept at computers, and a technical support person from Lands' End showed children and adults how we would be making journal entries for our Web site using water-resistant computers. Gerry Galuza set up a smithy under a tarp and pounded out iron rivets. Bystanders were allowed to whack out the rivet's head and marveled that these rough pieces of metal held *Snorri* together. Gerry's blacksmith shop had burned down a month earlier, and it was heartening for everyone to see him come out swinging.

Six days later, Memorial Day, with our final crew member, Elias Larsen, over from Greenland, we set sail for Boston. Elias had been around for only a few days, but his jovial attitude eased him into our company. He was extremely comfortable on *Snorri* and good with people. Elias had served as a community judge in Sisimiut, worked as a teacher, and run a number of cooperatives. He would, I thought, be our mature voice. Of course, when he showed up on board hopping around like a devilish elf in a multitasseled wool hat, pulling pranks, I had to wonder.

We had eight days before the boat had to be loaded on the container ship. The distance from Hermit Island, Maine, to Boston was roughly 110 nautical miles. We were counting on the trip taking four or five days. It would be a good warm-up for Greenland, testing our abilities to cook, get from point A to point B safely, and, maybe even more important, work together as a cohesive group. Rob, Jan, Homer, and Russell could not go with us. Jan had to go back to his law firm. Rob had to put in floats for the local sailors, and Homer had to drive back to Michigan for his stepsister's high school graduation. "I told her I'd be there," he explained to me, looking anguished. "But . . . I want to be with you guys." As we rowed away from the dock he stared at us teary-eyed, and then he ran from vantage point to vantage point to watch us until we were out of sight. I had no idea where Russell was and had thought he would have at least been around to take pictures.

I felt the usual pangs on departing, sad that Lisa could not be on board and worried about all the little details. This tension came onto the boat with me, and Trevor and I had a little spat that evening over propping the red-filtered flashlight against the compass. I had done so, and Trevor immediately said in an authoritative way, "Oh, you don't want to do that. It will throw off the magnets." Defensive, I replied that the person needing to see the compass would have to use the flashlight and should be able to find it easily. Once the light was lifted up, the compass would immediately go back to its proper position.

I was embarrassed about squabbling at such an early date but at least I was right. I had seen Gardner smiling at me in support, and it felt good to be right about something. I had not felt that way since first setting foot on *Snorri*.

The withy—the rudder line—was constantly working loose as we sailed downwind, just as it had during the sea trials. Like all of the standing rigging, it was made of imported tarred hemp. Hemp is fairly flexible, and it was stretching too much. It was also getting worn, although Gardner had methodically covered it with thick leather at the chafe points. We had to lower the sail in the early evening to tighten it—a laborious project entailing wrapping the line countless times around a lower crossbeam and then driving in wedges to make it snug. We were sailing again within a half hour.

Off watch, I lay on my back on the foredeck. It was a warm night and breezeless on board, since we were sailing downwind. We were averaging about six knots. At this rate, we could cover the entire distance from Greenland to Newfoundland in nineteen days. Even if we rested every other day and took an equal amount of days to sightsee, we would finish the voyage in roughly six weeks. Maybe, just maybe, despite all our difficulties, things would turn out as I'd always hoped.

I stared up at the tentacles of shrouds, the mast, and the billowing sail, and I felt as if we were in a fairy tale. Faint northern lights. A shimmering moon. Ahhh. We were successfully sailing a Viking cargo ship down the New England coast. This was the feeling that I had expected and hoped for all along. And, of course, the rich smell of *Snorri's* pine tar alone transported us all. It was heady and made me feel like a salty dog. I fell asleep feeling very emotional and finally at ease.

"All hands on deck!" Terry called out, although there is nowhere to be on an open boat except on the deck. "Yard coming down!" he boomed out. The yard, as I have pointed out, is very heavy and is a frightening object to have looming over your head or, even more so, dropped quickly in a rolling sea.

This was after midnight. I was standing by the tiller. After we hauled the rudder over the side of the boat to run a new line through it and then through the rudder boss, a carved block of wood holding the rudder away from the hull, I ended up in the bilge, wrapping and tightening the line around an adjacent floor timber. The seas were about five feet and the last place you want to be in a rocking, becalmed boat is staring down into the bilge. It makes you want to puke. It did not help matters that moments earlier I had watched Gardner adroitly lose his dinner over the side.

At some point I looked up to settle my stomach and saw . . . "A ship! A ship! It's bearing down on us!" I yelled excitedly. Everyone looked over as if in slow motion, and sure enough, I was right. It was about a hundred yards off, headed straight for us.

"Grab the searchlight" Terry said, and Trevor hurried to find it. There wasn't enough time. Instead someone grabbed John Abbott's headlamp and waved it furiously back and forth. Luckily, Abbott had not yet followed Terry's orders to cover the lens with a red filter, and the "ship" saw the tiny light. It turned away just in time. It was not a ship but a fifty-foot fishing boat—big enough to put a damper on our fairy tale, however, if we had collided.

"Turn on the radio," Terry requested, "but don't say anything. I don't really want to get in a discussion with them, since our running lights aren't working."

"Who was working on those lights last, anyway?" Abbott asked in a highly irritated tone.

"I don't know," Terry said.

"It was me," Abbott answered, smiling broadly. "Who else?"

We were sailing again within the hour—this time with the searchlight handy. The following wind continued throughout the night, to our collective amazement, and we passed Cape Ann, just twenty-five miles outside Boston, before sunrise. By that afternoon, May 27, we were anchored off Thompson Island—a Boston city park where Outward Bound runs a program.

We killed a few days at Thompson, since we did not have permission to tie up near the *Constitution* at the navy yard until the end of the month. The instructors at Thompson opened the grounds to us because of Terry, Abbott, and Trevor. We tried out the climbing tower for a little more team building and to pass the time. Elias, from a land where hardly a tree grows higher than a man, looked at me as though I were crazy when I suggested he trust us with his life while he climbed sixty feet in the air. He was so worried by this that even when it was not his turn to belay, he stood alongside the belayers, ever ready to grab the safety line if needed.

Since we were mostly idle during this time, we got to know each other a little better—enough to poke fun at each other's idiosyncrasies. One night as we lazed on board, cooking chili and drinking beers, Gardner, the boatbuilder, said, not for the first time, "Who has a better life than me?" He was no longer as quiet as he had been the first days out, and it was clear he liked to provoke things now and then to keep from being bored. He had his big smile on, and, looking over at him, I had to wonder. He had no obligations and could take off whenever he wanted.

Doug smiled and said, "Well, John, I was wondering about that." He moved in closer, circling Gardner in a catlike manner.

"I've heard you say that before." He paused. "My question to you is, do you really think you have a better life, or are you trying to convince yourself of it? Maybe you're not really confident of it. It sounds like you're trying to convince yourself of it." Doug was some kind of Viking therapist. He was going to help Gardner explore his own psyche and maybe roughen it up somewhat at the same time.

After a bit of verbal tussling, Gardner admitted, "Well, mainly I do say it to psych myself up just before I'm going to do something—like ask a girl to dance. But"—and here he smiled even more broadly than before—"I do believe it to be true."

When it was finally time to cross to the navy yard, not a hint of wind blew across Boston Harbor, and we had to row the entire day. Before heading out, however, we unloaded all of *Snorri*'s ballast. The idea of shipping fifteen tons of rocks to a land of ice and rocks seemed too ludicrous, even for me. At first we tried to dispose of the rocks surreptitiously, easing them into the water out of the island's view. The fun of tossing huge rocks into the water took over, however, and *Snorri* was soon soaked.

After a couple of days tied up next to the *Constitution*, during which we probably received as many visitors as Old Ironsides, we rowed *Snorri* to the shipping company's office in Watertown. A $6,000 steel cradle (not a sum I had counted on) built by a friend of Rob's named Red was lowered past *Snorri*'s waterline and then slipped beneath her. I swam around the boat in a wet suit, constantly exhaling through my mouth to keep any harbor water from trickling down my throat, checking on *Snorri*'s placement.

Snorri was hoisted out of the water. It was an odd sight, seeing a construction that was never meant to be lifted swinging twenty feet in the air. It all seemed very easy—very modern.

Then the insurance inspector arrived. He nitpicked every single thing we did, from the way we secured *Snorri* on the cradle—suggesting changes that we would have to comply with—to what we planned to eat while on the voyage. As a result, we had to drill more drain holes in *Snorri*, add more and more chafe gear, and tie extra line around the shackles holding *Snorri* to the cradle. The shipyard workers followed behind him, ridiculing every suggestion. A lot of his advice was sound, however, and to back up his points, he handed out a slick magazine his company published called *A Guide to Cargo*

Loss Control. It reminded me that the container ship could end up in forty-foot seas. As a result, the containers on board could swing a total of ninety degrees with each roll of the ship. That's a lot of bouncing around. Seemingly secured containers have been known to come loose and could demolish *Snorri* in a second.

The insurance agent also oversaw how we packed the container that held all of our equipment. Thanks to him, we had that thing so tightly bundled with cam straps and two-by-fours bracing all our goods into place, it would have withstood a hurricane.

After five days of preparation we finally loaded *Snorri* on the container ship, and as it cast off, headed first for different ports in the United States and Canada and then finally to Iceland, where *Snorri* would be transferred to a Greenland-bound ship, I felt relaxed for the first time in months. I still had to secure health insurance policies for the crew, give three talks in Wisconsin for Lands' End employees, and do nearly two dozen radio interviews from my home in one day. But this was nothing compared to the last few months.

Back in Maine, my family and I had a week alone in our rental home. Lisa and I went for hikes. We watched the girls eat sand at the beach. We focused only on our family, and things almost felt normal again. During this time, Russell Kaye finally admitted that he could not go. It turned out he had been saying as much to everyone but me. He had not been around during the sea trials—maybe a day or two of taking pictures, but staying pretty separate from everyone else. I called him one evening, prepared to needle him. *I understand . . . your family . . . it's a big commitment, but this is going to be a chance of a lifetime*, I was going to say. I was good at this kind of stuff now. But we started to talk, and he laid himself open.

"Hodding, I'm scared I won't come back alive," he said. "I've had these awful panic attacks. I can't even sit in the same room with my family. And I've been crying a lot. I need to stay home, sort things out." It was like a hard slap. I snapped out of autopilot and tried my best to console him. He told me he was confronting some problems he had been neglecting his entire life. I told him he really should stay home. He worried that he was letting me down, but I heard such relief in his voice, I soon found myself sternly saying he could not go.

A few days later I called Dean Plager and asked him to be our twelfth crew member. Dean was the fifty-seven-year-old sailor who had helped out at the launch and on a number of other occasions without much hope of being asked to go along. He had crossed the Atlantic solo, and Terry and I had grown to respect his enthusiasm. His age was a plus; it helped to round out the crew.

When I gave Dean the news, he belted out a loud "Yahoo!" and did a little jig. I could hear his feet tapping over the phone. "I only allowed myself the tiniest hope that I might get to come along," he said. "I thought that with so much time before Greenland, there just might be a chance." A statistician by profession, he had played the odds and won.

Lisa and I had decided that she, our girls, and Lisa's sister Jain would come to Greenland to see us off. We had not spent much time together recently, and we wanted to stay together until the last possible minute. As a result, the last few weeks in the United States were not sad, but they were a little trying. An agent for Royal Arctic, the shipping line that would be taking Snorri from Iceland to Greenland, left a message the last day we were in Maine: "I have an urgent message for Hodding Carter. Our shipping schedule has changed. Please return this call immediately."

It turned out the boat would not be leaving from Reykjavik, Iceland's capital, until July 14—two weeks later than the original departure date. This setback would cause us to be sailing during the fall season. We had wanted to be finished with the voyage before the fall storms increased too dramatically—gales, storms, even hurricanes—and I had still been clinging to the hope that I might get home in time for our baby's birth at the end of August.

Terry was quite calm about the matter and said we would just go to Greenland and wait. It was too late to try to change all our tickets. I suggested we try to sail from Iceland—with a chase boat, since we did not have many hours on board yet. Starting from Greenland, we would have weeks of sailing along the coastline, with ample opportunity to find an anchorage if something went wrong. Of course, leaving from Iceland would mean an immediate ocean crossing and involve maneuvering around pack ice that was currently traveling from east to west Greenland around Cape Farewell. Terry thought we were not ready for that and repeated his credo about chase boats: "The only reason you need a chase boat is to pluck people out of the water, and I don't want us to go into something thinking I'll need people plucked out of the water."

Lisa had an equally sane response in reference to my not wanting to be delayed: "This trip is not about us. There are too many people involved for you to make a decision based only on us. Having the baby isn't the hard part. It really doesn't matter if you're there for that. It's everything afterward," she soothed. "The baby won't be upset if you're not there. It's only us who care."

They were right, of course, but I still had to do something. I faxed Eimskip, the shipping company in Iceland that had picked up *Snorri* in Boston, asking if they knew anybody who could tow her to Greenland. While waiting for a response, we drove back to West Virginia and scattered our dogs' ashes in the New River. It had been their playground. They had ridden its rapids, chased squirrels and rabbits along its banks. We made a little celebration out of it with some friends who also loved our dogs, but the moment when we scattered the ashes our reverie stilled. They were missed.

A day later *Snorri*'s future looked a little brighter. Edda Geirsdottir, an Eimskip employee, shamed Royal Arctic into diverting another ship to Iceland that could pick up *Snorri* and the other cargo for Greenland. We were back on schedule.

Chapter Seven

The new Royal Arctic ship developed engine troubles off the Faroes on its way to Iceland, throwing us off schedule once again.

Thank God *Snorri* did not show up in Greenland when she was supposed to: Lisa, the girls, and I were granted two extra weeks just touring southwestern Greenland. Damn it to hell *Snorri* did not show up in Greenland when she was supposed to: We were weeks behind schedule, I had to argue with the shipping line nearly every day, and I had no idea what to do with my family.

We had a twelve-hour layover in Reykjavik, Iceland, on the way from the States to Greenland. While in Iceland, we visited *Snorri* where she was sitting on top of *Naja Arctica*, the ship that would be bringing her to Greenland.

Aarrgh! It was too frustrating.

We threw off our city clothes, donned our impervious rain suits, and set sail, bound for southwest Greenland. We were Vikings, after all.

Not really.

Actually, having taken off after midnight from the United States, we were so jet-lagged by that point I don't think the thought of sailing crossed anybody's mind. As Rob went through customs in Iceland, he had been asked what was in the two enormous plastic waterproof suitcases he was carrying that were stuffed with tools, rivets, wood, and God knows what else. "I have no idea," Rob had replied to the customs agent, who inexplicably waved him through without opening any of the cases.

So, instead of setting sail for Greenland, we gave *Snorri* a cursory inspection, patted her sides, ate some mutton (because that seems to be all anyone eats in Iceland), and headed back to the airport, leaving behind Rob and Gardner to accompany her on the container ship to Greenland.

We were flying over Greenland later that day, occasionally peeking through the nearly relentless cloud cover, beholding sights that frightened me to the core. Ice was everywhere, and it looked mean. As far as I could see, only the pinnacles of mountains and the ridge tops were ice free. We had stumbled upon Frankenstein's monster's Arctic hideaway, and we were surely going to suffer. People in an open boat could not survive in such misery.

I was wrong, of course, because as we bounced onto the runway in Narsarsuaq, Greenland, on June 30, we left the ice cap miles behind. It was seventy degrees out and would stay that way during the day for weeks to come.

Narsarsuaq is essentially an airfield with a few surrounding houses, a hotel at one end of the runway, and a youth hostel at the other. It sits two miles across the fjord from Brattahlid, Erik the Red's farm. Elias had arranged for an outfitter to ferry us to some accommodations in Narsaq, about twenty miles out along Erik's Fjord. The outfitter did not show. We were groggy and homeless, not a big deal except that my eighteen-month-old children were with us and Lisa was seven months pregnant. There were no vacancies at the hotel, and even if there had been, it was too expensive for us. Someone called the youth hostel. They had room.

Two young Danes, Michael Kreuzfeldt and Erik Larsen, ran the hostel, and our arrival nearly had them in stitches. They had been running the hostel for three summers by then and had grown weary of boastful claims. Greenland is an outpost destination. Wanderers, malcontents, and a few elderly northern Europeans on packaged tours trickle in throughout the summer. Many claim such goals as setting up a research station on the glacier, starting a new religion, or even retracing the Viking route. Most just seem lost. Arriving with no reservations, a pregnant woman, toddling twins, a teenage sister-in-law, and a cast of nine misfits, we fell into the lost category.

Since we did have money, however, they humored us, nodding with only a slight smirk at our proclamations that we would be sailing an actual Viking ship. They had read about us in the Danish and Greenlandic papers but remained unconvinced that we were for real. The twins scared them—drunken Germans and carousing Danes they were used to, but not squawking American children. We settled in.

The hostel became our base, and after a while Erik and Michael became our coconspirators. It was Michael who suggested I threaten the Royal Arctic officers with telling the press that all our plans were being ruined because Royal Arctic cared nothing for history, only for money. They were diverting the *Naja Arctica* five hundred miles north to Sisimiut because parts for a new bridge were needed up there, although the ship was supposed to go to Narsarsuaq first. Erik, who initially had been the most disdainful of our screaming twins, even took to holding them on his knees while he and I talked about the Vikings. Erik was quite interested in his ancestors and had crewed on a Viking replica for the last few years. He and Michael still did not believe that we were going to sail a real Viking boat anywhere except in our heads, but that did not keep them from getting entangled in our project.

Narsarsuaq (the name means "big plain") sits on a flat piece of land beside an azure fjord that ends about four miles farther inland. Small—and by this I mean house-sized—broken icebergs (called bergy bits) swirl by the town's runway, occasionally grounding out when they came to shore. Homer used one such occasion to lop off hunks of ancient ice, sharing iceberg cocktails of Scotch with members of the crew who were present. The Arctic drinks sparkled and fizzled like a mouthful of Pop Rocks. It was as if the ice, some of which could be centuries old, was rejoicing at finally being allowed to return to its watery state: *We're free! Yippee!*

Narsarsuaq was bulldozed into existence only because the American government convinced the Danish authorities that Greenland was needed as a strategic front during World War II, and on April 9, 1941, the United States was "given the responsibility for protecting Greenland." In truth, the agreement gave the United States virtually unlimited rights to establish military bases and installations in Greenland. On account of the war, the Danish ambassador to the United States made this agreement without permission from his government, but when the Danish parliament was able to meet again after the conclusion of World War II, the agreement was ratified.

Greenland was the perfect refueling stop for planes flying to Europe, and the Americans ended up building seventeen airstrips, bases, and installations there, including the one in Narsarsuaq.

Greenland is just awakening to its heritage, slowly shedding itself of its colonial past. Off and on, it has been a part of the Danish and Norwegian kingdoms since the 1000s, although it felt no lasting European effects until the 1700s. Depending on what authority you wish to believe, its status as a colony began either in 985 with the arrival of Erik the Red's group, making it a part of Norway, which would eventually fall under Danish rule for hundreds of years, or in 1721 with the arrival of a Danish missionary named Hans Egede. Either way, it stopped being a colony in 1953 when it was granted the status of a Danish county. In rushed an assortment of new rights, influences, and commercialism, and Greenland, formerly prevented from making its own decisions, became a confused adolescent. In 1979 Denmark granted Greenland home rule, meaning that it was self-governing but still a part of Denmark.

There are roughly sixty thousand people in Greenland, and five political parties represent them in the Landsthing, Greenland's parliament. Greenland also sends two representatives to the Danish parliament. The Siumut (Social Democrat) party holds the majority in Greenland and favors strong ties with Denmark, including remaining a part of Denmark. The Inuit Ataqatigiit (Inuit Brother Socialist) party holds about half the number of seats of the Siumut but is very popular with younger Greenlanders. The Inuit Ataqatigiit wants complete independence from Denmark.

Greenland, Vinland, and Canada had already had native populations when the Vikings came around, and because the Inuit populations in, for example, Canada are politically active, I wondered whether the next few months would be filled with heated arguments with young Greenlanders, angry that we were retracing some imperialists' journeys: This would not be the case. We had the occasional discussion over beers in various bars, but for the most part Greenlanders seemed as apathetic about politics as citizens in the United States or Denmark, unless the talk involved a recent scandal.

We spent most of our time outdoors while in Narsarsuaq. This was the land of the midnight sun*set*. Unlike the Arctic, where for a few days in the summer the sun never sets, in Narsarsuaq the sun would set around midnight, but there was never complete darkness. The hours leading up to midnight felt like early afternoon and the hours after sunset were merely a constant twilight. The sun would hang along the northwestern horizon for hours, swathing the hillsides with a golden glow. Walking in the evening felt like taking a sunlight bath.

With time to kill, my family, the crew, and I went on many hikes—to the nearby glacier and, for a couple of us, up the gorge to Narsaq, a distance of thirty miles. For those who stayed behind, a guide from the youth hostel showed us how to identify local edible plants, and we made a tasty salad of angelica and roseroot. Angelica, a part of the carrot family, is shaped like celery and has a strong flavor. Roseroot is fairly bland, a buttery green that serves to mellow the angelica. This ultrafresh produce was a godsend for us and the locals. The one store in town did not carry much in the way of fresh fruit and vegetables, since all had to be imported and Narsarsuaq was a fairly unimportant outpost for modern Greenland, except for its large airstrip. The store did have a large variety of frozen foods, soda, beer, and wine, plus boxed and canned goods at prices that were two to three times higher than in the United States. This was standard for a Greenland town, although larger towns boasted much more in the way of variety.

Lisa, the girls, and Lisa's sister went home before *Snorri* ever made it to Narsarsuaq. We debated changing their tickets, but it seemed best for them to leave. It meant that I would be able to focus on the project completely. Also, both Homer and Doug were smitten with Jain, and as a result, she was becoming an ineffective baby-sitter. Lisa gave me two gifts before they left: a polar bear claw, because Elias had told her it would bring good luck, and a journal she had been keeping for the last few months, with dozens of pictures of her and the girls glued into the back pages. Lisa and I had started this Viking project together, talking and planning for it as a team, but then, because it was my work and we were making a family, the project and I had drifted away from her. She was going back home to start a new job and take care of our family. Eliza started crying as we said good-bye at the airport, and then Lisa and Anabel joined in.

With my family gone, I felt empty, but I also could focus on important stuff, like learning how to play kapaka. Maybe to lighten my mood or simply to kill time as we waited for *Snorri* to arrive, Elias taught us how to play this card game from southern Greenland. The rules of kapaka (pronounced "kab-a-gah") appeared to be based on how Elias was faring at the moment. On one level, it was simply a game of crazy eights on amphetamines in which the loser is the first to reach two thousand points. Whenever Elias appeared to be in a bind, however, another card had some miraculous power: for example, a seven skipped the person next to you, a nine sent your entire hand to the person next to you, a five of spades made the next person pick up five cards. Then, suddenly, the five of clubs passed everybody's hand to the right, and a little later we learned that if you had to pick up a card but none were left turned down, you automatically took on another two hundred points. And so on. Elias had us clenching our guts with laughter, and tears came to our eyes as Elias sang out of tune, "Nearly kapaka, nearly kapaka," over and over again. The first night we stayed up past two playing; after that, kapaka became an addiction. If there was an idle moment, we would play kapaka. Even the hostel managers, Michael and Erik, were sucked in.

After that, Michael started posting signs. The first demanded 550 kroner ($80) for card playing. Then FAKE WIKINGS DOUBLE PRICE!! (NO TRANSPORT PROVIDED). And then, after Erik helped us secure new ballast stones, Michael posted STONES: 95 KRONER PER KILO. We believed he was joking, but there is something about Danish humor that is a little disturbing. You can never be too sure, because everything is done with such a straight face.

A reporter for the *Greenland Post*—a 140-year-old newspaper—told me it was illegal to take rocks out of Greenland. We were planning on exporting fifteen tons of stones as ballast. Elias thought this transgression was serious enough to put in a call to the regional office for technical and environmental affairs, which consented to let us take the rocks.

Over the next few days the crew dragged themselves back to Narsarsuaq, having dispersed throughout southern Greenland to kill time while waiting for *Snorri*. Most of them had spent part of their time in Narsaq, hanging out at the local bar. They told stories of people nearly driving trucks off the edge of cliffs and women busting each other over the head with bottles in a local bar. One crew member had to suddenly leave a woman's house, his pants around his knees, when her ex-husband came blundering into her room at 3 A.M.*

The boat arrived on July 12, and we spent the next three days monomaniacally readying *Snorri* for the voyage. We worked through rain, sunshine, and a temporary iceberg attack. Actually, when the iceberg floated up we stopped our labors long enough to push it away from *Snorri* and then bash it with extra ballast stones.

I was in love with those new ballast stones. They were clean and round, having come from a glacier-fed riverbed that had spent centuries smoothing them out. The ones back in Maine had been coarse and caked in dirt; although we had scrubbed each and every one by hand, they had been an embarrassment. No self-respecting Viking pretender would have been caught dead fondling them. But these new ones . . . well, a fellow could stand atop these gems and pound his chest like an Arctic Tarzan. Unless, of course, there were a few too many onlookers milling about.

We loaded the new stones in under three hours with the help of some touring kayakers—a far cry from the two and a half days it had taken us the first time. Supposedly, round stones were best because they would roll out of the bilge when the boat capsized, thus allowing *Snorri* to float to the surface. Rob delighted in pointing out, however, that on my instructions he had built a narrow catwalk that would hinder the rocks from tumbling out.

By the evening of June 16 we were ready to row across the fjord from Narsarsuaq to Qassiarsuk, site of Brattahlid, Erik the Red's farm. We did not leave the dock until six o'clock. We had six guests on board, mostly female guides who worked out of the hostel. They brought us a gold-painted ballast rock, a bag of gnawed reindeer bones, and a sheep's skull. We tied the skull to our bow. Erik also joined us for the crossing, and it was plainly obvious that he wanted to hop on board for the entire journey. Compromising, we asked him to sail with us to Narsaq, thirty miles out the fjord. Our guests lent the moment a festive air, and *Snorri* was alive with

* Okay, it was Jan.

DEAN PALGER

Snorri arrives in Greenland

laughter and conversation as we rowed the two miles across the fjord.

Thanks to the local glacier, the water in Erik's Fjord is milky blue. Rocks get caught up in the glacier, and as it advances these rocks act like grinding stones on the bedrock over which the glacier creeps. The particles that these scraping rocks create are smaller than sand and are called glacial flour. This flour is what was turning the water milky, and when the sun rays caught the water just right, it sparkled like a wave of twinkling stars.

Trevor, now our nominal first mate, started singing "Swing Low, Sweet Chariot" while rowing, and everyone on board joined in. We slowly passed a light blue iceberg off to starboard. The sun highlighted the maze of icebergs and bergy bits farther out the fjord. It seemed like an elaborate stage, or a dream . . . or better yet, a dream come true. Our voyage was beginning; this was what the last two and half years had all been about. Part of me was excited and overwhelmed with emotion, but my overriding feeling was one of relief. *Snorri* was leaving Narsarsuaq. Tomorrow we would depart from the shores of Erik the Red's farm. We were finally going.

As we rowed up to the town dock, Terry asked, "Do you think we'll piss anybody off by tying up to the pier tonight?"

It looked like Qassiarsuk's entire population of one hundred had come down for our arrival.

I yelled to Elias, asking if he could ask someone. Elias shook his head. He was already tired of translating, and this was only the first day. I had wanted a Greenlander on our voyage because I had always noticed that the Greenlanders were a mere afterthought in most discussions of the Vikings in Greenland—ironic, considering that the Inuit outsurvived the Vikings. But was sailing with a bunch of Americans going to be too hard on Elias?

"Well, besides," Terry continued, "who cares? We're Vikings! We're supposed to piss people off."

At that, a loud and resounding cheer rose from the crowd, although it had nothing to do with Terry's statement. Again Elias would not translate, but, judging by the widening smiles on the townspeople's faces, a good thing was happening. It turned out they were giving us the Greenland equivalent of three cheers. After we tied up at the town pier, we were asked to hike to Café Brattahlid, just yards away from the probable burial spot of both Erik and Leif. We had not expected anyone to care about what we were doing, and their generosity caught us by surprise. We walked up the short hill, every last one of us looking more than a little stunned. The new café held two tables piled with meats, cheeses, and bread, as well as an endless assortment of sweets.

Ellen and Carl Frederiksen, a Greenlandic couple, owned the Café Brattahlid. Ellen translated Carl's welcome and explained that the entire community had decided to throw us this party. She then translated again as her father-in-law, Erik the Red Frederiksen, gave a speech. Earlier this century, Erik's father had built the first house in Qassiarsuk since the age of the Vikings and began raising sheep, just as the Vikings once had. Sheep farming is one of the few agricultural enterprises in Greenland (others include reindeer farming and, in the past, even chicken farming) and is carried out only in southern Greenland. The animals are slaughtered and packaged in Narsaq, thirty miles away, and then shipped throughout the country.

Erik's speech was a delight: "We who live here in Brattahlid consider ourselves successors to the Vikings by farming sheep. Nine hundred years later we are finishing what Erik the Red started. The sounds of different voices can now be heard in Greenland: cows, horses, hens, and sheep, as well as the dominating sounds of women and men's voices. . . . Today you are here to follow Leif the Lucky's footsteps. By doing so, you are making clearer that which was fading. We will keep it in our memory. And we truly hope you will succeed in your journey to America."

I attempted to say something meaningful in return but managed only to mumble a few jumbled sentences before retreating with a heartfelt thanks.

Later, when Erik's daughter-in-law gave me a copy of the speech, I realized it had been recycled. He had planned on giving it to Ragnar Thorseth's group, but they had to pass up sailing to Qassiarsuk when pack ice blocked their way. No matter; everyone recycles speeches. His words were endearing. Afterward most of us hung around the café, talking with locals in broken English. Every grandparent, parent, and child shook our hands. They seemed a bit worried about us. If I had not been feeling so befuddled by all the attention, I probably would have felt as though this were our last supper.

I led a small troop—Dean, Rob, Russell, who had flown over to photograph us, and David Conover, the documentary filmmaker who was taping our departure—in search of Erik the Red's house the next morning. Terry seemed a little impatient with this idea, but I was determined to sit where Leif had once sat and dreamed of

sailing west to a land of trees. Having grown up in southern Greenland, where he was taller than the average tree, Leif must have
had an extraordinarily strong urge to see such wonders as trees as
tall as hillsides. I had a brochure that explained where to find the
trunk-case-sized stones that were all that remained of the original
outpost, but neither the Danish or Greenlandic governments had
done anything to mark or preserve the sites—no information station, plaques, or fences.

First we found a U-shaped mound covering the remains of
the first church in Greenland. Around 1000 Erik the Red's wife,
Thjodhild, had a small church built. She prayed there with other
Greenlanders who had adopted Christianity. Her husband, Erik,
had not converted, and as a result Thjodhild would not have sex
with him.

When I finally sat down on a stone that I believed to be part of
the old wall of Erik's house, and later Leif's, I felt a twinge of excitement. *This is good*, I told myself. *The right thing. I can feel the
past. . . .*

"Hod, I don't think this is it," Dean said, bending over our map.
"We should be on the other side of this creek." Thank God I had
said nothing out loud. Dean has Scandinavian roots, and it seemed
that finding the right site was very important to him. Rob tagged
along, saying, as he would often repeat during the voyage, "I just
like seeing where people used to live."

We eventually found Erik's home. It had been a nice-sized
house. A guy could cook up a mean bowl of barley and still have
room to bring his farm animals in on a particularly nasty winter day
at this homestead. Most likely roofed with sod (although in Scandinavia some houses were also shingled or thatched) and heated by a
central fire with poor ventilation, probably a hole in the roof, the
house might have been a little claustrophobic in the winter, but then,
cramped quarters probably helped get Leif all riled up to go somewhere new—somewhere that might not cause annual carbon-
monoxide poisoning. Also, things could get a little spooky in a
Greenland house during the winter. One story goes that three hundred miles up the coast, not far from present-day Nuuk, Leif's
brother Thorstein wintered in the western settlement. Nearly everyone in the community was taking ill and dying, and Thorstein died
as well. But after he died he sat up on his death pallet and called for

his wife, Gudrid (the same Gudrid who would later give birth to Snorri in Vinland). She wisely did not respond on her own but eventually went to his side with another fellow named Thorstein, who asked what the dead Thorstein wanted. He then foretold her future, which sounded pretty good, except that she would end up doing a lot of Christianizing.

With dead men rising to babble about the future and the copious amounts of smoke that wafted throughout a Viking house, I could easily understand lighting out at the first opportunity, which came for Leif when he was only as old as . . . well, I actually had no idea how old Leif had been. The sagas were so confusing and contradictory and the scholars all have such varied interpretations that I was no longer even sure when Leif was supposed to have sailed to Vinland. Most historians put it at 1000, but I had recently looked more closely at *The Greenlanders Saga*, the one that seems more accurate. It indicates that Leif went to Vinland in 986 or 987. But if that were true, then he would have been only a young child at the time, according to *Erik's Saga*, which by its name should be pretty accurate on the ages of various members of Erik's clan.

So there I was, sitting on the stone walls of Leif's dad's house (if it really had been Erik's and if there really had been an Erik the Red), trying to be overwhelmed, and I suddenly wasn't too sure if our voyage was about to begin 1,000, 997, 1,011, or 1,010 years after Leif's.

But I did know we had a long, long way to go.

Before heading back to *Snorri*, Dean and I debated whether it would be bad karma to take a rock from the site for ballast. In the end, we agreed it would be. However, Dean ran down to the creek just below the house site and grabbed a large stone. Maybe it could have rolled down from Erik's house. Hell, maybe Erik or Leif had even pissed on it one drunken night. Dean cradled the rock in his arms like a baby.

Back on board, we completed a few more chores and began our voyage in earnest at one-forty-five. With less confusion than one might expect—by this I mean no one was strangled by an errant line as the yard rose to the top of the mast—we raised the sail.

Although I was trying my best to hide from this fact, we were, at best, a dysfunctional family. In front of the crew Terry and I spoke in guarded tones, neither of us quite revealing all that he was thinking. It was as if we were always put out with each other. As a result, our family—the crew—was confused about whom to turn to. They knew Terry was the only one qualified to sail the boat, but they also knew that I had the overall plan. Most of them were there because they believed in that plan. As a result, they sometimes seemed divided into pro-Hodding and pro-Terry camps. Added to that was the tension created by Terry's unwillingness to accept Andy as the navigator. He did not like Andy's style, nor did he believe Andy could actually navigate. My relationship with Trevor, shared by a few others, also did not help matters. His behavior on board was often paternalistic, while his overly cautious nature seemed inappropriate for our endeavor. So not only were there pro-Terry and pro-Hodding camps, there were also pro-Trevor and pro-Andy camps. Yuck.

Our roles for the journey were cemented that first morning. Terry stood in the stern, giving instructions in a not particularly loud voice. He was full of confidence in sailing situations, although the volume of his commands did not convey this. He was unflappable, even when we were on the verge of catastrophe. Trevor then repeated the instructions to those who were on duty, telling them where they should be and what they should do. Sometimes he dashed from bow to stern to set them straight. Oftentimes the person was already doing what was needed. Trevor never worked on the foredeck, the forwardmost position on the boat, except when it came time to row. Then he would work harder than anybody on board, wherever he was.

Dean stayed as close to Terry as possible, perhaps due to the shock he experienced when he realized how little sailing knowledge the rest of us had. He was twenty years older than Terry, had crossed the Atlantic solo, and yet seemed unwilling to do anything unless Terry suggested it. Terry did not seem to mind, except when it came time to sleep. Terry hates snoring, and Dean sounded like what I imagined to be a walrus in its death throes.

Rob and John Gardner stayed on the foredeck working the beitiáss—the spar that helps the boat sail windward. They liked the action up there and wanted to have every little detail of how to work the sail ironed out. They practically refused to go on the afterdeck, the stern.

Because of the tension between himself, Terry, and Trevor, Andy stayed on the foredeck too. He and Terry could not seem to stand being anywhere near each other. Andy was good at working the lines and sail, so the boat benefited somewhat from his and Terry's tension.

Homer quickly took to hanging out with Jan, who for the most part could not assist with the sailing. Having eleven people to cook for, three times a day, was a little overwhelming. However, whenever an extra hand was needed, Jan was always there unasked, pulling in a line or hauling on a heavy object. Homer helped Jan with the meals, but he also worked on the foredeck and steered the boat whenever he could.

Doug, Abbott, Elias, and I were the only ones who roamed the entire boat, taking on various roles but not quite fitting into any niche. To the very end, though, Abbott always found a way to get in the middle of something and help out, even if it meant being the clown.

I still wasn't sure about my own role. Was it simply to take notes and work as a crew member? Or should I try to lead? What that even meant, I wasn't sure.

When we raised the sail that first day, a muddled cloud of division hung over the boat. One of my goals had been that we all have a positive, cooperative experience, and here we were, failing at it from the very beginning. How were we ever going to make it to L'Anse aux Meadows? I wondered. As if in response, the wind was blowing right at us, making forward progress nearly impossible.

We set the tack . . . and an hour later we were back at Narsarsuaq, ground zero.

Never mind, we'll just tack again! We'll tack our way out of this fjord! Charge!

The wind died immediately. We lowered the sail and began rowing. When we reached an iceberg where it had appeared that the wind had been blowing, the wind was no longer there. We rowed for an hour.

The wind returned. "Yard going up!" Terry hollered. We were off!

Not for long.

"Now we're really going backward," Terry lamented three minutes later. The wind had shifted.

Terry whipped off his baseball cap and thrust his head forward. He swung it from side to side. The wind hit one cheek, then the other, back and forth, and finally it landed directly on his nose. This was his never-fail way of finding the wind's direction, and he looked just like a dog joyfully sticking his head out a car window. Countless times in the future he would perform this same maneuver, looking as pleased with the situation as the windblown dog—but not today. Our sail was backed, meaning the wind was filling it from the wrong direction. Then the wind died. Both sail and crew sat there limply.

"There it comes," Dean stage-whispered ages later. "There it comes."

"Any chance you can get it?" Trevor pleaded to Erik Larsen, our youth hostel friend, who was steering.

"There she comes," Dean coaxed. The sail filled, and we were on our way again.

"Okay . . . ready about," Terry commanded too softly. No one moved.

"Ready about!" Dean yelled, and everyone jumped to his station.

Erik pushed the tiller hard to port. The sail was now supposed to swing around, but it was taking its sweet time. An avalanche of ice rumbled down the side of a distant iceberg. The harsh thunder filling the fjord sounded like a dump truck tossing out a load of rocks onto a steel sheet.

We hauled the sheets and braces around, picked up speed, and headed for another iceberg. It started to blow so hard that we reefed the sail to protect it and the hemp rigging. When our sail was reefed, it was lowered about five feet or so and the reefed material was tied up with square knots all along the bottom. We had three reef points, the third of which would be used only in a gale.

"This is what you call an auspicious beginning," Dean called out—prematurely. The wind died again.

We lowered the sail and began rowing. We repeated this process again and again—row, sail, row, sail. Five hours later—around a quarter to nine at night—we finally reached a point where the wind was blowing consistently on our starboard quarter (back right side of the boat). No sooner had we started screaming downwind, than we found ourselves in an icy soup of bergy bits and growlers, smaller pieces of ice showing nothing or very little above the

RUSSELL KAYE

Pickle barrels

ocean's surface. We were probably moving along at four or five knots, and at that speed even the basketball-sized ice chunks could crack our planking. Polar-bear-sized bergy bits, although floating free in the water, would stop us in our wake and certainly smash the bow. It would be like hitting a jagged, rock-hard shoreline. Sailing through this minefield was dangerous but glorious. The water sparkled with these bobbing deadly jewels. Off to our right, sheer cliffs grew dark with the approaching dusk, and on our left the far side of the fjord was speckled with a kaleidoscope of maroon, purple, and green hills.

Elias climbed onto the bow, and as he led us through the ice Jan began to cook our dinner: beef (bought at the small grocery in

Narsarsuaq) with Thai red curry sauce and rice. A real Viking meal. All right, so we were not replicating what the Vikings ate, except by accident and once or twice by plan. We had eleven four-foot-tall maroon plastic pickle barrels with gasket tops that Jan had procured in New York. Stacked amidships, they were filled with modern fare: dried papaya, almonds, pecans, grits, mix for hummus, jasmine rice, linguini, dried pinto beans, canned vegetables, quinoa, tahini, peanut butter, and many more treats meticulously packed and labeled by Jan, Andy, Homer, and John Abbott. Jan had also managed to smuggle in nearly a whole wheel of Parmigiano-Reggiano and about ten pounds of cured Italian sausages. We would not be roughing it foodwise, except for having to labor over a temperamental two-burner kerosene stove.

As Jan huddled in his cramped, makeshift kitchen area, an Icelander named Stefan pulled alongside in a motorboat and tied onto *Snorri*. Then he boarded us without asking permission. Some of the crew had met him in a bar in Narsaq. He was a reindeer farmer who liked to be thought of as a modern-day Viking. An oft-repeated-story began with a guy complaining to friends about Stefan. According to the story, Stefan heard about it and called the man up, explicitly threatening to rape the man's wife and kill his dogs if he did not shut up. Supposedly the man shut up, and this story made Stefan's reputation as someone not to mess with.

After strutting around on *Snorri* for a very short while, Stefan jumped back on his boat and handed over a reindeer leg, saying something about us needing real Viking food. Seconds later he was gone. Later I would cook that reindeer for breakfast, mouthwatering steaks tasting like a cross between veal and venison. Stefan may have been a vulgar ass, but he raised good reindeer.

We finally anchored at midnight, our minds and bodies content from our spicy dinner and arduous day. I began to congratulate us for holding up so well until I remembered it was only the first day.

If we were not holding up well at that point, then we were doomed for sure. I began inventorying my aches and pains. I had raised the yard twice, and thus my legs were cramped and sore. My arms were feeling tight, a precursor to the achy, bruised feeling they would insist upon exhibiting the next day. My palms were tender to the touch, but everything would be okay. We had, after all, made seven miles in twelve hours.

Seven miles in twelve hours?

At this rate, with roughly 1,893 more miles to go, the voyage would take 270 days. That's not the kind of calculation you want to find yourself making while moaning about your aches and pains and missing your family like a blubbering child. It was so ludicrous that I knew things had to improve. We would make plenty of miles the next day. I just knew it. And, even more on the bright side, we had sailed all day without hitting an iceberg or the hundreds of bergy bits that streamed by our hull. Not everyone on board hated everyone else on board. *Snorri* had not leaked much. The rudder had worked. The rigging had stayed intact. The sky had not fallen.

Chapter Eight

We had only thirteen or so miles to Narsaq, our next port of call. A person can paddle that distance solo in a canoe on flat water in four hours. Walk it in three hours. Hop on a pogo stick, if in shape and armed with extra springs, in two hours. Run in one and a half hours.

In a knarr, on the other hand, he might never get there.

A knarr, we discovered, was not made for sailing in fjords, especially a fjord in which the prevailing wind blew straight for the ice cap that is at the end of it. As the next day and dozens more like it unfolded, we espoused new theories about the Vikings. One theory explained why Erik had settled in Brattahlid in the first place: He had sailed around Cape Farewell at Greenland's southern end looking for a decent place to live. Bredefjord was one of the first fjords he came to where pack ice did not block the entrance. He headed into the fjord, shrieking downwind, and could never get out again.

A passage in *The Greenlanders Saga* was beginning to make more sense as well. When Leif decided to search for new land, Erik did not want to go, "reckoning he was now getting on in years." However, Leif persisted and "Erik gave way to him, and once they were ready for their voyage came riding from home. When he had only a short way to cover to the ship, the horse he was riding on stumbled; Erik fell off and damaged his foot. 'It is not in my destiny,' said Erik then, 'to discover more lands than this we are now living in. Nor may we continue further this time together.' " So Erik went home and Leif and his crew rode on until they reached their ship.

What were they doing riding horses? Erik's farm was only two hundred yards from the fjord. The whole lot of them certainly would not ride horses such a short distance. Given our troubles, I decided that the Viking Greenlanders did not keep their boats near their homes at the end of the fjord because they knew how impossible it was to get out. They kept them at the mouth of the fjord and carted everything overland to their houses, using the same trail some of my crew had used earlier in the month.

Chalk one up for experimental archeology, I thought, patting myself on the back.

Of course, this theory was full of holes—namely, I had no way of proving it—but it helped to take my mind off the fact that we were going nowhere fast. Our second day out, we still did not reach Narsaq but instead screamed back and forth across the fjord. We probably tacked three or four dozen times, sometimes coming terrifyingly close to the fifteen-hundred-foot scree cliffs that loomed above us. One belch too loud and all those rocks could have come tumbling down upon us.

We tacked until ten-thirty that night, a time more suited to snuggling under covers, and then took up the oars. A localized current was striving against us, and we tried to power-sail, simultaneously sail and row, against it with little success.

At this point things got a little testy on board. Jan, John Abbott, and I argued about cornmeal, grits, and polenta. Jan's polenta had tasted too grainy. Being a southerner, I took offense at his mishandling one of my favorite grains, pretending I knew everything about ground corn and telling him that his mush was too dry to be polenta. He must have used cornmeal instead. Somehow Jan became convinced of this but acted as if he had realized this on his own. Abbott then took offense with both of us, since he had ordered the polenta/cornmeal. I told him he did not know anything about corn, being a Yankee. He said he had never had any problems with it when he was cooking. Then I said . . .

Meanwhile Erik, our friend from the youth hostel, who had

only counted on a nice day sail to Narsaq, seemed fed up with us American Vikings. After midnight, when we were still rowing but no longer assisted by the wind, he began to question some of Terry's decisions. He wanted to pull over to the shore and drop the anchor, but Terry wanted to find a good anchorage. "We're going backward, Terry," he said as Terry passed up another anchorage Erik thought suitable. What it really sounded like he was saying was, "You ignorant product of a worthless civilization, do what I say now!"

Doug, who had challenged Gardner's bragging back in Boston, now questioned nearly every word that anyone else uttered. Admittedly when he picked on anybody but me, I did not mind it: For instance, if Trevor suggested flaking the sail, Doug would immediately ask why we should go to the trouble, since it was already one-thirty in the morning and we still had not found an anchorage. If he picked on me for acting too bossy, however, I did not like it.

Terry and Andy each approached me separately, complaining about the other.

At the very least this frustrating time did a wonderful job of supplementing the limited sailing experience we were afforded in Maine. In two days we had become very good at handling the sail both on the foredeck and aft. And we knew the boat's and our limitations. Jan said to me at one point, "It's amazing how much I've learned in twenty-four hours. You know, unimportant things, like how not to pack so that you don't find yourself wanting to toss every last item in your dry bag overboard because you can't find your toothbrush, or what the cooking problems are—like the stove not really liking to cook food in windy conditions—or even less important things, like how the boat works."

We were also still learning how to sleep on board. The first night we had not set up a tarp over the foredeck and we all woke up a little wet. It was too cramped on the foredeck (Vikings would have used their sail) for all twelve of us to sleep there, so Terry decided to sleep on the smaller afterdeck. Dean naturally followed suit, driving Terry a little crazy. The second night, when we were all up till a quarter to three, Terry, Trevor, and Elias did not bother to get out their sleeping bags and slept on the bare deck. They were all sore and a bit cranky in the morning.

We did make it to Narsaq on the third day, however. About a

hundred townspeople came out to greet us. Rob was by far the biggest hit. When a handful of schoolchildren gathered around, he handed out yo-yos and rubber balls. Later, as we walked around town, children came running up from all directions, screaming, "Yo-yo!"

In the afternoon, the town threw a barbecue in our honor. The mayor spoke. He was a young helicopter pilot for Greenland Air. He seemed very urbane but also very much at home in this small hamlet. After he spoke, the town choir sang four songs in our honor—beautiful, lilting Inuit songs. We had no idea what they were about—Elias was still not translating very often—but it was a very sweet time. Then it was my turn. This time I was prepared. I thanked everyone for making us feel so welcome. I rambled a little about the Vikings and why what we were doing concerned every-one, not just Scandinavians. Then, on my cue, a man from the local tourist office stood up and announced there was a special treat for the day.

"A very talented dancer is among these men, but he is a little shy. If you will all cheer him on, then he will surely perform," he said, looking back at us. "So, Mr. John Abbott, will you please dance?" I had no idea if Abbott could dance or not, but I was des-perate for us to at least attempt to entertain our hosts. Of all the crew members, I figured he would be the best sport.

Abbott's long ponytail already had many of the women gig-gling, but now, as he turned as red as a skinned seal, they burst out clapping and laughing.

I moved behind him and nudged him forward. "You asshole, no way," he muttered.

I pushed a little harder, and he was soon standing before the crowd.

They cheered, somewhat hesitantly. He turned back and said, "I'm gonna get you, Carter."

"Think of this as public service," I said. "My speech sucked. They need you."

The crowd cheered louder.

"Come on, John, I'll pay you back. I promise."

"I know you will," he said, then, "No way." He inched forward, however, and they cheered some more. The choir looked like they were on the verge of accompanying him in song but then thought better of it.

Abbott, seeing no escape, called out, "This is what my people do on a Friday night."

He then bent forward—an unseemly, arthritic bow. He extended an arm past his head, supporting it with his other hand at the elbow. It looked like a freckled, withered elephant's trunk. Suddenly his body ground into motion and he became a rotating, undulating, freakishly skinny elephant—an animal that had certainly never before set foot on Greenland soil.

An abrupt, awkward silence descended over the crowd. We were in the midst of a cultural crisis. He had to do something else, fast.

He spun around, smooth as blubber. Then he skipped toward a row of onlookers, who backed up in fear. He was going to fall into them. Suddenly he skipped back.

His hips began to rotate in a sexual pantomime. A few cheers escaped from the more lascivious spectators.

He flapped his trunk, never losing a sense of his inner rhythm, whatever it was. The crowd began to clap, and a few laughs could be heard.

Then, for his grand finale, he spun, flapped his trunk, and rotated his hips, all at the same time. Abruptly standing still, he bowed smoothly, and the crowd applauded. Laughter far outweighed the clapping. Later Elias' sister, who lives in Narsaq, dubbed him "Wind Dancer." Better yet, unbeknownst to us, Abbott's dance was broadcast on Greenland TV for the entire country to enjoy.

While walking around town after the barbecue, Abbott, who was still speaking to me, and I stopped at the house of John Rasmussen, a Danish photographer who had lived in Greenland for the past thirty years. His black-and-white photographs do justice to a land that is hard to capture. They are both alluring and reserved. His wife, Bolette, a native Greenlander and daughter of one of the early sheep farmers, brought out coffee and cake, making us very welcome. Bolette attempted to educate us on what to call people in Greenland. We were definitely not to call anyone *Eskimo*. People preferred being called *Inuit*, but since she was old, she said, she did not care. *Greenlanders* was the best thing to call them.

Rasmussen shattered our dreamlike perspective on Narsaq

during coffee, telling us that he had been mugged by a gang of youths during the past year. They had beaten him until he was unconscious and stolen the little money he had on him. Since Narsaq was such a small town, roughly two thousand citizens, he knew all his attackers by sight. Rasmussen bitterly complained about Greenland's criminal system, lamenting that his attackers would go virtually unpunished.

In the late 1940s Denmark sent a group of scholars to Greenland to study the best way to deal with crime. The product of their work was the Greenland Criminal Code of 1954, which for the most part preserved the traditional methods of handling crimes in Greenland. The most extraordinary aspect of the code to Western sensibilities is that there were, and still are, no jails in Greenland. In the distant past, most disputes were settled by drum dances, except for homicide, which was settled by revenge. In the drum dance, two enemies, or the alleged perpetrator and victim of a crime, encircled by the community, would attempt to belittle and lampoon each other in song. Since colonizing Greenland in 1721, the Danes had attempted to implement more modern punishments. Imprisonment, however, proved to be intolerable to Greenlanders, and instead convicted criminals are rehabilitated.

Depending on the crime, they are either confined to their homes or are put in a halfway house. During the day they take rehabilitation classes and work at a regular job within the general populace.

The hardest thing for Rasmussen to bear was not the crime itself but the daily pain and embarrassment of watching his attackers loaf around town, clearly unrehabilitated. "I cannot stand to see them," he said, shaking his head.

Equally infuriating to many Greenlanders is that rape is still treated as a minor crime, equal to theft. Earlier in the colonial period rapists were castrated, but more recently sentences for rape are usually only a few months of rehabilitation. A Greenlandic Justice Commission, appointed in 1994, is attempting to correct this situation.

The Greenland system seemed to work in the past and it was rightfully heralded as a landmark code in that it preserved traditional Greenlandic ways of handling crime. However, a recent increase in murder and violence, cases like Rasmussen's, and the awareness of rape as a serious crime are putting its effectiveness in doubt. The murder rate of late has equaled that of some of the United States' worst cities (Miami and Detroit in 1988), and as a result, convicted murderers are now sent to Denmark for imprisonment. Maybe prisons in Greenland are not that far off.

At some point conversation at the Rasmussens' turned toward a lighter subject, the Vikings, and I began to fantasize how Rasmussen might have gotten revenge a thousand years ago.

First of all, he would have had more options to handle the situation himself. If he were a timid Viking, he might express his grievances at a *thing*. If lawmakers at the *thing* found Rasmussen's attackers guilty, the attackers would have to pay him a fine, based on how much the lawmakers appraised Rasmussen to be worth.

If Rasmussen were more aggressive, say, like Erik the Red, he could kill his neighbor openly for insulting him. Under most circumstances, this would have simply been considered a lawful revenge killing and that would be that. In others, Rasmussen would have been found guilty of manslaughter. (Murder was defined as killing someone without owning up to it and was not an honorable form of killing for a Viking.) For manslaughter, Rasmussen might be fined and/or made an outlaw and banished from his land for a prescribed period. Such a killer usually was granted a certain number of days to make his escape, but from then on anyone could kill him, free of consequence. Erik the Red was such an outlaw when he decided to settle Greenland. If Erik had dabbled in witchcraft or thievery, however, it would have been a completely different matter. The community would immediately have killed him, hanging him if he were a thief and either stoning or drowning him if he were a witch.*

Obviously Rasmussen's best recourse would have been to label his attackers witches. While my mind was meandering in the past, Bolette, Rasmussen's wife, told us she had grown up thinking often about the Vikings. "When we would find a dead bird, we would bury it with some of the jewelry we had found that was from the Vikings," she told us. I was curious about this jewelry, but she was even more curious as to why a bunch of Americans were retracing

* For more on this, read P. G. Foote and D. M. Wilson's *The Viking Achievement*. It has a wonderful section on justice that includes many of the archaic rituals that Vikings had to go through to either escape or receive justice.

Leif Eriksson's route. My explanation (the reader is directed to the first chapter of this book) seemed to meet her approval.

There is a traditional Greenlandic story told about the Vikings' disappearance that explains why the Greenlanders might still be conscious of or care about the Vikings. According to the story, the Inuit and the Vikings lived harmoniously in close proximity to each other.* Then one day while the Inuit men were out hunting, the Viking settlers sneaked over to the Inuit settlement and slaughtered all the old people, women, and children. When the Inuit men returned, they were understandably enraged. They sneaked up to the Viking settlement with their kayaks disguised as icebergs and attacked the Vikings, killing all but one man, who was allowed to escape in a Viking boat.

We were allowed to escape the next day, too, thanks to Abbott's dance, or perhaps in spite of it. However, our progress did not improve. In fact, it got worse. Every inch in the week that followed was hard fought.

Much of our time on the water was spent rowing. Six men on, six off, at half-hour intervals. We argued and argued about the best rowing positions and ceaselessly criticized each other's rhythm, pace, and body odor. Some thought it better to row facing forward, others backward. Unlike a conventional seated rowing position, on *Snorri* we had to stand up because of the oars' length and angle to the water. No matter which way you were facing, you had to use your entire body to exert enough force with the oar. The rowing was not really that difficult, but it was interminable. Our top speed was not much more than one knot. We could row for hours on end and gain only a few miles. On occasion someone would attempt to lighten the burden by reading aloud. Doug's reading from *Moby Dick* was the most inspired:

"Pull, pull, my finehearts-alive; pull, my children, pull, my little ones. . . . Why don't you break your backbones, my boys? . . . Pull, then, do pull; never mind the brimstone—devils are good fellows

---

* According to archeological evidence, this would have been up at the western settlement, near present-day Nuuk.

enough. So, so; there you are now; that's the stroke for a thousand pounds; that's the stroke to sweep the stakes! Hurrah for the gold cup of sperm oil, my heroes. . . . Pull, will ye? pull can't ye? pull, won't ye? Why in the name of gudgeon and ginger cakes don't ye pull?—pull and break something! pull, and start your eyes out! Here! . . ."

Although Doug put his heart into the performance, he could not make us row any faster. It seemed we would never even make it to the open ocean before the summer ran out. The only possible good we could find in our situation was that the delay allowed the pack ice that had drifted from eastern Greenland to the mouth of our fjord to clear out—and the same was true for the pack ice along Baffin Island.

Also, moving at such a slow pace, we found one enviable anchorage after another. We would row or sail up to a narrow inlet, drop the sail if it was raised, and then row through a chute to a cove protected by hills on all sides. The rocks on the hillsides were covered with moss and lichen, painting them in reds, yellows, oranges, and browns. We spent many of those unending evenings walking on shore, saying what we hoped would be good-bye to the tiny willows and birches that fill every hollow in the south. One of my favorite coves was bordered by a thin, low-lying spit of land separating us from the fjord, across which we could watch towering icebergs float through the night—a parade of stately blue-and-white sculptures.

As a result of this quiet time, we fought less. The bickering our first couple of days had been opening-night jitters, evidently, and even some of the inherent divisions amongst the crew were beginning to dissolve. We were growing closer. Andy would often play his guitar, strumming out rock or folk standards that perhaps helped soothe our tensions.

One day I heard Doug complaining to Elias, "Hey, you just called him 'dear,'" referring to John Gardner. "I thought I was your dear!"

"No, you're my sweetheart," Elias responded, chuckling.

That same day, while a group of us worked the foredeck, setting the forward edge of the sail so we could try and sail windward, Gardner started to tell someone how to wrap the tack around the beitiáss properly. He always wanted everything to be done right, all the way from working the tack properly to getting up at the right time in the morning. Oftentimes after someone had cleated a line around a belaying pin, he would quietly recleat the line when the person was not looking—Captain Tidy strikes again. As Gardner was explaining the proper way to cleat the tack, Rob came diving aft from bowwatch.

"Wait a minute! Wait a minute!" he yelled, sliding across the deck on his knees. "Before you take his advice, I've got to tell you something. A short time ago, this guy was living in Hawaii, bartending, surfing whenever he wanted, and dating a model. Then he suddenly decides to move to Rockland, Maine. Do you really want to take advice from a guy like that?"

Bringing us so close together, perhaps, was kapaka. We played endless hands of kapaka whenever we were not moving. I think it was such a great stress reliever because the rules always appeared to be changing. You could not really be expected to be good at it, unlike everything else on our voyage. Terry and Dean, however, did not join in. Terry appeared to think the game was too frivolous and obnoxious. He would scowl ever so slightly whenever the cards were pulled out. Apparently Dean did not play because Terry did not play.

During one particularly boisterous kapaka game, someone farted loudly, and Elias confided in me, "When I was a little boy, I believed the Danes never farted. Then one day, I heard a Dane do that," he said, pointing at the farter. "Oh, I laughed and laughed. I could not stop laughing." His comment reminded me of something that often happened when I was a Peace Corps teacher in Kenya. I would be walking to my outhouse, not looking particularly ridiculous, when suddenly I would hear peals of laughter directed toward me. I would look around to see what was so funny but could detect nothing. After this happened dozens of times, I realized they were laughing because I had to answer nature's call, just like them.

What a strange image Westerners must project that other cultures think we don't fart or pee. The Vikings, on the other hand, were quite open with their bodily functions, at least while trading in the Far East. An emissary from the Byzantine empire recorded his time with a group of Viking traders called Rus who traded and lived in what is now Russia. Not only did the men of the community ravage their women in public, they also relieved themselves in broad daylight. There was no mistaking their humanity.

The gods knew we were all too human as well, and occasionally they showed us mercy by granting a slight following breeze. At these times *Snorri* reminded me more of a vacation cruise than a Viking ship. The wind was never strong and never lasted more than an hour or two, but we all had our own ways of handling this time. Trevor would have to fiddle with something, usually the computer because he seemed the most intent on getting our Web site journal entries sent out. Jan would read one of his cookbooks or a novel that had nothing to do with adventure, for example, *The Plague*. Terry might be "driving," as he called steering the boat, while Dean hovered within a foot or two, looking purposefully out to sea. When Terry was not driving, he was checking on the condition of different parts of the boat. While everybody else relaxed during these downwind interludes, Terry did not.

John Abbott would attempt to organize his gear, as his stuff had a tendency to get scattered across the boat. Otherwise, he and practically everyone else would kick back, staring at the water, the occasional iceberg, the undulating hillsides, amazed that we were sailing a Viking ship in southern Greenland.

Andy, no longer the navigator, would resplice a line that had been coming loose or work on some other aspect of the rigging. The rest of the time he lounged. He could sleep while sitting, standing, probably even hanging over the side of the boat. Meanwhile, Doug might whittle on a piece of wood or write letters to his girlfriend in his notebook. Rob spent most of this time on bow watch, praying that we anchored before the water turned rough. Elias would try the reception on his cellular phone or turn on the radio if it was close to the time for the nightly weather report. Homer might tell very long stories that none of us really believed, invariably involving a couple of girls, high speeds in either cars or boats, and cops.

I was usually either reading, or thinking about Lisa and my girls. Sometimes I would read the journal that Lisa had given me. In early May she wrote, "I'm just empty without you. It's never the same when you are gone. Today, I've been feeling as though we haven't talked or spent any time together in the past few months.

I'm not upset or angry or annoyed—just a little sad and feeling it's a preview of what's going to happen this summer." I thought about her biting her fingernails with worry and wished I could reach out to calm her hands and heart.

Once while inspecting a new wound, oblivious that I was thousands of miles away, Rob blurted out, "I myself think that life isn't led well without a good pus-filled wound. Something to squeeze and pick at."* Then he squeezed some pus out. "Without this, you've been hanging out in an armchair too long. What you need is a good Douglas fir splinter in you. Now *that* has a sting to it!" Earlier he and I had been discussing the buildup of bacteria in the poop bucket. He had concluded, "I do not believe in the germ theory." Perhaps his theory about pus-filled wounds was an alternative.

Sometimes Gardner would read aloud from *Arctic Adventures*, a colorful memoir by Peter Freuchen about his days in Greenland, while sitting on our drywall bucket outfitted with a homemade wooden toilet seat. Gardner had not yet reconciled himself to going over the side. It amazed me how quickly we all adapted to using the so-called bathroom in front of each other. Often someone would pull out the bucket or lean over the rail just a few feet from someone else, carrying on a lively conversation all the while.

At various moments Doug would suddenly announce it was time for push-ups, and half the crew would face off for a grueling series of push-ups called pyramids. Everybody did one push-up, then two, on up to ten or maybe even fifteen, and then back to one.

Every evening we would pick out an anchorage, usually row to the spot, checking depths with our lead line, and then drop the anchor. Although we might have been rowing for ten hours, this was not a time for rest. First we had to stow the oars. Someone would always get hit or bumped during this process. They were, after all, an ungainly eighteen feet long. Then most of us gathered around the lowered yard and flaked the sail, layering it on top of the yard. Sometimes Gardner would make us start all over again if the result was not pretty enough for him. Next we went about moving lines to the side of the foredeck to create a sleeping space. Three or four guys would set up the tarp that ran from the bow to

---

* We were always getting cuts on board, mostly from fast-moving lines, and Terry and I had a contest to see who could accumulate the most cuts before leaving Greenland. Since our hands were never dry, the cuts took quite a while to heal.

the mast—heavy dew and the occasional rain shower had taught us to appreciate the nighttime coverage. Meanwhile, Jan and two others would begin preparing dinner—coddling the temperamental stove, chopping onions and garlic, opening cans of vegetables and spices, and boiling water for rice or pasta. Then we could relax.

One evening I wandered around the deck, drifting in and out of the disparate conversations that ensued once the chores were complete. On the afterdeck Dean said to me, "You're quiet tonight."

"Yeah?" I answered. "I miss my wife."

"Me too. It'll be good when we get this e-mail stuff straightened out." We still could not get the computer to work very well, only occasionally getting a journal entry sent off and completely failing at receiving or sending e-mails. Then again, having a computer and satellite system on board a Viking ship was begging for such problems, and we had not expected much from them.

Meanwhile, Elias and Abbott were lounging on their bags, which were stored upright amidships beside the plastic pickle barrels, rolling cigarettes. "I think I would like to sleep in the tent tonight and write and read and drink tea and dream about sunshine," Elias said.

"Dream about naked ladies, you mean," Abbott added. Then he madly searched through his dry bag, his knapsack, his waterproof ammo tin, and his fanny pack for his lighter, but ended up finding it in the ballast rocks beneath the dry bags.

"You must stop that!" Terry said, exasperated, standing over Trevor, who was humming slightly off-key as he huddled over the computer.

"What?" Trevor asked, not looking up.

"You must stop that humming."

Trevor looked up, hurt.

"I was only kidding," Terry added, but Trevor did not resume his humming.

Up on the foredeck, Andy announced, "A girl gave me genital warts once."

"How do you get those?" Gardner asked, opening a can of corn.

"It comes from doing it too many times in one night, I think,"

Andy said, pleased with his explanation. Doug laughed out loud and said he did not think that was quite right.

Then it was time to eat. We all grew silent except for heartfelt praise of Jan's cooking. After working all day outdoors, we would have praised a nightly bowl of corned beef hash as haute cuisine, but Jan's cooking was really quite tasty, usually bursting with garlic and lots of fresh Parmesan.

Around ten or eleven o'clock we would go to sleep except for the person on anchor watch, who would be replaced after an hour by the next person, and so on until the morning.

That is how our time passed, day after day, for nearly two weeks, until one day Terry said, "See the ocean swell?" I looked toward the mouth of the fjord in vain. Then I realized he was talking about the mild swells beneath us. "It's very gentle and long— barely noticeable."

We reached the ocean proper that afternoon. Fog rolled in immediately, as if to say, *Not yet, boys,* but it cleared as we rowed around an island called Upernivik. Tall bergs stood, sentinel-like, out past the island, the echo of waves hitting their hard edges rumbling like thunder. This was the place we had been struggling to reach for so many days.

As we rowed past the icebergs Abbott remarked to me, "It looks like the end of the world." A moment later I overheard Terry say the exact same thing. And they were right. Staring out at the endless harsh ocean bordered by deafening icebergs, we were minuscule nothings. How could we dare to challenge this reality, this rugged beauty, in our little open boat?

As if in response, we chose not to. We could have stayed out there, but Elias knew a better way. We would take a cut behind a place called Cape Desolation. The water was supposed to be pretty tricky off the cape, and there was no reason to have our first offshore, out-of-the-fjord sailing experience right then and there. So we retreated. Also, when granted the opportunity to sneak by a place called Desolation, one should always take it.

Maybe to reward us for being so prudent, we were granted a following wind and actually sailed most of the way to Qassimiut, a small community a half dozen miles away.

After anchoring and cleaning *Snorri*—Terry and Gardner demanded we have a tidy ship whenever we came to a port—a group of us went ashore. Two dead seals greeted us as we stepped on the town landing, which was a huge slab of rock about half the size of a football field. The seals floated in a pool of blood, skinless, with bulging eyes. I understood eating seals—they were like cows to Greenlanders—but could not understand this waste. Seal meat was and always had been an important staple of the Greenland diet, yet these seals were obviously not going to be eaten by humans.

Except for some children, who had escorted us the last half mile to Qassimiut, and Anders, a young man I spoke with for a while near the community center, the town of ninety souls appeared deserted. No one came out to greet us. Anders, who was studying physical education in college in Qaqartoq, said everyone was eating dinner, but even after dinner nobody came out of their homes. It seemed as though they might be afraid of us. Or maybe they were afraid Abbott would dance. Anders said everybody knew about his dance.

Anders explained that the seals I had seen had been killed for their skins, which were sold to the cooperative in Narsaq. "If someone wants the meat, he can just take it. . . . No one needs it right now." I could not help wondering if this waste, much like the increase in crime, was a result of Greenland's rush to modernize. Or was I just expecting too much, assuming or hoping they would be better than us? Some hunters waste deer in much the same manner all over the United States. I probably had my answer when gazing at Qassimiut's houses, which were typical for Greenland. They were brightly colored wooden structures made with material imported from Denmark. Somewhere I had read the opinion that these red, yellow, blue, and green buildings looked out of place in Greenland, but they were so cheerful I had to disagree. Perhaps the author of this complaint wanted Greenlanders to remain quaint and live in sod houses, just as I wished them to use all parts of the seal, as they had done only twenty years back. I suppose I bring romantic expectations and notions to any place I travel to, especially somewhere considered exotic or less "developed" than the United States, and these notions often have nothing to do with what the people I'm visiting really need or care about.

✛

Over the next few days, as we got closer and closer to reaching the ocean for good, it became obvious that one of our crew members came with some rather odd notions of his own, and I felt slightly responsible. Trevor seemed inordinately apprehensive about offshore sailing, especially since he was the nominal first mate and an Outward Bound instructor. In retrospect, I think it was because he had been asked to join the voyage at a fairly late date and was thus less informed than anyone else as to what we were trying to do. Terry, I was finally gathering, had only outlined some aspects of the trip to him, and I had never gotten the chance to fill him in completely. As a result, Trevor was operating on completely different expectations than the rest of us. For example, one day he asked me if we were going to use the motor on our inflatable boat to push us when needed. No one else even would have thought to ask this. They all knew this was out of the question, especially so early in the voyage. The motor was for emergencies only. It made me wonder if he even knew what our route was. So it should not have come as too big a surprise when he began questioning our plans to sail up the coast. He thought we could inch our way up through a mazelike succession of islands that would afford us some protection from the ocean, as we were doing to get around Cape Desolation. This method could only add weeks to our journey, and sailing offshore along the coast had always been the plan, weather permitting.

"The truth is, I've been offshore just enough to make me nervous," he said one evening. "I haven't been off enough to make me comfortable with anything. That's why I'm questioning how we go about the next step."

I am not proud that I had taken to saying "Shut up, Trevor" whenever he suggested something that bothered me, which was often, but at least I refrained from doing so at this moment.

Terry stepped in and said, "You can't really explain what it's like until you've been in it," he told Trevor, "and you can only learn by being out there."

At this point we were anchored behind Cape Desolation. I glanced up to see Andy playing the guitar in the bow. Elias was pouring kerosene into the stove with a lit cigarette in his mouth while Rob held the stove unsteadily on a crossbeam. In this light, I could understand Trevor's worries, but they should have been brought up back in the United States, not the day before sailing offshore.

"I'm feeling like I don't know what we're doing. What's our next step? Have we planned it?" Trevor asked.

"We haven't planned a step since we left Narsarsuaq," Terry answered curtly. I felt relieved that Terry seemed to find Trevor's anxiety as unnerving as I did. Terry, however, remained calm. "We're going where we can, depending on the wind and conditions."

Trevor repeated his questions, apologizing for beating a dead horse but beating it nonetheless.

"I guess I try not to have any expectations about where we're going to stop or sail because of the kind of boat we have," Terry replied.

By this time the entire crew had huddled around. No one else expressed concern about leaving sight of land, but then again, only Dean had much experience in offshore sailing. Some of the crew chose this time to ask if we were still sailing up to the Arctic Circle. There seemed to be Arctic Circle fever going around. Terry and I had talked privately about being far behind schedule. We had tossed around the idea that making it to Sisimiut, Elias' hometown and our destination within the Arctic Circle, might not happen.

I tried to be diplomatic and inclusive during this discussion. A few days back, the consensus was that I had acted in too authoritarian a manner in the Hot Chocolate Incident. I had rationed the hot chocolate without first explaining that I was doing so because Jan told me it was being used up too quickly. Since it was just hot chocolate, I had not thought it would be a big deal. Trevor had gotten very mad. "Well, if we're going to start rationing hot chocolate, then we have a big problem. Food issues are a big problem." I think this is when I took to saying "Shut up" to him. It became an almost-all-crew argument. Terry said we had all been eating luxuriously—rationing a few items would not hurt us in any way. He also added that he thought decisions such as rationing food should be discussed ahead of time.

With that lesson learned, I tried to listen and answer questions as patiently as possible.

"All I want to do is cross the Arctic Circle," Homer said. "That would be cool. If the group has a consensus to do it, then I think we should."

Terry also tried to remain diplomatic but ended the discussion with, "Sometimes group consensus may not be enough."

Chapter Nine

Despite Trevor's concerns, we eventually sailed offshore as planned, but not before we had a few mishaps. One particularly bad day, Dean dropped the yard directly on Elias' head. The halyard had started slipping too quickly around the belaying pin and then, as Dean tried to slow it down, it completely slid off. Dean tried to stop it, but it just burned through his arm, scraping off a sizable patch of skin. When the yard hit him, Elias was knocked down for a few seconds and seemed slightly dazed upon standing, but he recovered promptly. Within a few hours we also ran aground for the first time. We were hugging a bold shore (a shoreline with a steep drop) to escape the wind funneling down a narrow channel. The shore turned out to be not so bold. Elias was on bow watch and waved Dean, the helmsman, to steer toward port. Dean did not respond. Elias waved again, more emphatically, but said nothing.

"I'm trying to keep us out of the wind and I've got this bow watch waving me out into it," Dean complained to Terry.

Elias waved some more, but it no longer mattered. We were grounded on a ledge. We tried rowing. Nothing. We tried shifting ballast. Nothing. We tried rocking the boat off by running from side to side, looking like extras in a Monty Python skit. We eventually got unstuck by shifting more ballast and raising the sail to let the wind back us off.

Once safely on our way again, we ended up on the northern end of Cape Desolation and explored the outer coast by foot for a few days, waiting for the right wind. Abbott and I gathered wild plants for salads, mountain sorrel and green sorrel and roseroot. Crowberries, growing on plants that look like juniper ground cover, carpeted the hillsides, but they were not sweet enough to waste time gathering. The roseroot, however, with its fleshy petals and light lettucey taste, was a good antidote to all the dried and canned food on board. One day Jan added a bowlful to a pot of barley soup—a meal the Vikings surely would have recognized. The mountain sorrel and green sorrel were even more of a treat. With tart green leaves that are rich in vitamin C, they taste a bit like green apples. When I figured I had collected enough for the crew to eat, I lay back and ate whole clumps of sorrel until it was time to return to *Snorri*. Later, I was delighted to learn that the Vikings had brought sorrel over from Iceland.

The outer coast was weather-worn and even more dramatic than the land surrounding the fjords. It was rough, uninhabitable land that dared us to step foot upon it, and we were all drawn in. One day as Homer and I lounged in a patch of reindeer lichen and cushiony moss, he told me, "I don't know what to write about this place. 'You gotta sit here where I am, then you'll know.' That's all I can come up with. Can't describe it."

It was as if we alone were given free run of a private nature preserve. Shore and ocean and snow-topped mountains and the occasional reindeer surrounded us without another human being in sight, although there was evidence that others had been there. We often came upon stone burial sites and old tent rings. In some cases, the stones used to hold down summer skin tents were covered with moss, unused for decades. Others looked as though someone had used them the summer before. At times a wave of melancholy spilled through these old sites; at others it was an exuberant rush of life.

The Inuit graves were almost always located on a peak, with a mound of rocks heaped around and over the dead. I have been told that they were buried on the high points because the Inuit prized a good view of the ocean and fjords. In some of the graves, the granite slabs had shifted out of place from years of frost heaves, rain, and snow, and we could see a skull or maybe just a part of a pelvis catching a ray of light in the shadowy chamber. I found a knife or harpoon point carved out of bone lying outside one grave and dropped it back in just in case it was needed in another world.

"Good move, Hod," Abbott told me. He was a delightful companion on these walks because everything was a novelty to him and because I never knew what he might say. "We don't want this to turn out like that *Brady Bunch* episode. Remember?"

I did not.

"They went to Hawaii and explored this cave. Mr. Hanilea, their tour guide, told them that if they took artifacts, it would upset the ancients and bring bad luck. Bobby took this thing and everything went wrong. They even got kidnapped by Vincent Price, playing a mad archeologist."

Um, thanks, Abbott.

At first some of us felt guilty walking around grave sites or trampling willows that were probably a hundred years old although no taller than a dandelion. These tough little shrubs are natural bonsai. Burdened with a very short growing season, they can't waste energy on getting tall. Nearly all of their resources are put into leaf and root production. We felt equally guilty about treading on the moss and lichen, which also have only a few months to thrive before closing down for the winter. I tried my best to walk around them, sticking to the boulders. Then I realized the boulders were covered with equally precious lichen. Eventually I gave in. Since there weren't thousands upon thousands of us trying to get a glimpse of nature, I figured it was all right to walk wherever we wanted or needed to go.

Reindeer would bound across a field a hundred yards from where we stood, or casually forage at closer range. Some of them had such improbably gargantuan antler racks that it looked as if they should topple over. They were picky eaters, snuffling at items they did not care for, nibbling at the good stuff, and then quickly moving on to the next morsel. I was curious to see if they were eating what is called reindeer lichen. Somewhere I had read that the Vikings ate it, and I tried some. It was pretty bland, like a mouthful of paper, and tasted a lot like dirt. It didn't look like the reindeer were eating it, either.

The government of Greenland had reintroduced reindeer to the area about twenty years earlier. Although we did not see any large herds, the reindeer seemed to be getting by, judging by the number of droppings.

When a southerly wind finally came, I did not feel as Trevor did—that we were not prepared to sail north—but part of me still wanted to linger. This land made everything less confusing.

Nevertheless, we headed out at the first chance. It was July 29, twelve days after leaving Brattahlid, and we had only a hundred miles behind us.

By early afternoon we had already erased twenty more miles, but the wind was letting up. Jan, now referred to as Cookie despite his protests, leaned heavily on the oak crossbeam to steady himself. He seemed deep in profound thought. Later he would tell me that he had been thinking, *I could just do ramen. These guys wouldn't know the difference. They won't care. . . . No, that would be too wimpy. It's time for risotto!*

He began his preparations for cooking by warming up with a few jumps carefully timed to miss the sail as it snapped across the foredeck. The bolt rope lining the edge of the sail was an inch in diameter. Pine tar had hardened it to a clublike consistency. Each of us had been whacked across the head enough times to be forever leery of it. After completing his warm-up successfully, Jan lit a cigarette, and I joined him, bumming my daily allotment. Dinner could wait a few more minutes.

I had been giddily prancing around the deck all day. We were offshore—four miles from Umanarsuk, "little heart mountain." After twelve days of sailing, rowing, and slogging our way out of Erik's Fjord and Bredefjord, we were finally free. Free! Soon enough we would be crossing to Canada! We would show the world that the Vikings really had sailed this route. I still might make it for my daughter's birth.

"Time to make dinner," Jan said aloud. "Come on, Doug." Doug and Dean were his assistants for the day, but Jan knew asking Dean would not be of much use. Dean had not taken well to kitchen duty. He was willing to help Trevor with the difficult task of getting the computer to work, but he tried his best to stay clear of KP, even when it was his turn.

Together Doug and Jan lifted the pine floorboards in the center of the foredeck and hoisted out the marine plywood kitchen box crammed with pots, pans, and utensils such as a cheese grater, whisk, and can opener. Their efforts were labored: a leg planted just so on a floor timber, an arm braced on a crossbeam, muscles tightened and expectant so that when they were sent tumbling into the bilge bodily damage might be minimal. Next Doug lifted out a smaller plywood box housing the two-burner kerosene stove.

The wind extinguished match after match. Real Vikings would have been grateful to gnaw on a hunk of *økkvinn hleifr, thungr ok thykkr, thrunginn sádum* (coarse loaf, heavy and thick, stuffed with bran) or, if they were lucky, a slice of cold dried *steikja* (steak). But we had to have hot food. Jan finally triumphed in lighting one of the burners and began heating a half cup of olive oil in a pot large enough to cook an entire seal. The wind simultaneously shifted direction and increased, and as we tacked, heading farther out to sea, the beitiáss crew reset the sail's leading edge. Doug hovered over Jan, trying his best not to let the beitiáss guys stumble onto the pots and pans. With nowhere else to go, Jan had set up his kitchen in the epicenter of the foredeck action.

Jan peeled the wrappers off a dozen bouillon cubes and plopped the cubes into the water that covered the ten cups of arborio rice. Rain slashed horizontally with the increased wind.

"This has got to be a local phenomenon. This is so bizarre," Terry said to no one in particular. The wind had shifted nearly 180 degrees and was now out of the northeast. "But then, the conditions are always bizarre here. So does that make this *not* bizarre?"

Jan began to feel seasick. He methodically exhaled hard, looking away from the stove, out across the sea. It occurred to him that making risotto on our first offshore sail had not been his greatest idea.

"Shouldn't we tack back now?" Trevor asked. He still had not reconciled himself to our destiny. "That low could still be on its way," he cautioned, referring to information we had received earlier about the weather. I was probably not as worried about the boat or us as I should have been, and I silently willed him to be quiet.

We were sailing as close to the wind as possible so as not to go too far out to sea. The steel blue water chopped at *Snorri*'s thin pine planking, and virtually frozen waves sprayed across the deck.

This was quickly becoming a miserable experience, but I felt we had to push north. I mentally urged Terry to keep us going, never saying anything aloud because I feared he might follow Trevor's suggestion if I did.

Terry chose to continue on our course. As a result, we were about to have a very good lesson in sailing windward through the night, something we had never done.

When the rain and wind decided to improve upon the lesson, increasing dramatically, we donned our Mustang suits, bright red, heavy foul-weather gear with built-in flotation. I loved my suit because it made me feel invincible: have ocean suit, will survive. That is, it made me feel invincible while balancing safely onboard *Snorri*. Its armor, however, was merely superthick nylon, and I did not take much comfort in the suit's built-in flotation. If I accidently fell overboard, it would only allow me a better view of my shipmates' vain attempts at rescuing me as I slipped into hypothermic unconsciousness. Unlike my emergency immersion suit, this outfit would be useless soon after I was tossed overboard.

Things had progressed even worse for Jan, and he now sorely regretted having chosen risotto. Not only could he not keep his hands warm, struggling with metal pot handles and herb flakes that twirled in the sail's vortex, he could not even cook the rice fully because of the size of the industrial stockpot. Also, the spice mix he added was too acidic. The guys were not going to like it. Ah, but the Parmigiano-Reggiano he had brought on board at his own expense would be so wonderful. Jan toiled on, an unlit butt dangling from his pursed lips.

Around nine o'clock the mushroom and sun-dried-tomato risotto was as ready as it would ever be. Doug and I dutifully passed out plastic troughs laden with risotto. These troughs, bought at a kitchen-supply warehouse, were each big enough to feed a family of four.

Within an hour Rob and John Gardner were puking Zabar's finest Parmesan into the Davis Strait. Although they had never tasted it before, they now forever hated risotto. Most of the other crew members felt the same. Besides being a little too al dente, however, I found it delicious. A good, hearty meal to carry us through the night. I reveled in my calm stomach.

It would be my last revel that evening.

As the sky darkened and I grew colder, my earlier happiness became a faint memory. We were not going very fast—probably four to five knots tops—but the combination of the rain, apparent wind speed, and waves created a tempestlike effect, at least to me. Unlike the last time we sailed on the ocean through the night, straight downwind from Maine to Boston, we now had to work to get anywhere. I became vigilant, not in navigating these roughened waters or anything else that might ease Terry's burden, but in trying to remain dry. Not vigilant enough, however. Around ten o'clock Terry barked at me to pull in an errant sheet, and I didn't have time to take off my mitts. A trickle of cold water leaked through the seams as I gripped the sheet tightly and hauled it in. *Aw, that's okay. Not much water. Nothing to worry about,* I calmed myself. I wanted more than anything, wanted it with close to a fanatical passion, to remain dry inside all my protective clothing. I felt that if water gained access to my inner sanctum, all would be lost. Ripstop nylon, Gore-Tex, neoprene, polypropylene, fleece, and pile—these were my gods. Pleading for them to protect me, I had no time for Odin, Thor, or Frey.

The wind increased, and Terry called for the first reef. Someone lowered the sail. We did not gather in the canvas quickly enough, so Rob, Andy, Abbott, and I had to haul it out of the icy water. My waterproof mitts and two layers of fleece liners were now completely soaked through. Misery. I tore them off to tie the reef points in a square knot. "Right over left, left over right," I repeated again and again, although I still managed to slip in a granny knot or two in my panicked state. My hands burned from the cold, and I muttered bitterly as I struggled to get the mitts back on.

Then we jibed. Jibing was supposed to be easier than tacking, since heading downwind would give us more time to work the sail into place, but we had jibed only back in Maine, in comparison to the hundreds of times we had tacked here in Greenland. The beitiáss crew successfully worked the beitiáss into place but did not secure the tack (the bottom point of the sail) quickly enough. The sail whipped the three-man beitiáss crew around like an enraged rodeo bull and lifted them four feet above the deck. Luckily, they wore harnesses tethering them to the jackline, which ran the length of the boat. That was Terry's rule while sailing beyond the fjords— one of his many anti-macho decisions that proved his confidence and expertise to me.

Back on the afterdeck, I released a sheet to help out the beitiáss crew. Then Doug handed me a brace—a line attached to the yard, which was now thirty feet above the water. I was hurtled forward in a poorly matched game of tug-of-war. The upper half of my body flailed over the ocean. Seconds later Doug pulled me back in.

As we struggled to regain our composure a few of us grumbled loudly about our leaky mitts. It appeared nothing—not the rubber fishing gloves some sported nor the Gore-Tex mitts—could keep our hands dry and warm.

At midnight the watches rotated, and although the sun had only just begun its four-hour tour below the horizon, rain clouds enforced a greater darkness. I scurried under the two-foot-tall underway tarp, doing my best to reach the middle and warmest spot. The tarp was set just forward of the mast and afforded very little protection.

Terry stayed on duty. He did not feel comfortable turning the boat over to anyone else. I realized with some guilt that he was paying a miserable price for the mostly unskilled crew. He would later tell me that he was suffering not only from a lack of confidence in *Snorri* and the crew but also from uncertainty about his own knowledge of this particular boat. It would be a miserable evening for him and also for me, but for very different reasons. I was obsessed with staying dry and warm. This was only the first of many overnight sails to come. How would I survive? What was I going to do when we crossed three hundred miles of the Davis Strait? Why had I been so exuberant only hours earlier? I should have sided with Trevor. I rolled onto my side to gather in a little warmth, but that only succeeded in cutting off the circulation in my arm. My hands grew icier, and then my feet began to betray me as well. They were turning numb.

The crew was divided into two watches, which we called port and starboard watches. Rob said that was the traditional term for them, what they would have been called on the old schooners or whaling ships. Like me, Abbott had been on port watch, and he also could not sleep, but for a vastly different reason: He was too excited. Here we were, finally sailing along the Greenland coast in the most authentic knarr to do so in at least six hundred years. He had been waiting for this moment for two years, ever since I first mentioned the project to him. Instead of snuggling under the tarp with me and whining, he was good-naturedly laughing and encouraging those on duty to keep warm. I was amazed at his resilience. I was proud of his generosity. I prayed that he would stumble over his insulated boots and his skinny ass would be smacked silly.

Somehow I fell asleep.

Two minutes later Abbott's frantic shout jerked me awake.

"You've got a big berg ahead!" he screamed back at Trevor, who was manning the tiller. "It's close."

The Vikings did not make boats capable of withstanding direct iceberg impact. Not even icebreakers are made to do that. Our precious replica was about to be smashed to bits. I could just see it. Upon impact, the crew would fly through the subarctic air, crashing on the slippery iceberg. *Whump.* Desperately we'd claw at its granitelike surface. *Klllhhh.* And then, even if we managed to hang on, just as we thought we were safe, the frozen bastion of fresh water would begin its slow, unyielding roll. Icebergs, we had learned, are not static, despite their stately demeanor. They roll, topple, or spontaneously break apart in resounding explosions.

"Which way should I go?" Trevor hollered back. He sounded steady and calm, as if he had been sailing these waters his entire life. At that moment I loved him.

"You could go left!" Abbott yelled. An interminable pause followed. "You could go right!" Another pause. "I don't know!"

Where's the real bow watch? I wondered. *Abbott really should be quiet. I really should get up.*

"You're not going to make it!" he screamed.

My other watchmates and I remained huddled beneath the useless tarp. Andy valiantly struggled to extricate himself from his zippered sleeping bag flopping around like a dying seal. The bag won, though, and eventually he lay motionless, resigned to our fate. What good could we accomplish? Either we were about to die and mercifully end this absurd adventure, or, worse, we would live to be tortured for another day.

We lived to be tortured.

To go Viking, I mused as Trevor managed to miss the unmissable iceberg, was not all that I had dreamed it would be. Vikings were obviously made of much tougher stuff than I.

Rolling from side to side and stomach to back, I failed to regain sleep. My hands were too damned cold, but it was my feet that tormented my enfeebled brain. Ignoring the fact that I have Raynaud's phenomenon had not worked. Raynaud's is a circulatory problem in which blood flow is diminished to cold fingers and toes. Like Robert Peary, I was going to lose my toes. Unlike him, I would whine and scream until the end. And I certainly would not be able to claim I discovered the North Pole or anything at all beyond learning that Viking boats were not meant to sail windward in anything beyond a duck pond.

Of course, I knew that I was not actually going to lose my toes—that in reality they were just going to hurt so much that I would end up wishing I had lost them.

I decided the best option was for me to quit. This whole project was the stupidest thing I had ever thought of. I had suspected it for quite a while, but there is nothing like pain and suffering to bring true clarity.

Strangely, the more I thought about quitting, the warmer I became. I had always embraced the idea of quitting, but now I wanted to marry it. It succored me where bravery and a stiff upper lip brought only tears. It was giving me hope when all else had failed. I would just hop off the boat in Nuuk, wish Terry and the crew a good voyage, check out the national museum, and fly home. After all, who could blame me? I was expecting a baby within a month. Okay, Lisa was, but I was clinging to any excuse I could. Our twins needed their daddy to be home, safe and sound. My heirloom tomatoes back in West Virginia needed harvesting.

Lying next to me, Jan was living the same fantasy, but with a nastier twist: *I'm going to quit when we get to Nuuk. Unlike Hodding, I can. This isn't my project. I'm not a sailor. I'm needed back at the law firm. Ha, ha! I can just call it quits!*

Reality drove the warmth of my fantasy away. I could not quit.

My feet went completely numb, and no matter how I tossed and turned I could not regain even a smidgen of comfort.

I decided I had been better off standing up. Carefully I made my way to the afterdeck, trying my best not to step on Elias, who was sprawled uncomfortably across the catwalk and some lumpy dry bags. I guessed he had decided he would rather die out in the open than stuck under a tarp. Wasn't he supposed to be on watch?

Terry was slumped in the stern. I didn't even bother suggesting he crawl under the tarp.

Trevor gripped the tiller with both hands. He was going to make sure we lived through the night if it took all his worrying and his strength. *Atta boy*, I thought. *I'll never tell you to shut up again.* And Rob, leaning over the boat he had so lovingly built, spewed messy chunks of risotto into the subarctic sea, ever marveling at the sparkling phosphorescence that danced in our wake.

I stood bow watch for the next three hours because in truth standing gave me a bit of warmth. During my watch we headed back to shore, since there was enough light to approach an anchorage. I probably fell asleep a dozen times for a second or two, but each lapse sent my heart racing. Once I heard my dad yelling at me to look alive, but when I opened my eyes, I realized it was just Terry, calling out instructions. I was scared into complete attention, however, when we came upon a sea of bergy bits. After safely negotiating them, we dropped anchor in yet another insular cove around nine-thirty in the morning.

We had made a little over four miles of northward progress during the night, traveling roughly forty miles to do so.

Lesson learned—for the time being.

Chapter Ten

We spent the next day sleeping and did not venture from the anchorage until the wind turned southerly a few days later. I felt somewhat heartened that the all-nighter had been as difficult for everyone else as it had been for me. "It was an eye-opener," Dean said. "It's amazing how much it took out of us—not being able to get out of the weather."

Waiting for the right winds was becoming intolerable. I desperately wanted to reach Nuuk by August 3 so I could call Lisa on our anniversary. It was killing me to think I would not get to call her. I was not sure if past adventurers or explorers worried or cared about their families, but I craved to be with Anabel, Eliza, and Lisa. I have read journals of Arctic, African, and American explorers from the eighteenth and nineteenth centuries, the great age of exploration, and I cannot recall a single one admitting the pain they felt over being separated from their families. In truth, writing about emotions at all was apparently taboo. If Peary, Elisha Kent Kane, Henry Morton Stanley, Meriwether Lewis, or William Clark wrote about their real personal worries, it was just a momentary affliction, lost in thousands of pages of facts and descriptions. These men had been my inspiration,* but they lent me no comfort as I yearned for my family. Maybe a real adventurer just kept quiet and bore his burden.

Our computer system finally began to work consistently. While waiting for a southerly, we sent out journal entries for our Web site and also received e-mails. While I had originally been ambivalent at best about having a satellite hookup, as well as a supposedly water-resistant laptop, it was nice to know that thousands of people were getting to learn about sailing a Viking ship up the Greenland coast. Their e-mails, filled with questions and statements like "What's it like to puke all day?" or "You guys are the coolest!" and "What direction are the Inuit graves facing?" were comforting and made us feel a part of something bigger than our daily suffering. E-mail was also keeping me abreast of my family. Lisa wrote that Eliza and Anabel had switched from cribs to "big girl" beds, and I knew I should have been there. It was almost worse hearing from her than not.

I was not the only one on board feeling such pangs. Abbott was constantly debating his recent separation from his wife, doing his best to see it as a good thing, talking about why he and Annie were not compatible. But we could all see his pain.

Doug's girlfriend had broken up with him just before we left, and he was still spending many hours penning what I assume were heartfelt, emotional letters. He had stopped picking at us the way he had done at the beginning, and he was fast becoming our romantic. We might be toiling along, rowing hour after hour, for instance, cursing our fate, but Doug would look up, notice a subtle but divine sight such as an unusual sunset or mountain, and point it out. He would often stare out to sea or head off on solitary walks. Every experience mattered to him simply because it was another experience. Although I knew he was in turmoil over his relationship, I felt jealous.

---

* Well, Peary was more of a lightning rod than an inspiration. I liked his determination but not how he treated the Polar Inuit. After one of his expeditions, he brought back six Inuit to New York and handed them over as exhibition material to the Museum of Natural History. Essentially, the museum neglected them and four of them died of pneumonia. Later, these people, who had traveled south with Peary as his friends, were used for medical studies and then their skeletons were put on display at the museum. Peary, while not taking a direct hand in all these matters, was responsible.

When we were not contemplating our fragile emotional states, we played kapaka, of course, went on walks, and collected water and edible wild plants. We had been told by a reliable source that giardia did not exist in Greenland, and it was such a unique experience to be able to simply dip a jug in a stream and lift it to your lips without a slow and cumbersome filter. The runoff was sweeter than any water I ever had tasted, except on the one occasion when it had trickled through too much moss and lichen.

Finally, we set sail again and, in just a few days, covered a miraculous distance—two hundred miles. The only hitch was that we had to sail in the rain the entire time. We were learning that whenever we wanted to get anywhere, it would rain. The only upside to this phenomenon was that we never had to deal with thunder or lightning. Thunderstorms need instability in air pressure caused by divergent temperatures. The cold water and cold atmosphere in Greenland, as well as the region's dryness, do not produce much thunder. While thunderstorms do occur there, they are highly unusual, and so at least we never had to worry about being blown out of the water by a bolt of lightning.

The nearly constant drizzle that accompanied our northern progress did not dampen our spirits, but it did lessen my enthusiasm for our Mustang suits. They had a fatal flaw: The inner cuffs, made of some ribbed synthetic material, wicked water up our sleeves. After a few hours in the rain our upper shoulders and sometimes even our chests were soaked. The water inside our suits was at the very least a nuisance, and it could have lead to hypothermia.

I was thinking—okay, worrying—about this problem while on bow watch as we headed to Nuuk the morning of August 4, the day after John Gardner's birthday and my anniversary. We had celebrated these events around midnight on the third after sailing and rowing all day. Gardner passed around a bottle of Scotch he had been saving for his birthday and a bar of Toblerone chocolate, grinning from ear to ear and repeating, "Treats for the boys!" Gardner loved to celebrate.

It was only ten in the morning but the sun had already been up for six hours. I still was not used to the nearly endless sunlight and my unconscious mind was convinced it was early afternoon. I fretted that we would not get to Nuuk in time to hit the marine supply shops, if there were any, to find a solution to our leaky rain suits and cold hands. Not really knowing my way around Nuuk, I also worried about everything else we needed to get: more hot chocolate, other foods, a gun for polar bears on Baffin, the latest ice report, and, and, and . . .

Luckily, something caught my attention to starboard, and I glanced over to see two of the strangest-looking creatures I'd ever encountered. They looked like headless sea otters, but there are no otters in Greenland. What kind of creatures could these be? I pointed them out to Elias, who said they were seals. "Sleeping seals. They're on their backs," he explained. I realized I had never seen a seal asleep in the water and had assumed seals always slept onshore, having seen them do so in Maine and other coastal areas. Although one should resist calling something in nature "cute," these seals undoubtedly were.

A light wind continued to blow from the south, accompanied by the inevitable rain.

"I think Elias is a direct descendent of Leif Eriksson," Rob blurted out a little later, while we scrubbed the decks. We had split into two groups, one to tidy *Snorri*, the other to sail into port. "The whole time he was criticizing south Greenland, didn't he tell us how nice it is in west Greenland?" Apparently Rob was about to point out that we were now in west Greenland.

Elias jumped in. "Yes, I said that," he said quite emphatically. He had a charming, half-joking way of talking with us in which he spoke every word with great emphasis. Some of us had begun speaking the same way. "This is not west Greenland. It is still lousy south Greenland." Elias was right. We had gone over three hundred miles since Narsarsuaq but remained in the bottom quarter of the western Greenland coast.

"Yeah, the sagas didn't say much about the shitty weather around here," Abbott added, ignoring the south-versus-west debate. "Nothing about drying out the wool and sealskins after each sail."

"Maybe that's because if that is the way life is, there was no reason to write about it. It wasn't out of the ordinary," Rob replied.

"Well, maybe you need to move the stove over," Trevor said, disregarding the conversation around him but noticing that Rob and Abbott were not cleaning under the stove. It was the kind of thing that Trevor usually said or did, infuriating most of the crew, even though he was probably right.

Rob laughed and looked up, saying, "Whenever you are going to say something irritating, just say it to me. I like to learn things."

Eight hours later we sat in Tulles Rock Cafe toasting our arrival in Nuuk with cold Classic Tuborg beer. Plates full of pizza, french fries, steaks, and ribs sat before us. Four TV screens were filled with MTV from Europe. I had showered and was still tingling, both from the heat of the water and from the blood that had returned to my benumbed regions. All the crew had either shaved completely or trimmed their beards at the very least. Their appearance was shocking.

A pretty waitress walked by our table. Terry's eyes nearly popped out of his head. "Having never spent much time with only guys on a boat, I never really understood it, but now I can see why sailors coming ashore want to marry the first woman they see," Terry said, doing his best to look away from her.

It was fun to watch the crew off the boat. They seemed much more awkward. At first everyone was quieter. We sat around the table, carrying on stilted conversations—stretching for something to say to each other. But some things remained the same. Rob was still Rob, for instance. I overheard him say to Jan, apropos of nothing, "I live in a world where there are no job applications. You just stand side by side, stare out into nowhere, and fart."

While Terry and the others, Gardner in particular, ogled the waitresses, I went down to the local Seaman's Home to call Lisa. Five Seaman's Homes are scattered along the western coast. They are clean, well-kept missionary hotels that serve meals to local fishermen. The meals consist of heavy Danish dishes, mostly meat and potatoes, as well as *smørrebrød*—open-faced sandwiches topped with local shrimp, herring, or unidentifiable sliced meat. There are eggs, bacon, and cereal for breakfast, accompanied by strong coffee. We had brought fifty pounds of coffee beans to Greenland but no grinder. There had been no local grinder in Narsarsuaq, so we coffee drinkers had been quaffing instant swill while we held our noses. For some of us, the coffee was the best thing about the Seaman's Home.

We were able to take endless hot showers in a room set up for sailors or other travelers. There was also a small laundry. Most of us had worn the same long underwear day after day, and we were grateful for the facilities. We had docked the boat just downhill from the Seaman's Home, and it became our central hangout as we got *Snorri* and ourselves ready to move on.

Lisa was doing well. Just hearing her voice lifted my spirits. I liked hearing her complain how huge she was and that the baby's kicking was making it hard to sleep. She had adopted a new dog—half dachshund, half basset hound—who had come with the name Ginger. Ginger, Lisa explained, would have been put to sleep by the animal shelter if she had not been adopted that day. Lisa sounded happy about Ginger and she said the girls were too. All her news was not good, however. The doctor had told her that she would have to have a C-section. She had wanted natural birth badly, and I could hear her sadness even though she said, "I just want the baby to be safe."

Given how far behind schedule we were, Lisa and I both knew there was now no way I would be home for the baby's birth, and as we talked, painful, interminable silences increased our separation. It did not help that there was a disconcerting two-second lag in the conversation, since Greenland's telecommunications are handled by satellite. Before we had even set down our phones, we both felt farther apart.

⁜

We stayed in Nuuk for four days. It is not a large capital, with a population of twenty thousand counting Nussuaq, its commuter town, but there was plenty to keep the twelve of us entertained. I took utter delight in walking through the tunnel from Nuuk to Nussuaq, for example, simply because it was the only road connecting two communities in all of Greenland and it reminded me of how ignorant I'd been back when I thought I could hitchhike from town to town to retrace Leif's route. I also liked going to the modern grocery to stare at the packaged goodies I take for granted at home. There was such bounty, and I easily identified with the many kids who appeared to be doing the same as I.

Homer took even greater advantage of all that Nuuk had to offer. In one day he fell into the harbor, had a filling replaced by a sadistic dentist, and was kicked out of a store for being a nuisance. The day began with an aching tooth. The deputy minister of cultural affairs was visiting *Snorri* and offered to give Homer a ride to the dentist. As they approached the clinic he told Homer, "Now, understand that they won't speak English in there and the first thing they'll want to do is pull your teeth." Not knowing what to make of this comment, Homer mumbled a hasty thanks as he left the car.

Inside the dentist's office, everything looked clean and orderly. Homer was promptly put in a chair, and the dentist came in. He wore a seemingly permanent frown and, although Danish, looked to Homer like a Nazi. This was when Homer started to worry.

Homer, very slowly and carefully, said, "I have a hole in my tooth and it hurts." Chances are he used his deep voice. Whenever Homer wants to be heard, be taken seriously, or sing, his voice drops as low as Paul Robeson's.

The dentist cranked Homer to the reclining position, looked inside his mouth, and immediately began drilling. Not a word, not a spot of Novocain.

"It was fine at first," Homer later reported. "Then he hit a nerve. Wham! I made a noise. He stops drilling. Smiles. Looks at his assistant, laughs, and says, 'Viking!' and immediately goes back to drilling. I was out of there in six minutes and they wouldn't let me pay a thing."

While relating this story, Homer dropped his coffee cup overboard. He tends to get a little excited when he is telling a story (and in the opinion of a few of the crew is a little too liberal with the facts). The cup immediately sank to the bottom of the harbor. When he tried to retrieve it with a boat hook while standing on a slippery dock piling, he stumbled, snapped the boat hook, and fell into the water.

It didn't stop there, however. After showering and warming up at the Seaman's Home, Homer decided to grind our coffee beans. Earlier he had noticed a local market with a large coffee grinder in its window. He asked if he could use it, pantomiming what he wanted to do. They did not see his fifty-pound bag and said sure. Soon enough, beans and ground coffee were spewing all over the store. He was kicked out after only a few pounds were done.

Homer was treated to quite a few beers that evening to make up for his bad day. There are only a handful of bars in Nuuk. As is the case everywhere else in the world, the purpose of bars is to get people drunk, and drunk people hang out in bars. I had read much about drunkenness being a problem in Greenland, but the reports had always seemed a form of cultural snobbery. So, yes, we saw drunk people in the bars there and sometimes on the street, but you can see that in my hometown. However, a lot of Greenlanders also complained of the problem to me and the government has enacted laws addressing it, limiting times when liquor can be bought as well as the amount.

We did most of our socializing and drinking at the Kristinemut Restaurant and Bar. The first time we were there was after dinner one night around nine-thirty. Mainly elderly couples in groups of four sat at wooden tables in a room decorated with America's Wild West paraphernalia: cowboy ropes, saddles, bull's horns, and so on. A scene developed at a table next to us. An older man, dressed smartly in a button-down shirt and a checked sweater, started to get a little loud. Others at his table tried to hush him. He continued unheeded, and suddenly a man at his table jumped up and smashed him across the temple with an elbow. The loud man and his chair toppled backward onto the floor, where he lay stunned and finally silent. At least a minute went by, and then a couple from another table helped him to his feet and escorted him out of the room. I did not see another scene remotely like this while in Greenland, but it served as a reminder that Greenland, as well as other northern regions, have something of a problem with alcohol abuse. Considering our own drunken behavior while there, however, I would have to say that alcohol abuse is not solely a northern problem.

That night, the older patrons gave way to the young, for the most part, when a two-man Sri Lankan band took to the stage a little later. They played reggae, calypso, American pop, and some Greenlandic tunes as the dance floor remained crowded past two in the morning. A couple of the crew found women friends for the evening, and Jan met a sixty-year-old woman who found his Italian Dutch-boy looks too irresistible.

After the bar closed, we learned that after-hours parties in Nuuk popped up at different apartments throughout the city. Although I never actually made it to one of these parties, most of the crew did. It seemed that some kind of free love reigned there. John Abbott met a woman to whom he talked most of the night. He went back to her place with some other people, including, it turned out, her boyfriend. After a while it became quite clear that the woman wanted to go to bed with Abbott, and although Abbott was willing, the boyfriend was sitting right there. Then the boyfriend told John it was okay, and something like "It is a part of the culture." John thought the guy looked sad in spite of his words, and he made excuses so no one felt bad.

When not partying or shopping for truly waterproof mittens and boots, we worked on *Snorri*. We put on new chafe gear, tightened the rudder line, and replaced lines that were not working adequately. During our downwind sails, oatmeal-like globules of the mast had splattered on the deck from where the rakki lines chafed the yard.* This and other places where there was too much friction had to be fixed or at the very least protected better. Meanwhile, Trevor and Dean worked on getting improved weather reports over the computer. So far, a man named Herb Hilgenberg, who provides free weather advice to sailors (though usually in more southern climates), had been e-mailing us reports. We also wanted to see the weather maps for ourselves, and Dean and Trevor were trying to obtain them from a service in the United States. Jan inventoried our food and then went shopping for more supplies, including fresh butter, havarti cheese, more granola because nobody liked oatmeal very much, cabbages, canned potatoes, fruit, and, of course, more hot chocolate.

Elias did not sleep on *Snorri* with us, taking the opportunity to stay with friends. But each day he would ride down to the boat in a taxi, find out that we were not leaving, and then take off. He eventually grew angry, fearing, it seemed, that we would never go to Sisimiut, his hometown.

His fears were not unfounded.

We received an ice report from the Canadian Ice Service that cost $200 for three faxed pages, showing detailed positions of pack ice and icebergs along the Baffin Island coast. Cape Dyer, directly across the Davis Strait from Sisimiut, was clear of ice, and only

---

* The rakki is a crescent-shaped wooden yoke that loosely holds the yard to the mast.

two-tenths coverage blocked the shores about a hundred miles south of the cape. All of southeast Baffin looked to be completely ice free.

On the afternoon of August 7 we held a *thing* to discuss the situation. Originally we had hoped to be leaving Baffin, not Greenland, by early August, so things did not look good to Terry or me. Before the *thing*, he and I had talked. I knew that he did not want to go to Sisimiut. He had never thought it practical. I also knew he wanted to skip Baffin. This was intolerable to me. My stomach twisted at the thought of it. I could not believe he did not understand this. A captain of the *Bowdoin*, a teaching boat that sails north most summers from Maine, had suggested to Terry that we skip Baffin and stay well clear of the Hudson Strait because he felt the tides between Baffin and Labrador might be too difficult for us to handle. The *Bowdoin* has a long and glorious history of sailing and motoring the Labrador coast and also crossing to Greenland. This captain's words were probably like the voice of God to Terry. I made it very clear, however, that I could not sacrifice Baffin. To skip Baffin would have been like skipping the Continental Divide when retracing Lewis and Clark's trail. We danced around the subject, being fair and respectful of each other, but obviously more at odds than ever before.

During the *thing*, a lot of the guys expressed frustration with the idea of not making it to the Arctic Circle. Homer, Dean, and Andy really wanted it, but Dean also thought it best to head straight for L'Anse aux Meadows. Homer added, "I'd like to be in the States for Christmas. Other than that, I'd like to ride the south wind as far as we can."

Andy pointed out that we had known the conditions ahead of time. "I don't think it's a surprise to anyone that these are the factors we face," Andy said, clearly bothered by the thought we might retreat. "I personally would like for us to do what we set out to do." In the course of the discussion, Andy and Terry argued over a minor issue. Although it was a little tense and embarrassing, it was probably a good thing, since they had hardly spoken to each other in weeks. Andy still had not been navigating, and now even I had to admit that their philosophies were incompatible.

I still felt a strong pull to continue north, despite Terry's arguments in favor of heading straight out from Nuuk. It is not known where Leif began his crossing, but it always made sense that he might have taken the shortest route, which was from Sisimiut to Cape Dyer. More important, it is roughly Karlsefni's route as described in *Erik the Red's Saga*. Karlsefni was the cool, Marlon Brando–type figure of the westward-seeking Vikings who I fancied emulating—more than Leif, even. It was a known route. I also worried that if we aimed for southeastern Baffin, we might just end up missing it altogether. Skipping Baffin at this point would be like going to McDonald's but not ordering any fries—you just would not do it.* And going to Sisimiut had been our starting point for getting to Baffin from the very beginning. It was, according to Helge Ingstad and other historians, the way the Vikings went: "Near Holsteinsborg (Sisimiut) the Davis Strait is at its narrowest, no more than 200 sea-miles across, and a crew would not need to sail far out to sea before sighting the lofty mountains of Baffin Land," Ingstad wrote in *Land Under the Pole Star*. "From the higher mountains near Holsteinsborg [Sisimiut] one may also glimpse the loom of the Cumberland Peninsula [on Baffin]. In short, it is more than probable that at quite an early period the Norsemen had knowledge of the coasts of Baffin Land, and these pointed the way to other parts of North America." It could be—and has been—easily argued that this is a lot of crap, but this was not the moment to do so.

Then Gardner spoke up. He had refused to speak when first asked how he felt about things, and he had been yawning during much of the discussion.

"You say we want to be in Newfoundland by the middle of September—to stay clear of fall storms," he reiterated. "That's five weeks from now. Given how long it has taken to get here, there is no way we could be there by then if we also go north."

Gardner and others who had voiced the opinion that we were running out of time were right. Sisimiut should be sacrificed for our own good. Neither Terry nor I said anything conclusive at the *thing*. Terry politely did not want to announce a decision without first talking with me. Afterward I approached him and suggested he tell the crew that not only were we skipping Sisimiut but that even going a little farther north made no sense. They were all edgily

---

* Yes, I have a lot of metaphors for skipping Baffin.

milling about *Snorri*, obviously discomfited by the state of limbo. The minute Terry announced our plan, everybody seemed relieved—not that we were headed straight out from Nuuk but that we had made a decision.

"We're going home, boys!" Doug shouted, and his words rang true. It felt good not to be working ourselves farther and farther from home. Even Elias appeared content with our decision.

Chapter Eleven

Rob woke at 5:38 A.M. and started untying the boat before the rest of us were even out of our sleeping bags. We were off by six-thirty—our earliest start ever. Headed for the New World!

Wrong. We spent the next five days anchored just twelve miles west of Nuuk, nestled between some short hills. Gale after gale pinned us to Greenland.

We were anchored on the east side of an island that Hans Egede of Denmark settled in 1721. Hans eventually became known as the Apostle of Greenland but at first must have seemed more than a little crazy. Ostensibly his mission was to find the stranded Vikings, who were believed by some to be alive and reverted to heathen ways in Greenland. Although he found no trace of the Vikings, he decided to stay to convert the Inuit, and he established the relationship between the two peoples that has lasted nearly three hundred years.

Although Hans eventually moved to present-day Nuuk, his original settlement lasted two centuries. As a result, we all, and especially Gardner and Rob, who loved looking for signs of the past, came upon troves of artifacts. Gardner found an oval soapstone dish used as a candle holder. In this Inuit candle, rendered seal blubber fuels dozens of tiny wicks made from dried lichen. Peat and

HODDING CARTER

Waiting (Homer and Jan)

tent homes were lit by such candles for thousands of years, until the middle of the twentieth century.

The waiting revealed how comfortable we now felt in the role of wanderers, which is what we were. As such, we adapted to our surroundings. In towns we fanned out, met new people, and caroused. In the countryside we hiked, gathered wild plants, and slept as late as possible. We were not there to change or improve anything. We were not trying to actively learn anything or check off another item on our must-see list. We were there to listen, look, and then move on. This island was a foreign setting, but we were comfortable. We found a minke whale carcass decayed on a rock beach, a cold-smoke oven used for curing cod or char (which we first thought was some sort of foxhole), a solitary strip of salmon twisting in the wind in a drying shack, and a fishing/country shack, open for all to use as they wanted, just a few hundred feet from the whale carcass. These things made up our world.

Elias explained that the cabins of mismatched construction were individually owned but free for all to use. "I have two of these myself. Anybody can stay there, of course." Jan and I had to sleep in the cabin one night after our tent blew into the harbor, thoroughly soaking our sleeping bags. The cabin was decorated with crates used as coffee tables and a cupboard. The beds were mere foam pads, but they had dry bedding. We hung our sleeping bags in the fish-drying shack, where the wind funneled through, drying them within a day.*

After five days the gale winds let up and we headed out again, bound for Baffin Island, Canada. This was it. We rowed out of our anchorage filled with emotion.

The wind we needed never materialized, though, and a fog rolled in. Foiled again. By late afternoon we were drifting sound-lessly in the current, skirting dozens of rock islands that passed like spooky figments of our imagination. A desolate, tiny island would suddenly appear out of the mist, just a few feet to port. A moment later there was only white. We anchored between these islands.

I jigged for cod and caught two. Elias sneered at them and said they were fjord cod, good only for dog food. After I cleaned and gutted them, Abbott made vegetable and cod soup. Abbott had a knack for brightening somber moments, and his soup did not fail him. All, including Elias, licked their bowls clean, it was so good, and some of us howled at Elias as he ate.

Finally, the next morning, August 14, it appeared we were truly on our way. A light wind blew from the northwest. We took to the oars at eight-fifteen, needing to navigate through the clus-tered islands before we raised the yard. This time was for real. Baf-fin or bust!

Five minutes later Rob called from the bow, "Hey, Terry, Elias says it's getting pretty shallow. You might want to slow down a bit." As we were under oars, slowing down would mean coming to a complete halt, since our top rowing speed was a knot or so. Terry looked around, puzzled and possibly disbelieving. The charts showed enough depth, but we had learned not to trust them. Some-times they would show entire islands five miles from their actual location.

A few seconds passed. The rudder scraped something hard. Terry quickly released it from its set position. Then *Snorri* came to a shuddering stop. We were on a ledge, again.

Despite all our efforts, we could not free her. We tried sailing

---

* Of course, they never really stayed dry after that, being inundated with salt, which is hygroscopic, attracting every bit of moisture around it. Think of a salt shaker without rice in it.

off, rowing, rocking, even dropping an anchor and hauling on the line. All that did was free the anchor. We had to wait for high tide—a good six hours away.

By two o'clock we were free of the ledge and had power-sailed past the barrier islands. A few of us made offerings to the ocean to protect us on our crossing. Jan solemnly flipped in a dried sausage and a hunk of Parmesan. Doug threw in a small golden elephant given him by a waitress at the Thai restaurant in Nuuk, where, oddly enough, we had eaten some of the finest Thai food I've had outside of Thailand. Gardner, who was now known for pulling out a drink whenever the occasion seemed worthy, poured a hefty shot into the ocean. We were all then obliged to take a swig. Homer, ever generous, dumped in half a pouch of tobacco.

I had once been instructed by a Navajo healer, as he watched *Robin Hood—Men in Tights* over my shoulder in a dimly lit living room, that I should offer tobacco to the gods overlooking a particularly treacherous river in northeastern Manitoba. I followed his advice and lived through the adventure, despite forest fires raging along the river's banks and a real threat of polar bears. Ever since, I had taken to the notion of offering something precious before a journey. Since I had already involuntarily offered over the past month the lid to my coffee mug, an insulated glove, a pair of underwear, and a package of Hob Nobs (a crispy oatmeal cookie that succored us on particularly bad days), I too resorted to tossing in most of my cigarette tobacco, which was a paltry amount in comparison to Homer's munificence.

A light fog enshrouded us, but for once we sailed without rain. The wind's direction was killing me a bit, however. I desired a north or, better yet, northeast wind, but it currently blew from the northwest. With this wind, we would miss most or even all of Baffin Island.

I tried my best not to fret, and by nine that evening we had covered thirty miles. Even more important to me, despite the less-than-perfect wind, we were headed straight for Hall Peninsula on Baffin Island.

This was the moment I had been waiting for without even consciously realizing it: crossing Davis Strait in an open boat. No chase boat. No land to be seen. The thought of this moment had scared me the most and had always seemed unattainable.

Each swell that rocked *Snorri*, each wave that slapped her across the sheer plank and sprayed over the foredeck—I cherished them all. We were finally attempting something ancient. We had left the safety net of land and civilization. For the Vikings, this had been *the* moment as well. Inspired by blind faith or sheer determination, they had taken this same leap of faith a thousand years before us. For the first time I felt that we had breached the gulf of time and understood a little of what they were about. We were finally like them, but would we be equal to it? How would we compare?

I felt unbound. "This is *the moment,*" I kept telling myself. I suddenly fell in love not only with sailing but also with the ocean. I liked being at its mercy. It no longer felt like the end of the world but instead the beginning. The sun appeared to be conspiring with us, giving us a wink and nod of encouragement. It glowed a mustardy gold wherever it struck *Snorri.* The water shifted colors again and again, from blue-green into purple-black into an improbable rosy purple.

Sounds competed for attention. The rakki creaked like a tree swaying in the forest. Our inflamed wake gurgled, swooshed, and churned past the hull. The sail snapped to attention as it emptied and then filled with air as *Snorri* dropped down the sides of swells that were substantially increasing in size. I knew then why Leif and the others sailed west—not for wood or new land, but merely to feel so much at once.

I could not sleep that night, although I knew it would be a long crossing. I steered, did bow watch, pumped the bilge, kept the log—whatever I could in order not to let the moment slip away.

It did anyway.

By seven the next evening we were more than 130 miles from Greenland, adrift. All that bashing and groaning I had so cherished had taken its toll. Some of the crew were falling apart. Rob was retching wherever he stood. Others were nearly as sick.

Snorri was faring even worse.

Our huge rudder had loosened a supporting crossbeam, a thigh-thick piece of wooden framing, by constantly pulling forward on it, instantly creating four holes in the bottom of the boat. Water gushed in. As we rolled abeam (sideways) in the six-foot swells, Trevor and Gardner patched the holes with aluminum tomato-

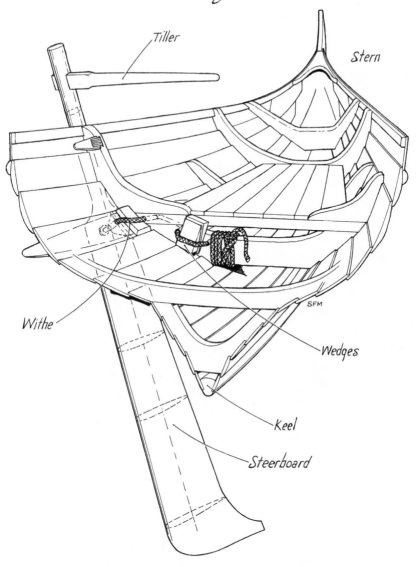

Tiller

Stern

Withe

Wedges

Keel

Steerboard

sauce-can lids and scrap wood. Even worse than the holes, however, was the now useless crossbeam. It had been a crucial piece, helping to keep the stern intact.

A couple of the guys rigged a come-along from the rudder line to a crossbeam farther forward and placed an oak plank athwartships to keep the stern from falling apart completely.*

Elias stared at the work being done and then looked up, disgusted. I knew he was lamenting that we had not gone to Sisimiut—that many of our problems could have been avoided if only I had given us enough time. I turned to hear him out.

"I got to pee," he said, grimacing, and then motioned to the nether regions of his foul-weather suit. "But first I have to take all this stuff off."

Even in crisis, we had to take care of the day-to-day crap.

The ocean, which I had so wanted to embrace just hours earlier, now scared the living hell out of me. The sun, unfettered by any filtering clouds, highlighted the no-longer-so-picturesque whitecaps, the harsh light lending them the menace of roving demons sent to destroy us. The wind whirred in the hemp shrouds, recalling every disaster at sea I had ever imagined or seen in a movie.

We raised the yard, and for a few hours everything seemed okay. We had decided, however, to fall off the wind and run straight for Labrador. Skipping Baffin no longer seemed like such a big deal. The swells were thick and looming. Every time we raced to the bottom of one, the rudder would creak and bang against the side of the ship.

Then at midnight the withy, or rudder line, snapped in half. Since it was made of steel and polypropylene and was attached to wood, this seemed impossible, but because of the way it had been attached to the rudder, it happened. The bottom half of the rudder broke free of the boat. John Abbott, on the helm, struggled to keep the tiller upright. A wave caught the four-hundred-pound rudder and suddenly raised it horizontally, crashing the tiller onto the deck and snapping it like a toothpick.

The sun had just set, and blobs of ethereal green light bloomed across the heavens. The blobs grew into curtains that danced above our heads. An eerie greenish yellow glowed on our faces as we labored to haul the massive rudder over the gunwale and safely aboard, where it could do no more damage to the boat.

Damn that Cleopatra rudder! Damn the Danes for not giving us more information! Damn me for not allowing enough time to get things working right!

---

* A crossbeam essentially runs port to starboard and keeps the hull from collapsing inward. *Athwartships* just means across the length of the ship. A come-along is not a nautical device but is a heavy-duty manually operated ratchet, strong enough to pull a truck out of a ditch.

The moon rose nearly full, and a convoy of falling stars raced above us. The aurora borealis continued to tempt us away from our troubles, swaying to some rhythm I thought we had been a part of but now knew had been only an illusion.

Throwing out our sea anchor, a parachute-type device that allows a boat to stay pointed into the wind and thus the waves, creating a more stable boat, we bedded down for the night. I looked over an e-mail Terry and Trevor wrote to Herb the weather guy, to be passed along to Coast Guard Canada. It described our situation but said we did not need assistance. We felt Rob could fix things well enough until we made it to Labrador. I fell asleep around one-thirty, still marveling at the most unique night sky I had ever seen.

Terry woke me an hour later. He sounded very sweet and gentle. "Hodding, can I talk with you for a moment?"

We huddled in the stern away from the sleeping crew. Coast Guard Canada had written back. They wanted us to contact them by telex every four hours—something we discovered we could do with our computer.

"I don't feel confident we can fix the rudder well enough while we're out here to finish this crossing," he said. "I think we should tell them to come get us."

In truth, despite our earlier analysis of our situation, Coast Guard Canada had already decided to come pick us up. We didn't know it, but they had diverted an icebreaker that was two hundred miles north to rescue us.

I agreed with Terry, and we officially asked the Canadians for their assistance. I couldn't sleep after that, my head tossing with thoughts and worries just as *Snorri* tossed in the rolling seas. I hoped that the boat would sink and everything would be over. I hoped that the weather would not worsen, since we were dead in the water. I hoped that I was just having a bad dream.

The following morning the wide-open ocean was affrontingly beautiful. It was one of those extremely clear days where you might see a gnat flying a hundred yards away. The seas were tall, maybe six or seven feet high, and the sunlight danced over the cresting whitecaps. This harsh beauty only seemed to punctuate the overwhelming despondency aboard *Snorri*. We milled about, readying *Snorri* to be towed by the *Pierre Radisson*, the Coast Guard icebreaker, and consoling Rob that our situation was not his fault. Now and then a shot of gallows humor attempted to break the prevailing mood. While making a bridle for the tow line, Trevor announced jokingly, "At least now we'll have more time for kapaka!"

I spent most of my time firing off e-mails in a desperate attempt to have the *Pierre Radisson* tow us to Baffin or even Labrador. If we could just get to shore on Baffin, Rob could certainly find a way to make things work. I knew he could. Nuuk, back in Greenland, was the closest port of call, however, and we had been told the Canadians had orders to take us there.

As the *Pierre Radisson* lumbered into view around two-thirty that afternoon, the captain radioed that they would, as predicted, be towing *Snorri* to Nuuk. I decided to board the ship to convince him to head for Canada or at least get him to check with his superiors one more time. Most of the crew opted to leave *Snorri* for the tow back to Nuuk, but Terry, Homer, Trevor, and Abbott volunteered to stay on board. Somebody had to make sure *Snorri* did not sustain any more damage.

On the *Pierre Radisson*, the captain obliged me and contacted Halifax about my request, but they still said no. I had to sign some official papers and then was set free on board.

As I roamed around for the next twenty-four hours I could not decide who was more miserable: the guys on board *Snorri*, bashing unnaturally into the ocean swells and strong headwind, or those of us on the *Pierre Radisson*. I asked the captain if we could trade places, but he did not want to risk operating a transfer in the rough seas if it was not absolutely necessary.

Besides worrying about those on board *Snorri*, I also had to listen to a barrage of comments from the Coast Guard officers.

The chief engineer, in particular, kept chastising me for not having the right "stricture." As he said this again and again I nodded, figuring it was a nautical term I had not yet learned, having to do with some piece of equipment that might have helped us. "The Vikings, one thousand years ago, they had the right stricture. You did not!" We were in the ship's bar, listening to Jewel, En Vogue, and the Doors on a CD player, drinking beers and smoking pre-rolled cigarettes. Out on *Snorri*, Homer was probably swinging from a shroud, puking his guts out.

Later it dawned on me that the chief engineer's French Canadian accent had mangled the word *structure*. I was sitting on a dock in Nuuk at the time, so my impulse to strangle him was pointless.

It took less than thirty-six hours to get back to Nuuk. The days following our arrival were like swimming through a bad dream. The first thing Terry and I decided was the most obvious: The trip was over. We had failed. After that, I had to figure out what to do with the boat and how to do it and then get back to the United States as quickly as possible. The baby had not yet been born. After working the details out, most of the crew chose to remain and help store the equipment and ready *Snorri* for the winter. She was going to spend the winter in dry dock at the local shipyard. I was going to fly home for the birth and then fly back a few days later to finish putting *Snorri* away.

The night before I left, we held a cookout behind the Seaman's Home. It was meant as a pat on the back so that no one would feel bad about the situation—an impossible goal, considering how defeated we all felt. A few of the guys were actually scowling at our failure, mainly Gardner and Homer. It evidently had never occurred to them that we might not succeed. At some point I reminded several of them of what had happened when Erik the Red colonized Greenland. Twenty-five ships set out from Iceland, but only fourteen reached the new land. The rest either turned back or perished. My little history lesson did not seem to help much. I tried consoling them by reminding them our voyage was more of an experimental effort, not just a masculine adventure at sea. Terry nodded in seeming agreement but then blurted out, "Yeah, experimental archeology gone bad." He was so morose, I wanted to kick him in the butt or at least put him on the next flight out of town. I felt the same but did not want any of them to feel they had failed. I knew I was to blame. I had not taken Fletcher Abbott's advice about letting time slow down.

During the cookout talk inevitably turned to our rudder problem, and everyone had a theory, even Jan. He seemed to think that running aground that last time, just before heading out to sea, might have loosened things up too much. Everybody's notions made some sense, and I tried my best to listen. The only obvious thing to me, however, was that I had not allowed enough time to figure out any problems *Snorri* might have. Was the rudder too big? Was it the wrong shape? Had the Danes sneaked into our last anchorage and sabotaged the rudder system in a fit of envy and spite? It would all have to be figured out later.

We stood around our dwindling charcoal fire amid hotel effluvia and a gray sky. Doug recited a poem he had written earlier in the

day. I kicked at a disintegrating cigarette butt as he asked pardon
for his first attempt at composing a sonnet. It was entitled "Helen,"
after my daughter-to-be:

> *Helen, unthinking, knows more than any one mind*
> *Ever contained, and is in her watery dark berth*
> *Closer than Thor to the levers of Heaven and Earth*
> *Free to just be, unburdened even of time.*
>
> *Helen of Troy, they say, looked pretty good*
> *And launched a ship or three, but if you ask me*
> *And still if you don't, I'll say more terrific is she*
> *Who unlaunches ships under way, tears metal, cracks wood.*
>
> *Nor was all the work of one mighty babe:*
> *To Helen, add magical twins and spellbinding wife*
> *Square in the throes of living and coming to life*
> *They said "Go ahead," and meant it, but still came that wave.*
>
> *Hodding, when plotting more glory, ought reckon that power*
> *That said to the* Snorri, *"I'm sorry, but nigh is my hour."*

Not only did I like the poem but I appreciated the way he was
looking at our situation. I mumbled my gratitude. As I was leaving for
the airport the next morning Trevor handed me a bone pendant for
Helen and gave me a big hug. He was such a contradiction: annoyingly
whiny but competent one moment, lovable and comforting the next.

I landed in Iqaluit, Baffin Island's capital city, just a few hours
later, unamused at the irony of this effortless crossing.

While I was laid over in Canada that night Lisa told me she
thought labor was coming on. Since her doctor had told her she
would be unable to deliver naturally, this would probably only make
things more complicated. "Even if I do go into labor tonight," she
said, "I won't let them operate until you get here—as long as my
water doesn't break." Lisa had always been selfless, but she seemed
to be transforming into some kind of saint. I felt like the returning
cad. Absent father, absent husband. Failed adventurer.

Lisa's water did not break, and we had time for a frantic reunion,
with the girls, Lisa, and the cad forming a massive ball of hugging
family. It was a sweet time, completely unmarred by the project's

failure. Anabel and Eliza both kept repeating, "Daddy on Viking boat? Daddy on Viking boat?" hour after hour. The cad brought home an armful of presents and massaged Lisa wherever she ached.

Two days later Helen Miranda was born, shuddering and cooing from the start. Her dark hair and bright blue eyes were a delightful miniature of Lisa's. She was breathtaking enough to sink a thousand ships, let alone defeat one lousy Viking tub. And to top it all off, she was probably the best nurser in West Virginia.

The cad slept on the hospital's pull-out chair and tried to be helpful when Helen woke with hunger every two hours. The cad even tried walking with Helen to calm her during one of her crying bouts, to let Lisa sleep, but it did no good.

The next morning the cad sneaked out to buy a baby book for Helen and ten gallons of pine tar for *Snorri*. During the night he had realized that he had two babies to take care of, a world apart. He stayed home for but a few days, then flew back to Nuuk to finish storing *Snorri* for the winter. Lisa gave him a book of poetry called *West Wind*, by Mary Oliver, and the cad read it enroute. He was only going back to Greenland for a few days, but it was too much for him. His emotions rose within him like a man bursting through the ocean's surface for the gasp of air that just might save his life. Lisa had marked a stanza, and the cad cried uncontrollably as he read it.

> You are young. So you know everything. You leap into the boat and begin rowing. But, listen to me. Without fanfare, without embarrassment, without any doubt, I talk directly to your soul. Listen to me. Lift the oars from the water, let your arms rest, and your heart, and heart's little intelligence, and listen to me. There is life without love. It is not worth a bent penny, or a scuffed shoe. It is not worth the body of a dead dog nine days unburied. When you hear, a mile away and still out of sight, the churn of the water as it begins to swirl and roil, fretting around the sharp rocks—when you hear that unmistakable pounding—when you feel the mist on your mouth and sense ahead the embattlement, the long falls plunging and steaming—then row, row for your life toward it.

Chapter Twelve

While floating rudderless, waiting for the Coast Guard, I had momentarily fantasized about the icebreaker barreling to a halt beside us, loading all on board, and departing—sans *Snorri*. Or better yet, maybe the captain would decide to blast her with a cannon so she would not drift into any shipping lanes. When that did not happen, I debated writing a book called *Quitters*. It would be the most unusual first-person adventure story ever written. When things got tough, the intrepid men chose to . . . quit. Rob lit up at the idea and added, "Yeah, and the ending could be, 'Just as the Vikings never really made it to America, neither did we.' "

In truth, I did not give quitting much thought beyond a few lighthearted daydreams, and I immediately went about enlisting Lands' End's involvement for a second year. They had spent a lot of money to have it end so abruptly, and I tried my best to assure them that we would be returning wiser, better prepared and, perhaps, more committed. Within a few months, Mike Smith, then president of the company, decided to support us for a second year—if we promised to do a better job of keeping the Web site up to date. It was obviously not an unreasonable request, and I made that promise for the crew and myself.

A lot of other things had to change besides the rudder system and our sporadic Web site entries, however. I needed an attitude adjustment, Terry needed one, and so did the crew—those who were still going. Trevor's question back in Maine during the sea trials—"So what do you see as your role in this whole thing?"— haunted me. I had been afraid, or at least hesitant, to be a leader back then, and I think this had helped seal our fate. It had certainly made things odd between Terry and myself. While he may have been the better leader and certainly called the shots on the water, I was the one who had to try to direct the entire venture to success. It was my job. There was no getting around it, and we needed someone to push us now. Hard.

Soon we were down to nine crew members. Elias, Trevor, and Andy all bowed out. Elias was simply tired of wasting time with us and had to go back to work, it seemed. Trevor had some stronger reasons that he never told me but was steadfast in his desire not to return. Even though Trevor and I had clashed on a number of occasions, I had always appreciated his capabilities and his willingness to work hard. I asked him to reconsider, but he wouldn't.

Andy and Terry had been a constant source of friction, for each other and for the entire crew. Even so, Andy might have returned except for the fact that he was feeling a great pull to make a living. He had quit his job working for a photography studio to go on the voyage and he needed a new job, so he reenlisted in the U.S. Coast Guard. And Jan was on the fence. The trip had thrilled him mightily, but he was not so sure his New York law firm was going to allow him to take off another summer. So we were only eight for sure.

Meanwhile Terry needed to be massaged. He was understandably disgruntled—with the crew and probably with me. He was talking about not returning. While at one time I had contemplated replacing him, that option was no longer conscionable. Replacing him would be like getting rid of Captain Ahab. No, that's not right. *I* was more like Ahab. Replacing Terry would be like offing one of your parents. So I decided to send him off to Scandinavia. I figured that if he studied how they sailed their boats a bit and simply immersed himself in what we were doing, he would return a happier captain. He might even be able to put up with us for the whole summer.

I also devised a fitness and sailing Olympics, the Viking Games, to be held in Nuuk on the summer solstice.

I sent the following letter out that January:

I know some of you think I'm being a hardass as far as this being-in-shape thing goes. I guess I am, but it is only because I want everyone focused and ready to go when we get to Greenland. Unlike last year, when we had the boatbuilding to keep some of you excited and the sea trials in Maine to thrill the rest of you, this year we're going straight from our regular lives to Greenland and the voyage.

Also, not all of the events test your physical prowess.

The events will showcase either your physical abilities or your nautical skills. Everyone will be taking part. If you don't score high enough (1,000 on the twelve events), you won't be sailing to Canada on *Snorri*. That's the hardass part, but if I don't make that a condition, then I know a few slackers (Rob and me) won't work on the skills needed to score 1,000.

Here are the twelve events, not in order of importance. Each is worth 100 points (a few can earn you bonus points):

1. Run three miles in twenty-four minutes. Every minute (or fraction thereof) above twenty-four minutes subtracts 10 points from your score. If you run it in twenty-four minutes flat or less, you score 100. If you run it in twenty-four minutes and fifteen seconds, you score 90. If you run twenty-five minutes fifty-nine seconds, you score 80. Et cetera.

2. Twenty pull-ups in two and a half minutes. These do not have to be done without resting, but each set cannot be less than five pull-ups. All twenty must be completed in two and a half minutes. Every pull-up less than twenty subtracts 10 points from your best possible score of 100. Do nineteen in two and a half minutes, you score 90. Eighteen, you score 80. Et cetera. Instead of doing pull-ups, you can opt for climbing a shroud to the top—without using your feet or legs. If you make it, you get a bonus 10 points—110. If you make it more than halfway, you get 50. If you don't make it halfway, you get zero.

3. Fifty sit-ups in sixty seconds. For judging reasons, this will be done the old-style way—someone holding your feet, your knees bent, your hands behind your head. Your elbows must touch your knees and your upper back has to hit the floor. If you do fifty, you score 100. You lose 10 points for every two less than fifty. If you do forty-eight, you score 90.

Forty-six, 80. Et cetera. *Sixty* sit-ups and above gets a bonus 10 points.

4. Coil and becket a sixty-foot dock line in one minute. This will be judged and scored by John Gardner.

5. Coil a sheet in your hands and becket it in under one minute. This will also be judged and scored by John Gardner.

6. Properly set a Gerry Galuza rivet in a plank in under one minute. This will be judged and scored by Rob.

7. Plot your position by dead reckoning. Sightings made, lines drawn, position noted in less than five minutes.

8. Answer a moderately difficult question on the Vikings. This will be prepared and scored by me. Hint: Read the sagas concerning the Viking voyages to Vinland (the New World) and a general history on the Vikings.

9. Swim complete length of *Snorri*. All or nothing. One lap around *Snorri* will receive a bonus 10 points.

10. Tie a one-handed bowline in ten seconds. Every two seconds (or fraction) above ten seconds subtracts 10 points from 100. Do it in less than five seconds, receive 10 bonus points.

11. Tie a bowline behind your back in ten seconds.

12. Sing a complete sea chantey. There must be at least two verses to your song. Each individual's performance will be judged by the entire crew. However, the most you can lose for being off-key is 10 points. This will be performed at the end of the day after a few beers (or mead) provided by the New Vinland Foundation.

In my heart, I knew that I would not kick anybody out for failing the games, but I faked it as best I could. I was motivated to do better, make good on our promises, and see our voyage through to the end. I was as full of clichés as a country-western love song. I wanted us to row our hearts out, and I needed a crew who felt the same.

During this time, I staked out my territory with Terry. I wrote a succinct e-mail to him that we were going to Baffin Island no matter what—that we could not change this part of our route. I knew with Terry that I had to stand my ground. A mutual friend of Terry's and mine said to me, "If you don't stand up for Baffin, nobody will." So I did, although I was worried what this might mean in the long run.

The boat was another matter. I could not just say what I wanted and that would be that. How could we make the rudder work and be true to the Viking design? Obviously, departing from it and using that powerful, modern-design rudder had failed. Rob and I wanted to go back to the Viking design and build it right. He was sure he could get it right with our windfall of extra time.

Rob found a scholarly book on rudders, *The History of the Rudder*. While it mostly concentrated on Mediterranean rudders, it did provide some useful information on Viking rudders and where we had gone wrong. "A large, heavy rudder could break or damage a poorly designed mount, and during a storm, vibration and the working of the mount itself could harm the hull," the writer warned.

We held a rudder conference at Rob's boatyard in early February. *NOVA* was interested in filming an episode on our adventure and decided to record our meeting. They flew in a self-styled naval archeologist from Wales named Owain Roberts. I liked him from the moment I picked him up at the airport. He would say things like, "These Scandinavians are full of rubbish, aren't they?" and then give me a look that said everything was going to be okay. He had built a replica of a small Viking boat in the 1980s and written a report for *Sailing into the Past*, the Viking Ship Museum's book. The book is a bible for Viking boat enthusiasts, so it was refreshing to hear him speak somewhat irreverently of the subject. At the same time, he was a proponent for going back to the beginning: "The replica builder aims to produce an exact copy but knows that he never will do so. Compromises are made. These must be few and well reasoned since it is not good enough to build in the style of a particular ancient boat. He must subjugate his own techniques, methods and prejudices to the one aim, that of creating, above all else, an honest replica."

On the opposing side, we had Mark Fitzgerald. He was the naval architect from Camden who had designed the Cleopatra rudder for us. He had also written an article about our project for a magazine called *Maine Boats and Harbors*, and it was clear he would be on Terry's side of the argument. I liked Mark and some of his ideas, but it was clear the only thing important to him was that the rudder work, no matter how modern the design.

These two newcomers plus Rob, Terry, and I stood around a makeshift table and argued for a few hours. I came armed with a letter from Max Vinner. I had written him about our problems, and

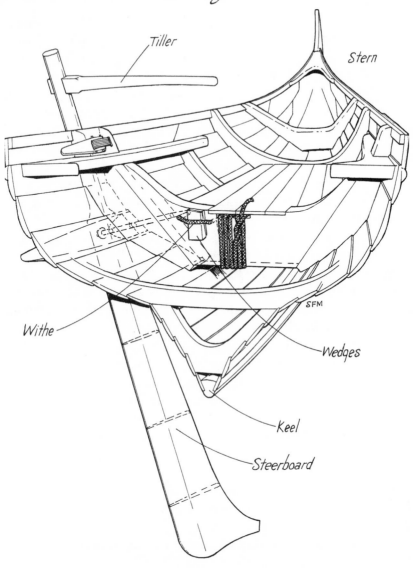

second year's rudder system

his response understandably stood on the side of Viking technology: "The snag about the Vorså rudder is that the rudder was found alone without a ship, and the snag with Wreck 1 is that it was found without a rudder . . . but the Vorså rudder is the most refined side-rudder design we know—and the best preserved apart from the Gokstad and the Oseberg. Personally, I think the slim Vorså belonged to a likewise slim longship of a smaller size. The knarr being a bit heavier in a seaway might very well in my opinion have a slightly (but only slightly) broader rudder board. Under no circumstances [use a] modern plastic thing."

It was clear that Max did not like our Cleopatra rudder, although calling it plastic was a little extreme. But his message was clear: Stick to the Viking design.

At first our rudder conference felt slightly awkward, since the conversation was being filmed. We were civil and restrained. But as things heated up we forgot the camera was there. It was hard to get a word in, even. Mark was insistent that the Viking rudder could not work. Owain argued the opposite point of view but conceded it might need to be broader or even longer, always maintaining that the original shape would work. No one convinced anyone of anything, but we all agreed that the framing—the crossbeam that had been pulled out of place—had to be beefier. We also all agreed that the withy should be threaded through the crossbeam. Originally it had come through the hull in front of the crossbeam to which it was tied, and thus the rudder was constantly pulling the crossbeam forward. If the withy was led directly through the crossbeam, it would pull the crossbeam into the planking and help keep the boat together.

After the meeting Rob and I decided that he and John Gardner would make two new rudders but that they would not be modernized, as Mark and Terry had hoped. Rob's argument was that the very first rudder simply had not been built correctly. I cheered from the sidelines but also knew we had the Cleopatra rudder just in case. With the beefier framing that Rob was planning on constructing, *Snorri* would probably be strong enough for the Cleopatra rudder if we had to resort to using it again.

Rob went off to Scandinavia soon after the rudder meeting to measure, study, and talk with the experts some more. While there he confirmed our decisions on the rudder and also decided to move our rudder back about a foot with the notion that this would give us more turning leverage.

Although we were moving forward and I was spending much-needed time with my family, there was a sadness we could not escape. Bob Miller, the cheerful boatbuilder who had done so much to calm me and at times counter Rob's moodiness and tendency toward being a loose cannon, had died in a carpentry accident. While working on a building for a local school he fell from the rafters, suffering traumatic brain damage. When I spoke with his widow, Allison, she reminded me that working on *Snorri* had been Bob's all-time favorite project. I had known Bob for only a little more than a year, but he had been so warm and funny that I felt as if an old friend had died.

Rob and Bob had been best friends. For a long time afterward Rob appeared empty and a little lost. While he laughed and put up a good front, he seemed very remote.

I had already realized something, and Bob's death somehow made it clearer: We could not trifle with this project. To anyone looking from the outside, it may have seemed like we had been deeply immersed from the beginning, but I could not help feeling this was not true. Lisa and I had talked a lot about it, and together we decided that I would go deeper. I would try harder to know the Arctic, the Europeans' and Inuit's past in the region, and even more about the Vikings. I read, read, and read. In this light, David Conover, the documentary filmmaker from Maine who had come to Greenland the previous summer, challenged me one day with, "You've gone to all this trouble to replicate the Viking sailing experience, but you don't really know what that felt like on board, do you? You need to dress like a Viking. Wear the same clothes. Feel what they felt."

I responded with a derisive "Yeah, sure." Reenacters wear replica clothing, and I did not want to become one of them. The idea gnawed at me, as David knew it would, and I finally agreed to have some Viking clothing made. I decided I would wear them for only a week, however.

In reality, I already was a Viking nut by this time, so I might as well dress the part. The clothes, though, had to be based on clothing that had been found at archeological digs. I did not want to wear anything based on conjecture. Sadly for my warmth, this meant I would have no furs. Owain Roberts led me to a man named Tich Craddock, who forges Viking tools and weaponry. Tich is also a reenacter. Given this, when I discovered that I very much liked him, I had to reconsider my view of reenacters. Maybe they are all likable, normal fellows like Tich and me.

Anyway, his wife, Di, agreed to make the clothing, but everything would have "provenance," as Tich put it. Tich's thick Welsh accent and my slight drawl meant that hardly a word was understood between us, but we had a grand time guffawing over the phone for a few months. The helmet, knife, and ax he fashioned would have made Leif proud, and the clothing Di created was simply beautiful. The first layer was linen undergarments. The kyrtle (I kept thinking Tich was saying *girdle*) stretched down to my knees. The next layer was a thinnish green wool kyrtle and dark green wool drawstring pants. The final layer was the same, a kyrtle and another pair of pants of much thicker wool. The last kyrtle was plaid. (Okay, so maybe not every single item had provenance.)

I also had a sheepskin cap backed with leather. It looked like a rugby ball ripped in half. A similar hat had been found in what is thought to be a wealthy merchant's grave. Over that I wore a pointed hood, making me look like a cross between Papa Smurf and a Druid. A thick, pale gray wool cape draped the whole ensemble. There was also a leather kyrtle to break the wind and resist rain. It looked as if half a cow had been used to make it, and it smelled that way too. The shoes were wraparound leather affairs that looked like city attire. This did not seem too inappropriate because the Vikings, despite their violent reputation, were also accused of being dandies. A certain John of Wallingford complained in one of the English annals that the Danes of England combed their hair, took a bath on Saturdays, and changed their woolens at frequent intervals to entrap English women. (The *Oxford English Dictionary* does not know where the word *dandy* comes from, so henceforth I'm asserting it is derived from these much-hated, clean Danish Vikings). Tich threw in a leather water bottle lined with beeswax.

All suited up, with battle-ax in hand, I felt like an extra in a B movie. I pranced about the house, demanding that Lisa and the girls admire me. Actually, while in my head I pranced, I could barely move. The clothes weighed nearly thirty pounds, and in West Virginia I was sweating profusely. I felt like a multicolored marshmallow. I think I even knocked over a lamp with my added girth.

Eliza and Anabel trailed behind me, screaming, "Daddy go Viking boat? Daddy go Viking boat?"

Lisa appreciated the clothes' comeliness but asked, "Weren't you miserable enough last year? Are you really going to wear this?"

"God, no," I said, amazed that she would even bother to ask. The Vikings may have survived in this stuff, but they were tough. With all the rain up there, I'd get frostbite in a second. "You know

I'm too wimpy. I'll just put it on the first day and then we will take turns wearing it at each new town. The kids will love it."

In recognition of my own shortcomings and the approaching Viking games, I worked out like a good berserker and also practiced my knots. In fact, I became devoted to knots. My knot book suggested, "The only way to gain the necessary confidence is to practice the knots over and over again until the movements become completely automatic and instinctive, for in uncertain circumstances, hesitation and doubt can make the knot an enemy." I took it to heart. I could not do anything without making bowlines, sheet bends, clove hitches, and carrick bends. I tied them in bed, while at the dinner table, and even while driving. Eventually I began tying them in my head. Lisa and I might have been having a conversation concerning, say, when the girls should start nursery school, and even before we really got into it, I would have tied four dozen bowlines in my head. I grew to love knots, and I saw Lisa growing jealous of my newfound affection.

"You are obsessed," she said, enunciating each word, one afternoon after happening upon me and my knots. "Everything in moderation, Hodding—even knots." I couldn't help noticing that her twisted auburn hair resembled an endless series of lovely half hitches at that moment.

Knots have such lovely curves. You can follow them round and round again like an endless roller-coaster ride. I sometimes found myself absentmindedly caressing my latest creations. There was something so reassuring in the shapes and the silky feel of the two-fathom length of climbing rope I used for my daily bondage sessions. A person, I realized as I tied my chair to my desk or my leg to a convenient lamppost, could spend his whole life devoted to knots.

Rope, my knot book told me, was one of man's first inventions, predating even the wheel. And there is nothing better to do with a rope than tie a knot. I began wondering what sorts of knots the Vikings had used. If I read my newly purchased copy of *History and Science of Knots* correctly (my ability to understand it was in doubt given the book's highly academic tone), the first physical evidence of knots accompanied the 1991 discovery of the Ice Man, the corpse frozen solid in the Italian Alps for 5,400 years. The knot-bearing articles on his clothing consisted of single hitches, overhand knots, a reef or square knot, an overhand bend, and a strap knot, as well as others that have not been identified. I did not yet know the overhand bend or the strap knot but would soon attempt to master them. If the Ice Man could do them, so could I. It was fascinating to me to imagine this solitary guy trekking across the Alps with so much knowledge strapped to his body.

My knot history book did not mention any Viking knots, but it did note that the Vikings were the first known traders of cordage. According to one author, the Vikings shipped walrus hide from Greenland throughout Europe because it was highly prized for its natural strength. Another author cited a find of a 3,500-year-old granny knot tied by Viking ancestors in Denmark. So while the Ice Man temporarily had me beat, at least I was equal to a pre-Viking.

By this point, even the girls were getting sick of my knot mania. One morning while watching the end of *Barney*, Anabel sat in my lap. Helen dozed at my feet. Eliza climbed off the bed, walked over to where I sat, and told me, "Shut dis, Daddy!" taking my *Morrow Book of Knots* out of my hand and shutting it for me. She then kicked my rope away. "No do dis, Daddy. No do dis." She plopped down in my lap beside her sister, and that was the end of that—for the time being.

I took a short break from knots to take a navigational course in Annapolis at the Annapolis Sailing School with John Abbott, Rob, and Doug. It was funny but inexcusable that we still could not even tell the difference between a small-scale chart and a large-scale one.* We had to become more adept at navigating or at least be able to pass the test Terry would give us during the Viking Games.

The Annapolis Sailing School structured a special no-frills weekend course for us that pounded home the finer points of dead reckoning. We learned mnemonics like "True virgins make dull companions," a memorization technique for the terms *true course, variation, magnetic course, deviation,* and *correction*. Our instructor, Dan Daniels, seemed nonplussed by our lack of understanding and sometimes would grow so distraught that he himself would forget how to navigate. Rob, however, did earn some praise early on: "You seem to understand the concept of the round compass."

---

* Of course, now that I've got it firmly planted in my brain it's easy: A small-scale chart represents a large area and a large-scale chart represents a small area. It's the counterintuitiveness of the words that makes it so hard.

"What are we looking for here, fellas?" soon changed to "This is the ABC's of navigation, fellas!" Dan was retired from the Coast Guard, and truthfully, I worried a little about his heart when he became apoplectic over how slow we were (except for Doug, who had a knack for figures and navigation, it turned out). We would have tried Job's patience. When he finally realized we were a hopeless lot, the classes went more smoothly. He asked John Abbott how he came up with a certain dead-reckoning position that was as far wrong as a person could get.

"I did the math right," John explained, looking simultaneously exasperated and dumbfounded. "I just had east and west flipped. . . . It's okay."

Dan bent over laughing and sputtered, "It's *not* okay. The math's the easy part."

His drilling did sink in, however. Near the end of our two-day overview, Dan stood beside Rob and me saying, "You can start a new DR from a fix but not an EP—generally speaking." Unbelievably, we understood him. We were certainly not a crack navigational team by the end of the weekend, but we could ease Terry's burden a little, if nothing else.

At the end of the class Dan asked me, "If you were steering zero-two-zero and wanted to go three-four-zero, whichway would you turn, right or left?"

Everything had been so theoretical up to this point that the blatantly pragmatic question threw me for a loop.

"Um," I stalled, "west is best, east is least. . . . You'd go right?"

"No, no, no," he cried, grabbing his head. "You'd turn left. The compass doesn't move."

As we walked out the door he handed us our official navigation certificates and said we would do a fine job—but added, I assumed for veracity's sake, "Saints preserve me for lying!"

My only remaining chore was to find a replacement crew member. Originally I had wanted Terry to replace two of the four crew members who dropped out. Jan's mother was ill and so he could not join us after all. For various reasons Terry did not find anyone. For starters, I think he wasn't expecting it to be so difficult; I had learned over the last few years, however, that while a lot of people say they want to go on a Viking expedition, hardly any really mean it. As we got closer to leaving the United States, we decided that we would bring on only one new crew member, and I called Erik Larsen in Denmark. Erik was one of the guys who ran the youth hostel in Narsarsuaq, Greenland, and we had all grown fond of his company. His credentials far surpassed all of ours combined: He had crewed on another Viking replica in Denmark, had sailed since his youth, and knew Viking history as well as the rest of us knew the words to the *Gilligan's Island* theme song. Thirty years old and preferring the buzzed haircut of an expatriate Dane, he was gentle, thoughtful, and open-minded. Yes, a Lands' End representative had seen him running naked down the hallway of her Narsarsuaq hotel the year before, but that only was because the ex-boyfriend of a woman Erik had been sleeping with was in the process of beating him up. That, however, just further illustrated Erik's resourcefulness.* Erik would be a great crew member for all the abovementioned reasons, but even more to the point was that Erik spoke Danish. This would be most useful, since with any luck we would be working our way up the coast of Greenland to Sisimiut before heading across to Canada. Erik immediately agreed to join our voyage.

On June 1 Rob, Dean, Terry, and I headed back to Greenland. I could not believe I was leaving Lisa and the girls behind again. Lisa cried a lot the morning I left. It was not simply our being apart that troubled her; she had always believed I had a good chance of dying on this trip, and that thought never left her.

On my part, I could not stand the thought of being separated from my family yet again. Helen smiled at me as I loaded the car. Anabel repeated, "Daddy leave? Daddy leave?" holding up my waterproof briefcase. Eliza stared at me as if she knew I was going away for a very long time. I started crying too.

But this year I was ready. Things were going to change. Gwyn Jones' words played in my head: "For the unbreakable will . . . triumphs over the blind injustice of all-powerful fate, and makes man its equal." I will forever be a sucker for that kind of stuff. We had that kind of will. I knew it. We were going to give it our best. We had to.

---

* Yes, a similar thing had happened to Jan, and this coincidence helped Erik's case greatly. Also, I, too, had almost gotten in a fight with this same neanderthal ex-boyfriend, who wanted to beat me up because my daughters were being too loud while he gabbed on his cell phone. So I empathized with Erik.

Chapter Thirteen

We went back to Nuuk to begin where we had left off. It was, after all, where our boat had been towed, and it made the most sense to begin at our last landfall, just as the Vikings would have done if they had been lucky enough to make it back to shore with a broken rudder.

We were renewed, invigorated, ready to go.

Ha.

Dean, Terry, and I went running our first day in Nuuk. Rob, the other crew member already in Greenland, refused to join us. He proclaimed he was going to prepare for the Viking games by resting.

During the run I felt awful. I felt as though I had not run in a year, although I had been training for six months, and Dean dropped out when we got to the closest public rest room. Terry alone looked and seemed to feel like a young gazelle—well, more like a giraffe, on account of his inordinate height.

The second morning was all that I had feared, featuring Rob the procrastinator. Rob stood around the boat, hemming and hawing. Running his hands along the planking. Sitting down, staring out into space. Talking about what he was going to do.

I wanted action. I wanted the boat ready before the rest of the crew even left the United States. I told Rob what I wanted. I urged him on. I rode him, and I assume he wanted to swat me like a pesky blackfly, which are not as bad in Greenland as one might expect them to be—they hover more than actually bite. In truth, Rob was incredibly understanding. While Terry, Dean, and I did the mindless chores—cleaning, scraping, and pine tarring, checking old food supplies, cleaning gear—Rob had to make the boat work. He had to repair his creation. He loved every inch of that boat and did not want to do anything wrong. You could see it as he stretched out in her like a bear in its lair. He had to get it right. The framing had to be strong enough and set in just the right place—not because he felt we had to make it to L'Anse aux Meadows but because he owed it to her.

As I pushed him for the twentieth time in an hour he turned to me and blurted out, "Hodding, I'm afraid to start. Okay?" I backed off but continued to worry we would not be done in time.

We worked long days, not bothering to stop at all for the first weekend. *Snorri* had survived the winter well, but once things warmed up a bit in the spring, her mast suffered badly. John Gardner and I had built a roof over *Snorri* in the fall, erecting rafters and covering it with strong, clear plastic. It was hot and dry under the roof, like a sauna, and this had caused the mast to check—huge cracks ran up and down the forty-three-foot spruce pole. Rob said he had never seen a mast check so much and worried that it had been fatally compromised—that it might split apart at any moment. We would never know for sure until we made it safely to Newfoundland.

The men at the boatyard mostly ignored us except when we asked to borrow a tool or use their workshops, and then they were absolutely accommodating. Rob kept saying you would never see such benevolence at an American boatyard.

Visitors straggled by. Elias drove up in a shiny new truck. He had been working in Nuuk for the last few months but was moving to Maniitsoq. He had been asked to run a small-business development organization and could not pass up the money or the opportunity. We could not believe that he was leaving his home town of Sisimiut, however. He had always said everything south of Sisimiut was a pit, worthless. Rob was convinced that Elias' wife, Karen, had kicked him out of the house—that Elias was merely putting up a good front. Elias' hatred of everything beyond Sisimiut was so profound that Rob's hunch felt true, but Elias insisted that everything was fine between him and his wife.

A woman named Benedikte "Bendo" Thorsteinson from Greenland Tourism stopped by. We had exchanged a few e-mails over the winter, and now she wanted to see what her government agency could do to help us. Together over the next few weeks we hatched a plan for the Viking Games that upped the stakes quite a bit. The event grew from a private competition for the crew to The Viking-Inuit Games, to be held the same weekend as Greenland's National Day. Not only would we be tested and timed on the functions I had laid out, but now Bendo and I added a quiz on a traditional Inuit story called Kaassassuk and a couple of traditional Inuit rope games that the crew and I would not get to practice. I knew this last test would (and did) upset John Gardner, who always likes to do everything right. We were going to make total fools of ourselves, but at least a few Greenlanders would probably join in too. I met with two members of the kayak club, cosponsors of the Games. They were going to set up the rope games and would help run some of the events. The men seemed serious and absolutely did not want any beer to be sold to the public. I had stumbled across a few kayak clubs over the last few years, and there seemed to be a political bent to them. It was not just about sport and making traditional dartlike Greenlandic kayaks. They seemed to yearn for the past—to make a Greenland for Greenlanders, not Danes and Americans. Bendo and I were both happy that they had agreed to work with us.

One day as I cleaned rotting cheese off my hands, marveling that Jan and John Abbott had thought twenty pounds of soft Danish cheese stored in a pickle barrel would be okay unrefrigerated in the heated boatyard supply shop for the winter, a young man appeared by my side from nowhere. I didn't shake his hand, for obvious reasons, but he nevertheless launched into a nonstop series of questions about our voyage and statements about what he was doing.

His name was Thomas, and he looked a bit pasty. He was a Danish bookbinder by trade and therefore could work anywhere, he said. Evidently people always needed bookbinders. He was traveling through Viking territories because he was a Viking fanatic. He had been in Greenland for nine months and would stay for another year, scouring various Viking settlements for artifacts, between bookbinding jobs. Then he planned to visit Iceland, the Faroes, and England. He had found many precious items at Sandnes—one of the sites that made up the Viking western settlement, just fifty miles down the fjord from Nuuk. He tracked us down again a couple of days later, reiterating that he would like to be a crew member if we needed one and showing some of his finds: a broken rivet, a spindle whorl, shards of soapstone pottery, a stone with seemingly runic etchings, and rectangular fist-sized stones with holes bored in them that Thomas believed had been used as loom weights. He gave me a Thor's hammer he had carved out of stone found at Sandnes, and one of the loom weights. Thomas' hoard consisted of more artifacts than had been found at L'Anse aux Meadows, Newfoundland, after years of excavations. I did not really want to have him as a crew member—one Viking fanatic was enough.

As I worked ineptly beside Rob, I grew to respect his work more than ever before. In the past I had not had time to think about all the decisions he had to make or the new knowledge he had needed to gain to build *Snorri* properly, but now I was getting that chance. Rob never ceased to amaze me with how much he knew. Even if half of what he spewed was bullshit, he still probably knew more about traditional boatbuilding than anyone alive.

I was pounding in some trunnels—the wooden nails that attached the planking to the framing. I did not know what I was doing but was gamely proceeding because Rob seemed to want me to. He wanted me to learn what it was like, and I felt honored. I asked him how hard I should hit the trunnel—that way I could gauge whether or not I had made the trunnel the right size.

"How do you know how hard to hit these things—how much force it should take?" I asked.

"Well, back a hundred years ago, it was an inch a blow," he answered without hesitating or even looking up from the crossbeam he was shaping. "On the video of *Saga Siglar* being built, though, Sigurd was just tapping them in with a small hammer. . . . But I'd make them an inch a blow."

If Rob said it was supposed to be a blow instead of a tap, then that meant I had to really whale on it to get that inch. So I pounded one really hard until its head began to splinter. I looked up to see Rob smiling at me.

"It's no big deal, Hodding," he said. "It only has to hold the rudder in place." I pounded it back out and reshaped another one.

I was realizing that I could ask Rob almost anything about building a Viking ship and he would know the answer. These were things he had thought about long and hard.

Rob showed us how to use his adz (an axlike tool used for dressing or planing wood) so we could thin down a naturally curved limb of a tamarack tree to make a knee. We had to shape two new knees, which would support the aftmost crossbeam. I was thrilled. Dean, Terry, and I were making a crucial piece of the boat's framing that we would be able to sit on, forever remembering that we had shaped it. Dean and Terry took to adzing fairly well—so well that they hardly let me do it—but when I did try, I nearly sliced off my foot. The blade tore through a quarter inch of leather and insulation, just shy of nicking my big toe. When I finally got the right rhythm, the wood peeled off like slices of cheese. It was divine, like eating the perfect peach or skipping the perfect rock. Although I was frighteningly inept and still shudder at the thought of my poorly made trunnel holes, I finally understood all I had missed while Rob and his crew carefully crafted *Snorri* for all those months in Maine.

As enlightening and entertaining as our days were, our nights were even better. We had moved over to the city's sports center, which was also a bunkhouse. Dean, Rob, and I shared a room. Terry, needing to be alone and away from us snorers, slept by himself. Every evening, when we were finally settling down to sleep, Rob would begin his daily exercises. We were still intermittently running and doing push-ups and sit-ups in preparation for the Viking-Inuit Games, except for Dean, who had inexplicably decided he only had to practice his pull-ups. I guess, being so old and wise, he knew I was not going to kick anybody off the voyage.

First Rob would start breathing heavily, as if he had climbed halfway up the Empire State Building and was on the verge of a heart attack. I think the mere thought of what he was about to do brought on these spasms. Then suddenly, like some freakish robot, he would begin popping his knees toward his chest, again and again. Next he thrust his arms back and forth twenty times like a decapitated chicken, launched into a dozen knee bends, and followed up with some straight-arm rotations. By this time the slapping of his naked flesh upon itself made it sound as if a huge animal, a walrus maybe, was being flensed in our fetid room. Rob would also have turned bright red and looked as though he were going to expire at any moment. Oddly, loud yawns punctuated his every move. His breathing began to sound as if the walrus were being not merely flensed but flensed while still alive. Then came the push-ups, sit-ups, side leg lifts, running in place with his palms on the ground, and, lastly, some exercise that I could never identify but which looked like the mating dance of a beast that with any luck will never be discovered. I was always belly-laughing by this point and could not stop until he zipped out the door for his half-mile run, which eventually increased to over two miles as the Games drew nearer.

One of these evenings, as I lay laughing in my bed, Rob tossed a plastic bag with three film canisters onto my chest.

"Film," I said brightly.

"No," he answered. "Bob." Bob Miller's widow, Allison, had filled the canisters with Bob's ashes, and Rob had brought them along so Bob could see the Arctic. He eventually put some of the ashes into a bucket of pine tar, and so Bob became a part of *Snorri* forever.

The remainder of the crew showed up on the thirteenth of June. They seemed psyched. Our banter was endless and only grew more out of hand when we had a reindeer-and-fish barbecue at Poul and Jeanne Holm's house. A couple of us had met Poul the previous fall, and he and Jeanne had been making our life easier ever since. Poul worked in everything in Greenland—boat repair, pipe work, and welding—and so he knew how to get things done. If we needed a part, he would stop what he was doing and drive us around town until we found it. Many times he just turned his van over to us. He had looked after *Snorri* all winter and stored some of our gear at his house.

During the barbecue Jeanne told us that the newspapers, TV station, and radio were exhorting people to clean the streets. All the snow had finally melted away, and the winter's trash needed to be cleaned up. Trash bags were lined up throughout the city for this purpose. Poul talked about hating the Danes, although Jeanne was pure Danish and Poul's dad was Danish as well. Poul mostly seemed to be joking, but there was obviously some truth to what he had said. He did not like the control that the Danish government still exerted over his country nor the superior attitude of the expatriate Danes, most of whom kept to themselves unless they were in a racially mixed marriage.

The minute we got back to the bunkhouse that evening, the talk turned toward a more normal, ridiculous level. Abbott was reading an article in *Details* and quoted aloud, "Circumcised men are thirty-three percent more likely to receive oral sex."

"What?" Gardner asked, sounding disturbed.

Abbott read it again. "Fuck that," Gardner said.

"Circumcised?" Homer said disdainfully. "I don't even know if I am circumcised."

Incredulous, the two Johns tried to explain to Homer how he could tell.

"I can piss," Homer responded.

They explained some more, and Homer finally allowed that yes, he was indeed circumcised.

Two days later, when the crane showed up to lift *Snorri* onto the railway that would be used to launch her, we were still getting her ready, pounding in trunnels, tarring rigging, and vacuuming the bilge, even as the straps were being run beneath *Snorri*. Not a big surprise there. Dean attempted to console me, explaining that this was always the case with any boat. At least the new rudder framing was almost complete.

Abbott was probably the most strung out of any of us. The day before, he had volunteered for the onerous task of filling in the cracks on the mast and yard with epoxy to strengthen them. The glue got all over his clothes. On launch day Abbott got stuck, along with Gardner and me, scraping the excess dried epoxy off the spars, and he was not pleased. Abbott looked as though he might whack the next guy who made a wisecrack, and more than one of the crew commented that he seemed much more stressed out than the year before.

However, *Snorri* was successfully launched that afternoon and did not leak much for having dried out and shrunk over the winter.

After launching we spent equally long hours working on *Snorri* in the water. It was a good opportunity for us to get used to each other again, and I was pleased to see how well Erik slipped into the group. He seemed a little more serious than I had remembered, but that, I soon realized, was because he was trying to learn everything we knew and did before we set out.

We had to keep postponing our first sailing day because everything was taking a little longer than we had hoped. We wanted *Snorri* to be ready for the entire voyage when we took to sea, so we labored over every little detail. Gardner took the job of storing our gear to a new level of compulsion. He had lists, charts, and diagrams for every item going on board, including the poop bucket, and was constantly searching for the perfect setup.

Homer was his stow boy and took to muttering aloud, " 'Move it here!' I do that. Then it's 'Move it here!' I do that. I've moved the same rock a dozen times.' " But he seemed more amused than annoyed.

Then the rains arrived. Nuuk receives more rain than anywhere in the country, and although we would be living and sailing in rain for the next few months, our progress slowed down. We were still used to living indoors. Being soaked and miserable was simply not a part of our lives—yet.

In our bunkhouse on a rainy Friday, we completed the part of the Viking-Inuit Games that would not be open to the public, testing ourselves on the saga, knots, coiling, and navigation. Everyone passed most of the tests, except the questions on the saga. I had even made photocopies of *The Greenlanders Saga* to help them out, but some of the answers showed that the whole Viking thing still escaped a few of my crewmates. Half of them blew my trick question, "What land did Bjarni Herjolfsson set foot on before reaching Greenland?"* Terry failed his navigation question created by Rob, not knowing that a raven can see two hundred miles when flying its highest. Since I had prepared the saga test, Rob quizzed me on Viking boatbuilding techniques. I passed only because he threw in a

---

* If you send me the correct answer, you might win a hand-forged iron rivet, or maybe just a pat on the back.

bonus question on how many strakes, or rows of planks, a knarr has: twelve.

Two days later we held the first-ever Viking-Inuit Games. The crew had trained in preparation for the games—some more than others—and several seemed eager to show off. Luckily, Bendo from Greenland Tourism had given us a short translation of the traditional Inuit story upon which we would be quizzed. Erik made a full translation, and here it is:

(Actually, it's too long to repeat here, but Erik's translation is full of wonderful anecdotes about poor Kaassassuk, an orphan boy who is mistreated by nearly everyone in his village. He was kicked out of his first adoptive family's house because his excrement was too big. They made him sleep in the passageway. When it was time for him to come inside, he was lifted by his nostrils. He was mistreated even worse by the village children, who stuffed excrement into his nostrils. Eventually Kaassassuk had had enough and battled the Lord of the Force on top of a mountain. He gained superhuman powers as a result and returned to his village, where he performed some heroic feats, such as killing three polar bears with his bare hands. His fellow villagers suddenly treated him with great respect, but it was too late. He killed them all, except for the three people who had always treated him well. After a while Kaassassuk heard of a man who no one could defeat in another village, and he went to battle him. Kaassassuk was sorely trounced and was covered in mud and weeds at the end of the fight. Everyone laughed at him, and from that day forth, Kaassassuk never fought another soul. He had found his superior.)

The moral of the Kaassassuk story, apparently, is that no one should get on his high horse, and it seemed like an appropriate cautionary tale for us, although we already had the previous year's experience to serve the same function.

No one proved himself to have the strength of Kaassassuk during the Games, but then, no one embarrassed himself quite as much either. For expediency's sake, I ditched a couple of the competitions, including the sit-ups and fastening an iron rivet. Regrettably, not a single adult Greenlander entered any of the competitions.

It was, however, a lot of fun, and about a dozen young people joined us for the run, which Terry won handily. A crowd of a hundred or so came down to watch us make fools of ourselves and cheered heartily during the pull-up competition. Doug performed his like a machine, completing seventeen full pull-ups without stopping. The crowd cheered even louder when we attempted the kayak rope game. A doubled-up rope was stretched between two poles. A contestant had to straddle the rope and then spin himself around in a full circle, as if he were rolling a kayak. I am still amazed that our genitalia remained intact. We also tried a two-man game of tug-of-war in which the contestants place the soles of their feet against each other and then tug on a toggle separated by a few inches of rope. Homer ripped the skin off my middle finger, but that feat was topped by Rob, who stood and lifted Terry off the ground in an attempt to shake him off the toggle.

When it came time for our swim, only one Greenlander, a brave teenage boy who had done nearly as many pull-ups as Doug, was crazy enough to join in, and the crowd, which I expected to be uproarious by this point, remained subdued. I was later told they had suspected one of us would die. We had to swim out and back twenty-five yards to a buoy that Poul Holm had placed for us. Poul and two other men donned wet suits, and a safety boat was ready for any calamity. Homer was cursing me before getting in, seriously mad that I was enforcing the swim. He had seen his stepbrother cramp up in cold water, and I think he believed the same was about to happen to him, or worse. He had told me the story three times the week before the swim.

Luckily, neither Homer nor anyone else was injured, but the cold was awful. The water was a little under forty degrees, cold enough to kill in just a few minutes. I probably covered the distance faster than I have ever gone since swimming for my college team. Most of the guys could not speak when they struggled out of the water, their jaws clenched shut and bodies a seemingly blood-less pale yellow. The swim accomplished its intended goal, however, and no one ever went overboard, except for extremely short swims.

Huddled together on a sloping boulder after the swim, still shivering, we sang our chanteys. We were miserable, but nearly all of us sang our tune to the end. Some covered their ears as Rob and I sang, but we tried our best.

The Games more than served their function. Not only could everyone now tie a bowline as easily as walk down the street, but there was a pervasive camaraderie among the crew that had been missing the previous year.

A few days later, we finally began our sea trials. Terry gave the crew a very clear talk on our objectives for the trials—trying out the rudders, making sure all parts of the boat and us were still functional, getting used to working together again—and then we took off on a sunny, breezy afternoon. In truth, the following weeks of sailing up the coast to Sisimiut would constitute sea trials. These first days on the water were merely a chance to have some fun and kill time until our official launch day, June 28. Lands' End and Bendo from Greenland Tourism wanted us to have an official launch, and so I had arbitrarily picked the twenty-eighth. It did not really matter what day we left Nuuk, because we probably had a month before the pack ice would clear up along Baffin Island.

We tacked and jibed across the fjord, frolicking in the light wind. The conditions made it easy to relearn the techniques we had practiced the summer before. We put the motor on our inflatable boat and took turns taking pictures of *Snorri* under way. I had never seen *Snorri* under sail, and the sight was stunning. It seemed as if the actual past were sailing toward me—not just a square-sailed work of art. Something about the way the wind filled *Snorri*'s sail and the hull barreled through the water was so powerful and eternal. Back on board, I stood in the stern, tears flooding my eyes. I wanted to hug everyone. We had come back and not given up. *Snorri* was sailing beautifully. Rob's new rudder seemed fine, and with a little work it would be perfect. For the time being, it could turn the boat, a big improvement over the first Viking rudder. I ran forward to where he stood on bow watch and gave him a big kiss. He seemed embarrassed, but pleased that his rudder was indeed working.

A little later, manning the tiller, I told Doug I wanted to scream out loud, dance a little jig. "Then do it," he responded. So I did.

As I looked around the boat, I saw all smiles. Everyone was pleased with how *Snorri* was sailing, even Cliff, another insurance inspector sent by Lands' End to make sure *Snorri* was sound. Many of the crew still had their worries, of course. Terry was still concerned about my insistence we head to Baffin, especially in light of the most recent ice report we had received. The report showed it was a typical ice year, which meant there was ice up to fifty miles offshore of eastern Baffin Island. It would clear up, I believed. It had to. Meanwhile, Doug was fighting hard to remain happy; he and his girlfriend had broken up again. Also, John Abbott and his wife had divorced, and although he was seeing someone else, it was not filling the emptiness he clearly felt. Maybe that was why he seemed more on edge, not as light and carefree as the year before. Rob and his wife had separated. Gardner's girlfriend would not speak to him. Erik's girlfriend had started seeing another man while on a skiing vacation. It was a ship of broken hearts. Even if we did not make it to Newfoundland, the time away would certainly do them all some good.

Erik walked around the boat, memorizing how we had everything set up. Rob was spending a lot of time sleeping. When he wasn't sleeping he was arguing about rowing with John Abbott. Rob believed it was better to face forward, and Abbott believed it was better to face the stern, or maybe it was the other way around. The argument had begun the year before, and it threatened to continue until our last day together. Abbott was still strewing his gear all over the place, driving Gardner crazy, especially since Gardner was suffering from tendinitis in his forearm and could barely lift any of Abbott's stuff out of his way. Luckily, since Abbott's messiness was obviously chronic, Gardner's tendinitis would clear up in a few days. Dean was already growing frustrated with the computer, but I guessed he secretly liked hassling with it because it sometimes excused him from more physically grueling duties. Doug was still trying to learn something new every day and perfect his skills. Terry was spending more time teaching, no longer quite as upset that he was not sailing in a boat of his peers. And Homer . . . well, Homer acted like a nineteen-year-old, slightly unreadable, sulky, happy, belligerent, giddy, and sleepy—all within one hour.

We were more of a crew than ever before, and as if to highlight this fact, spontaneous rounds of chanteys would arise throughout the day. I liked Homer's the most: "Haul Away Together." It had a robust tune and included such disparate subjects as King Louis and moldy lips: "When I was a little boy, my mother she done told me / Away, haul away / We'll haul away together / Away, haul away / We'll haul away, Joe / If I did not kiss the girls, my lips would grow all moldy . . . Louis was the King of France before the revolution . . ." Sometimes two or three guys sang together, and then the entire crew would join in. It seemed as if we were drifting back in time, or at least back into a movie from the 1930s in which we all played sailors.

This was how I had always wanted it to be.

During that first night on the boat, as if to remind us that we had not completely escaped into our fantasy world, a slew of Jet Skis and speedboats trailing wet-suited skiers spun circles around our anchorage in Nussuaq, Nuuk's suburb. There were even a couple of people parasailing.

Homer and I put together the tandem collapsible kayak, which I had gotten along with a solo kayak for those days when we would have to sit and wait for the right wind. It took about an hour and a half to get the wood, nylon, and rubber boat together, but we figured we'd soon have it down to less than thirty minutes. We paddled to a nearby island and climbed the tallest hill. After nestling into a corner of spongy moss, we rolled some cigarettes and stared out at the ice-covered mountains surrounding Godthabsfjord.

"After I tell people about last summer, they always ask me why I decided to come back this year," Homer said, shaking his head. He had lopped off his long mane over the winter because of a job at a Montana ski resort, and he now had a bouncy, impish hairdo that seemed to trouble him greatly. "There was no way I couldn't come back. Don't really have a choice. I mean . . . look at this!" He swept his arm across our view.

I think all the crew was feeling the same, despite their troubled hearts. Rob told me while we had been lowering the anchor, "This is a great bunch of guys. Boy, I'm glad I came back." And Doug, who shared his diary with me from the second year, the next day wrote, "The snowy mountains seemed more vivid last night at bedtime, as did the blue-green water and the rocky cove. The sleeping bag more heavenly, the sleeping bodies more dear. The whole of this notion felt great and inspired."

Chapter Fourteen

The night before our departure, Bendo threw a dinner for us at her house. Earlier in the day, while sailing around the fjord, we were escorted by a herd of fifty seals. They were apparently corralling fish. Every time they rose to the surface in unison, swimming fast, it sounded like surf crashing on a beach. They would twist their heads high into the air, as if trying to catch a beguiling scent, and then arch onto their backs as they headed below the surface.

"Hey, boys," Gardner called, "aren't they cute?" His grin was wider than ever. "That's what you're having for dinner tonight!"

Bendo and her mother were cooking us a traditional Greenlandic meal of *suassa*, seal soup. Our feelings ran the gamut from indifference to fear, but most were concerned with how it might taste. Surprisingly, no one seemed too squeamish about eating seal even though the animal is protected back home. We knew Greenlanders regard seals the way we do cows, as livestock. Who were we to condemn this or turn up our noses? I had recently read that the world has long been divided between those who abhor eating sea mammals and those who don't. The Romans ate dolphins, whales, and just about anything they could get their hands on, while the Greeks revered dolphins and whales, even sculpting them, and today we all know about the division between those who do and those who don't. Although I had once been disgusted at the idea of eating seal and would never have ordered it at a restaurant, I now felt ambivalent but willing to try the Greenlandic cow.

We straggled into Bendo's comfortable home. No one owns land in Greenland—a notion unknown in the Inuit culture—but they can own the houses and buildings. The back of the house had a small greenhouse/porch attached to it, and Bendo was growing a tomato plant. Nuuk has one florist shop, and Bendo had fresh tropical flowers displayed on a table in her living room. Her home was immaculate and adorned with lovely European and Greenlandic artwork. One painting in particular, by a Greenlandic woman named Aka Høeg, intrigued me. I had seen the artist's work at Katuaq, the Nuuk cultural center, and found it very moving. She managed to capture the longing and beauty of Greenlandic women. Her work made the Greenlanders more approachable to an outsider. So many pictures and old photographs of Greenlanders make them seem vastly different from other North Americans, almost otherworldly, but Aka Høeg's artwork dispelled that stereotype. It made them real and brought us closer together. And dinner that night at Bendo's helped do the same.

I had expected us to eat buffet style, with plates on our laps, but the table was set for all to sit together. I was pleased to see that most of the crew had at least made an attempt to clean themselves up ahead of time.

The seal meat itself was quite strong-tasting, at once gamy and fishy, but the soup was delicious. We devoured everything, to Bendo's amazement. She had assumed we would barely taste the meal, and she and her mother seemed flattered. After the meal, Bendo brought out tubs of ice cream and coffee. Then she set out an assortment of cognacs and liqueurs. Appropriately enough, we dispatched a bottle of something called Viking cognac in less than an hour. We laughed and talked for a few hours with Bendo, trying to clear up our foggy knowledge of Greenland. She was the perfect hostess and went a long way toward making us feel more welcome in Greenland than we ever had. She had a beautiful daughter named Inga, who was also the vice mayor of Nuuk. All of us had crushes on both of them.

Bendo had arranged a farewell party for us at the cultural center

DOUG CABOT

The Vikings are coming

the following afternoon, and Inga spoke in her official governmental capacity. Doug had the inspired idea of wearing the Viking clothing to the party, and so he and I dressed as Vikings from head to toe. Terry wore my Viking cape. Erik wore the leather tunic and the Viking helmet. A group of white people are not usually an oddity in metropolitan Nuuk. Lots of tourists come through on cruise ships and packaged tours, and thousands of European-born residents live there. Our Viking garb, however, lit up the face of everyone we passed on the walk to the cultural center. People stopped their cars and stared, smiling or laughing heartily.

The party at Katuaq was touching. A long table stretched thirty feet across the banquet room, covered with slices of whale, seal, shrimp, other meats, and open-faced sandwiches. Not many guests attended, but a choir sang about rowing, warm weather, and a higher power. Some of the choir's members had also sung for us in Narsaq the previous summer. They, of course, remembered Abbott's fabulous dance, and he obliged all by performing it again to resounding applause. TV cameras caught him once again, and his dancing was surely a highlight of the evening news.

Bendo spoke briefly, explaining why the party was being held.

Then Inga spoke about the Viking past in Greenland, our aborted attempt, and our current effort, and wished us luck. I tried my best to give a meaningful thank-you speech with Bendo translating. We wanted to thank the choir for their singing and sang a chantey Terry had taught us—"Bound for South Australia." We changed the words to "Bound for L'Anse aux Meadows," and Terry peppered the song with a few more changes to fit sailing in the Arctic.

At last, at three o'clock that afternoon, we were ready to depart for the north. Bendo, her children, and Thomas from Denmark came along for the first few miles. A small crowd cheered as we rowed away from the dock. For once the wind favored us, and after just a bit of rowing, we raised the yard and sailed downwind. A few minutes later we rounded the harbor exit, with more than a dozen kayaks paddling alongside *Snorri* to send us off Greenlandic style. Most of the boats were traditional Greenlandic boats paddled by both young girls and boys, as well as a few men, but one or two modern plastic kayaks showed up too.

I decided to stay in my Viking clothes. It was a warm, sunny day and I figured I should get my week of wearing the clothes out of the way. This way I knew that on at least one of the days I would not be miserable. Abbott laughed every time I happened to catch his attention. The wind shifted even before Bendo and our other guests departed on Poul Holm's boat, and John and I were manning the beitiáss on the foredeck. My tunic was a little cumbersome, threatening to trip me up as I wrestled with the sail, but I managed all right. I surmised that the Vikings would not have worn such long kyrtles on their boats, and I fully sympathized, to a degree that I never had before, with my wife's hatred of tailored dresses and skirts. Anything that hems in the action of your knees sucks, no matter how sexy billions of women in the world, a handful of Scots, and I might look. Of course, the kilt has one up on the kyrtle because it is loose and nonrestrictive around the knees. I remedied my problem by doubling up more of the material above my belt. I no longer cut as dashing a figure but I didn't fall on my face quite as often.

The shoes, however, simply would not do. They were a dandy's shoe, meant for strolling down the streets of Dublin, which the Vikings transformed from a tiny Celtic settlement to a thriving trade center in the late 800s. They did not keep water out, and they were too tight, so their poor insulation could not be supplemented with extra pairs of wool socks or grass. Both the Inuit and the Vikings stuffed their boots with dried grass for insulation, but even they would have been flummoxed by these shoes. To make matters worse, the soles were slipperier than Ishmael's unctuous spermaceti. So even when I wasn't working on the foredeck, I was falling down. After I fell on my ass for the third time in half an hour, I tore them off and put on my modern insulated rubber-and-leather boots, appropriately made by a Canadian company called Baffin.

The experiment was over as far as my feet were concerned.

Not so for the rest of the clothes, however. I wore them again the second day and the same for the third. Making a total of about eight miles during this time, there was not much strain on the clothing or me, although it rained lightly on the third day. The leather tunic easily repelled wimpy droplets of water.

The fourth day was altogether different. We were tied onto a rickety dock outside the abandoned town of Kangeq, just a few miles from where we had begun our crossing of Davis Strait the summer before. The previous day we had explored the decaying buildings, swum in warmish fresh-water pools, and run around naked while the sun was out. Now we were preparing to head out of the fjord and onto the ocean. Although it was raining and it is never fun to break camp or begin a sail in the rain, the winds were from the south. We could definitely make some distance north.

Huddling under the tarp in my sleeping bag, thinking about all the dry, warm, waterproof clothes packed away in my extremely dry waterproof bag, I certainly had no intention of wearing my Viking clothes. It would be ridiculous and obviously unfair to my shipmates. If I could not perform my duties because I insisted on wearing the ridiculous Viking garments, they would have to cover for my mistake. A real leader would not think of pulling such a stunt.

Rationalizations droned on and on in my mind. As the others were getting dressed I still contemplated my fate; both Terry and Abbott approached me individually and suggested I not wear the clothes. "Everybody will understand not wearing them in this weather," Terry said kindly. He mistakenly thought they were merely farmer's clothes, but extensive research by the Viking Ship Museum suggests that the Viking sailors wore clothes like mine.

(The museum is currently making some, but with an added twist—a full protective leather suit.)

I knew Terry was concerned for my health and worried about having to deal with a hypothermia victim. He and most of the others did not seem to want me to wear them.

That was all I needed.

Being the contrarian that I am, I hopped out of my bag and jumped straight into my Viking clothes, minus the linens. Rob advised that I not wear the linen underwear, since it would act the same way as cotton if it got wet, keeping the cold water against my body. I told Terry that I would change into modern clothes the minute things got bad enough.

They never did.

It rained all day. We sailed forty miles in rolling swells and frigid spray. Erik puked. Rob did too, of course—despite the assurance of new pharmaceutical patches under each ear. Everyone except Homer wore their heavy-duty, bombproof ocean rainsuits and their supposedly waterproof mitts and gloves.

I wore wool and leather. As the rain continued, my clothes grew heavier, increasing in weight from thirty pounds to probably way over forty, but they kept me warm. Actually, although I wore no mittens, my hands even felt hot at times. Heat from my torso funneled down my billowy sleeves, constantly warming my arms and hands. Something about the superiority of these ancient clothes thrilled me to the core, especially since I had been such a skeptic. I dashed around the boat like a caped Viking crusader, filling in wherever I could. I was Viking Man!

Erik was sick and could not cook? No matter, Viking Man could do it. A sheet was trailing through the water, hampering our progress and looking unseemly? Not a problem, this was a job for Viking Man!

Best of all, I was proving the unthinkable—the never before even imagined or considered: Vikings were not so tough after all. As I have undoubtedly demonstrated thus far, I am a wimp. I get cold easily and I moan about it. Loudly. But here I was rejoicing, even while soaking wet all over except where the leather tunic covered me. If I could feel good in these clothes, anybody could.

My conclusion: The Vikings were wimps too!

Viking Man

I determined that from then on, until the end of our voyage, I would remain in Viking garb whenever we were sailing. Although on this day we were getting wet from the rain and occasional ocean spray, we were sailing downwind—nearly ideal conditions. It would not be so easy if we were on a beam reach with the wind blowing perpendicular to our boat, or even if we had to sail into the wind, but I had a hunch these clothes would not let me down even then.

That first day along the coast was full of other surprises as well. Late in the afternoon a universally dreaded cry escaped Terry: "Yard coming down!"

We had tied a stopper knot in the withy to keep it from being pulled through the hole in the rudder. We had read that on another replica boat the force on the rudder had been so great that such a knot was pulled through. Although we had believed we had made enough allowances to keep this from happening to ours, we were wrong, and the rudder was flapping loose against *Snorri*'s starboard quarter.

It did not take long to fix, since we had had ample experience fiddling with the rudder the previous summer. Terry had prepared three withies in advance, and we slung the steel-and-polypropylene one into place. Later we would replace that with a flexible, Kevlar-type rope that would be used until the end of the voyage. Just for the sake of experiment, Terry decided to use the smallest rudder, our original rudder that we had never used beyond the first week in Maine. Besides this rudder and Rob's new one, we also had John Gardner's and the Cleopatra rudder with us. If nothing else, some-day we could have an awesome bonfire.

The wind appeared to be petering out in the early evening, and since we were in no hurry to get north, we began heading in toward an anchorage. I cooked up some curried chicken and vegetables. Although we missed Jan's culinary skills, our meals had improved tremendously thanks to Dean's suggestion that I order canned meat from a farm-based company he had discovered in Ohio. Dean had gone as far as to send some of their canned turkey to me in West Virginia to convince me. It was just cooked meat with no additives beyond a little salt, but it had an unexpectedly fresh taste. I had or-dered about eighty cans of chicken, pork, turkey, and ground beef, as well as a few cans of unsweetened pork and beans. We could have a can of meat nearly every day if the four cooks—Abbott, Doug, Erik, and I—rationed them properly.

As we ate dinner we passed two enormous whales apparently feeding in the transitional waters between Fiskefjord and the ocean. They breached less than a hundred feet from us, and we were awestruck by their gargantuan grace. Terry, who had captained a boat studying humpbacks in Alaska, was sure they were humpbacks.

The rain did not return for a few days, which meant that we did not leave our anchorage during that time. If we were going to make progress north, we had learned, it would only happen if it were raining.

Ravens ruled this spot. We saw one white-tailed eagle fly over us one morning, but otherwise ravens cawed from every vantage point. One day I hiked onshore toward a nest perched on a steep cliff. Crab shells carpeted the ground as I approached. I was curious to see what a raven's nest looked like in such a remote setting. Back home, you might find household items like necklaces and even silver-ware. Would there be any such items from Atangmik, the village a few miles across the fjord? Maybe an old Viking bracelet, even?

I glanced up to where I had judged the nest to be and saw I had fifty feet to climb. As I reached my hand over the first ledge, readying to pull myself up, a terrifying *caw* burst right in my face. Just before falling, I had the unfortunate luck to look up and find myself staring into a raven's mouth as it screamed at me to get lost. The inside of a raven's cavernous mouth is a revolting red. Somersaulting backward and grinding my face into a rough patch of lichen, it occurred to me that half my head could fit in that angry bird's mouth and that a person such as myself would be wise to respect a raven's living quarters, or at the very least be sure to approach a nest from above. Struggling to my feet at the bottom of the hill, I congratulated myself on not following through on procuring ravens for our voyage. When I first began researching the Vikings, I learned that ravens had been used by Floki Vilgerdson to navigate to Iceland in the 800s. Traveling with family, livestock, and ravens, he lost one daughter to the water near the Shetlands and another to marriage in the Faroes. When he was first at sea off the Faroes, he let one of the ravens go. It flew straight back to the Faroes. Sometime later he let the second one go and it rose as high as it could, saw no land, and returned to Floki's boat. Later Floki let loose a third raven and it flew straight ahead, which was not in the direction of the Faroes. Following the raven's path led him to Iceland. Floki was one of the first Vikings to make it to Iceland and was responsible for giving Iceland its current name, although he hated the place and never returned. For a long time I thought using ravens in such a manner on our voyage would be interesting, but after my little encounter on the cliff, I yearned no more for ravens.

Reassuring noises bathed *Snorri* as we passed our nights at Raven Point: water lapping against the hull, half the crew snoring, one groaning in his sleep, and Dean squeaking out a high-pitched fart whenever he rose to pee.

We did not spend all our time listening to each other snore and pass gas, however. Terry had decided that neither Rob's rudder nor the original was working satisfactorily. Maybe from being moved farther aft, both rudders turned the boat, but when left in a neutral position, they would eventually kick, or be kicked, toward port. The effect on the helmsman was like being yanked forward by a wild horse. We had long discussions about the rudders, and one day

A man and his rudder

Terry determined we should attempt a "push test" to see if *Snorri* was plumb. To conduct the test, we hitched the outboard motor to the inflatable dinghy and pushed *Snorri* around in calm water without any rudder. While the test was in no way perfect, it did show us that *Snorri* appeared to veer slightly toward port.

Rob had been flattening the inside of his rudder ever so slightly but now changed tactics and began to make the inside slightly convex. He did this in the belief that it might correct the rudder's lift away from port. I had always assumed that rudders worked by simple mechanics, in that they were mere levers. Perhaps I was wrong, but *The Development of the Rudder* made me feel less a fool for my assumption: "The fact that a rudder is a lifting surface has long been established by both theoretical and empirical methods. Unfortunately, this body of work has not completely put to rest the notion that the rudder acts as a lever because of water pushing against it. This idea was first advanced by Aristotle."

Rudders, despite what Aristotle and I believed, are foils, like an airplane wing, and supposedly the main forces that affect them are lift and drag. So Rob figured he could fix our current problems by adjusting the lift. Terry danced around the subject, not able to be direct because of his fear of offending Rob, but he believed Rob was wasting our time. The rudder needed some sort of dramatic change. Rob pretended to not quite get what Terry hinted at. He felt his reputation as a builder had already been besmirched by the push test. There was no way Rob was going to turn his rudder into a non-Viking rudder. A palpable tension rose between the two, to which most of the crew remained oblivious, because neither said much out loud except perhaps in some asides to me. Their positions were at such polar opposites that holding a *thing* would not do much good.

And, in truth, I did not really want this particular disagreement resolved. Like Rob, I wanted a Viking rudder, so I urged him to stick to his ideal, but I also wanted to kill a little more time. Up to that point the ice along Baffin had not yet broken up enough, although in just the past few weeks the change had been quite dramatic, and I knew Terry would opt for Labrador if given the chance. For the time being, the less chance Terry and I would have to fight over Baffin, the better. For the first time I was pleased by Rob's painfully slow pace.

On July 4 the wind finally turned in our favor, bringing more rain, of course, and we headed north. At first it seemed our only celebration would be the fact we were making northward progress, but then we saw three humpbacks lolling at the surface. We nearly ran over one that apparently did not hear us, as we sailed within thirty feet before it sounded. It is one thing to see a whale on TV or from a whale-watching cruise and yet a completely different experience to watch them from a serenely quiet sailboat. They don't look any different. You do. You have more time and sense to appreciate them.

A few hours later three apparently brand-new red-and-white double-enders built in the Faroes motored out of a small coastal settlement and circled around us. The ocean swells were too much for them to come alongside, but as we sailed along we talked by radio and screamed to each other. On board were Greenlanders, plus a Faroese film crew. They had motored from the Faroes after buying the boats for shrimping.

I asked Erik to ask them if they had any shrimp. Within minutes he had negotiated ten pounds of shrimp in exchange for one of our Viking Voyage 1000 hats and a piece of soapstone that some local fishermen had given us the day before. We accomplished this peculiar exchange in the large swells by throwing lines from boat to boat and attaching the items to the ropes.

The wind increased to beyond twenty knots and we were going to feast on shrimp. What could be better? A few hours later, as I slept in the underway tent (unlike the previous year's tarp, the new underway tent, made back in Maine by a friend of Terry's, actually afforded some protection from the elements, and so we were able to get a little sleep when off watch), I was suddenly woken by shouts and curses.

"Fucking hell! This fucking thing!" Abbott screamed. Then he slammed a pot against the stove, just inches from Rob's head. From inside the tent we could not see what was going wrong, but John's unbridled anger found us struggling to control our laughter. A few seconds passed. "Aw, motherfucker! I've gone through this two damned times already. Fucking hell!" Then, realizing the entire boat was listening to him, he tried to explain: "The stove's gone out again!"

Abbott's shrimp alfredo was worth all his troubles. Thanks to a competitiveness brought on by our rotating schedule of cooks—and also, in this case, Erik's artful negotiating—we were eating better than anyone has ever eaten onboard a Viking boat. Abbott's sauce was made from powdered cream, butter, garlic, capers, and a little lemon juice. It was heavenly. Although Rob passed on the alfredo and, as usual, puked throughout the sail, even he must have felt some envy before the first wave of uncontrollable nausea struck him down.

We journeyed late into the night. Everyone except Rob remained hale, although the conditions were miserable. When we had to put in two reefs, always an uncomfortable task but even more so in enlarged seas and rain, Erik joked, "Imagine doing this on a cold and rainy night along the Greenland coast!" We stopped six miles short of Maniitsoq, the largest town before Sisimiut.

Terry had not wanted to go all the way to Maniitsoq because the rudder still needed work. It would not stop clunking to port. Most of the crew wanted to get there and party for the Fourth of July. "It's not that it bothers me that getting completely wasted is of equal importance to say, the rudder, but . . . actually, what I am saying is that it does bother me," he told me as we discussed where we would anchor that evening.

At our anchorage we played kapaka and did some shots of whiskey to celebrate the Fourth. Despite Terry's efforts, getting wasted won out even though we did not go to town. I suggested, under the influence or maybe just out of misplaced optimism, that we gamble for anchor watch. Whoever lost first at kapaka had to do the winner's anchor watch as well as his own. Fittingly enough, I lost and had to do watch from one to three in the morning.

Never, ever gamble while playing kapaka.

Rob did no work on the rudder, despite Terry's hopes, and we rowed into Maniitsoq the following evening.

Brimming with four thousand souls, Maniitsoq is Greenland's fourth largest town, yet it was currently losing its prized distinction of having the longest bridge in Greenland. At what I judged to be not more than a couple hundred feet, the bridge connected the ferry landing to the town. It was nothing special except for its length, and even that triumph would soon be in the past. The company that Bendo Thorsteinson's husband worked for was completing a bridge in Sisimiut that dwarfed Maniitsoq's by a quarter mile.

Maniitsoq's name means "the rough place," and the local cliffs and surrounding hills proved this name apt. The buildings were like those of other towns we had visited, either prefabricated constructions imported from Denmark or stark concrete monoliths. Nothing unusual there, but there was a certain roughness, or edge, to the people that we had not encountered before. They were less accepting of European influence, and Erik soon realized that being Danish was not of much use in Maniitsoq. A radio reporter explained to Erik and me as she interviewed us for the local station that it was a more traditional town. For instance, although she was interviewing us in Danish and a little English for my benefit, she would have to translate everything into Greenlandic. The people of Maniitsoq were Greenlanders first.

Even so, we were a big hit with the kids. Dozens played on board as we took turns touring the town and replenishing our perishable food supplies. The kids taught us Greenlandic words. Gardner and I, while watching the boat, learned that a knife is called *savik* and that an anus is *ituk*. They were especially delighted to teach us *ituk*, which endeared them to me. The kids, both boys and girls, swung from our rigging like pirates, blew on Terry's conch shell, which we used as a horn, waltzed around in the Viking helmet, and thoroughly enjoyed themselves. With tides around ten feet, they imitated the way we boarded *Snorri* by leaping from the dock onto the shrouds and then shimmying down to the deck.

We handed out kazoos and bouncy balls, and the children, clearly not on board for handouts, gave us candy in return.

Kristina, the radio reporter, told me her five-year-old son, Kim, had been uncontrollably thrilled after being on board and wearing the Viking helmet. "He couldn't sleep last night," she said, laughing. "It was all he could talk about. 'Mommy, I want to go with them. I'll be big and tough and I won't even cry.' "

The local Seaman's Home, just like the one in Nuuk, became our hangout. We showered, washed clothes, and ate eggs for breakfast, a treat even though we occasionally had eggs on board. We worked on the computer, using free electricity; on *Snorri*, we had to either run our gas generator to charge the computer's batteries or pray that the wind generator created enough power, which it never did. The Seaman's Home was clean, slightly antiseptic, and wholly uninteresting architecturally, a strictly utilitarian design. But we loved its chairs and tables. A few of us had collapsible camping chairs on board that we took turns using, but it was a real luxury to sit in a chair whose seat rose two feet off the ground and use a table you could set your plate on. Eventually we would no longer expect or count on such conveniences, but we were still easing ourselves into a more rustic lifestyle. The people who ran the Seaman's Home bent over backward to assist us, carting our groceries around, doing our wash, and allowing us to loaf about as if we were actually staying in their rooms.

Elias Larsen, our Greenlandic crew member from the previous year, would be moving to Maniitsoq in about a month. He had told us, before he knew he was moving there, that Maniitsoq was an ugly town. There was a slightly oppressive feel to the place, because each building seemed to loom over the next on account of the geography. However, this same geography made the area outside of Maniitsoq enticing. A local company takes people on ski tours to the ice field about twenty miles from Maniitsoq. Abbott had brought his skis the previous summer in hopes of skiing at Maniitsoq but had not brought them again this time. Even so, I could see him debating tossing down a lot of money to dart out there.

The cliffs near the head of Sermilinguaq Fjord were filled with birds. Tens of thousands of kitty wakes, awks, and mers used these cliffs for summer nesting grounds. When no wind appeared on our second day in town, we took a motorboat tour to the rookeries. As we floated beneath the cliffs the captain tooted the horn, causing the birds to fly about in dismay. The sky was literally cloaked with birds and feathers, reminding me of descriptions of similar rookeries farther north, near the very top of Greenland.

Guillemots, which were also nesting in the cliffs near Maniitsoq, at one time provided an unusual meal for the Inuit. "In 1950, a hunter netted an average of five hundred birds," Jean Malurie relates in *The Last Kings of Thule*, a sociological study based on his yearlong stay with the Polar Inuit north of Thule. "He did not pluck or clean them, but simply stuffed them into bags made of sealskin from which half the fat had been scraped; he stored these bags under stones, where the sun could not reach them. The fat melted slowly in the heat, and as the birds' flesh rotted it was bathed in the fat. . . . After it had time to decompose and ferment slowly, the whole bird, feathers and all, was served up as an exquisite dish. Every house stunk with a fetid smell like that of an overripe cheese."

Oddly, this description of *kiviaq*, the Inuit name for the bird as well as the cache, made my mouth water. Malurie says that people get a hankering for strong-smelling, tainted meat in the cold months of the Arctic. Maybe this was true year-round.

We had no *kiviaq*, but back in Maniitsoq, Erik and I went shopping for ingredients to make mead. I had taken a recipe for mead off the Internet before leaving the United States. It was called Halfdan's Mead, and its list of ingredients called for such novelties as a newt's tail. Closer inspection of the recipe revealed that its most essential ingredients were honey, water, and yeast. We bought some fresh ginger, apples, and lemons to spice it up. The mead recipe said it should be ready in three to four months. Since it was early July, we hoped the mead would hurry up and ferment by the time we reached L'Anse aux Meadows in (we expected) early September.

On the walk back to *Snorri*, Erik directed the subject to Gardner and how he was always trying to keep everything in order, including himself. Since Gardner's gear was next to Abbott's, this was a Herculean task.

"Have you ever read Kierkegaard?" he asked. If anybody else were to have asked me this while out playing Viking, I would have laughed in his face. But there is an unassuming quality to Erik that makes the introduction of philosophy into a conversation that had previously been about, say, pooping, quite unremarkable. Or perhaps a Dane asking about Kierkegaard was like an American asking about *Peanuts*. They are just so urbane.

I muttered no but added that I was quite fond of Rousseau.

"They still read Rousseau in America?" he scoffed. "Anyway, Kierkegaard said there were two types of people: the ethos and the statos. Terry's a good example of the ethos. He sees principle as what you live by. Gardner might be more of the statos. The statos likes order. What you see before you is—"

"Ya, ya, ya, ya!" screamed some lunatic on the cliffs above us. I looked up, half expecting stones hurtling toward our heads. Hanging by one hand and feeling quite pleased with his antics, Abbott loomed over the road. "You yo-yos having an intellectual discussion? Some Vikings." He climbed down and walked back to the boat with us.

Our life wasn't just rudders, sightseeing, and discomfort. Cut off from our everyday lives, we reflected on each other's natures and our own. We were much like philosophers in that we had time for these intensive inner examinations. Abbott, although he laughed at us that moment, often carried on long conversations about relationships, discussing in great detail what it meant to be in one. Doug inwardly struggled to live for the moment and not to allow his loss of love to inhibit his Whitmanesque approach to life. "Amazing how I can feel alone even when thrown into such close quarters with eight other guys. And that I can feel that one small but critical step removed from direct experience even as I am thrown into such unbelievable surroundings," he wrote in his diary one day.

Nagging me still was the concept of leadership. When I began the project I didn't even know what a leader was. I now was leading, often without anyone but Terry knowing it. He and I would have a talk and then he would present the subject to the crew. We needed and wanted them to be looking toward him for the answers. It made sense. Our voyage was on a boat, and on a boat a captain is the leader. Except in this case it wasn't so simple. As a result, I found myself allowing him to step on my toes, thinking it would keep everyone happy. I wondered again and again in my journal if this actually made me a leader and if I could keep it up.

In truth, together we created a healthy balance. I was impulsive. Tallyho and all that stuff. I thrived on making mistakes, somewhat unconcerned about our welfare, always figuring we could pull it off. He was Mr. Ambivalent, weighing every decision, nearly unwilling to make a mistake, feeling that if anybody was injured or killed, it would be all his fault.

There were many times when each of us wished the other was not on board, but the combination of Terry and me seemed to work. Could I captain the boat? Not really. I had been navigating and taking on the role of watch captain, and the crew and I might limp our way to Newfoundland—if we got lucky. Could he lead the voyage? Yeah, but it would not be the same trip.

Coincidentally, Malurie wrote about this same subject in *Last Kings*. "When you talk about an expedition, you are talking about a team. A leader's primary qualification is the ability to recruit his partners," he explains. "A leader is defined by the group he chooses. The mediocre leader attracts and keeps only mediocrities."

I knew that Terry and the crew were far from mediocre, but I still could not say I was a good leader. Cut off from everyday life, I found that this question continued to haunt me. One thing I did know, though, was that we had changed as a group. Unlike the previous year, we all felt close, or "tight," as Doug put it.

Would our closeness see us through whatever was ahead? Would Terry and I continue to balance our coleadership roles effectively without bickering or backstabbing? Would the pack ice clear up in time for us to land on Baffin Island? Had Homer, as claimed, actually seen Bigfoot when parked at the edge of a forest in Michigan, guzzling beers with a buddy?

I found myself wondering about these questions nearly as much as I missed Lisa and the girls, which is to say I was consumed by them.

Chapter Fifteen

We celebrated the birthdays of Doug and Homer, who respectively turned thirty-two and twenty within a few days of each other, by eating a store-bought cake artfully decorated by Erik and singing a painfully off-key rendition of "Happy Birthday." Then we were off once again.

The wind was not blowing in the right direction, which should not have come as a surprise since the sun was shining, and we were low on toilet paper. However, the gremlins of civilization had taken hold, lulling us into inaction. In town, we had been growing fractured and undisciplined. Okay, we were never disciplined, but it just did not feel right staying in town for too long. The boat was becoming a mess. The guys were staying up until all hours at Moby Dick, the local bar. No projects were getting done. We had to leave. Terry was most adamant, and I readily agreed.

As if in response to my questions about leadership and captaining the boat, I manned the helm for the afternoon. We had all done this often enough, but this time I would be making the calls and deciding when and where to do something—until Terry decided I was screwing it up too badly.

I cleared my throat.

"Ready on the foredeck!" I called out in as deep and penetrating a voice as I could muster. This is the signal to the crew that I was heading into the wind to perform a tack. I had to repeat it, having insufficiently cleared my throat the first time around.

The foredeck crew came to attention, amazing me that they were actually listening, ready to handle the swirling interchange of tacks and bowline. But then, by this time they could and did perform most of their functions without needing or listening to the captain.

"Foredeck ready!" Gardner responded. He had uncleated the tack, leaving in one wrap.

The sail began to luff as the boat pointed directly into the wind. Was it luffing enough? I secretly glanced at Terry, but he was hidden behind his sunglasses. I was on my own. "Um . . . release the tack!"

The tack was set free. The boat continued to cross the wind. "Ease the bowline!" I called. This would let the front edge of the sail catch the wind in the opposite direction, helping us to turn more easily.

I was then supposed to wait until the boat turned well past the wind, so that it was forty-five to sixty degrees off the wind.

This was the tough part. If I made the next call too soon, the sail would get backed and everyone would hate me. If I made it too late, then we would blow the tack and everyone would hate me.

Everyone except Terry was looking at me, both waiting for and urging me to make the next call. I couldn't take it. I felt their beady little eyes boring into me. I screamed out prematurely, "Release the bowline!" and "Let go and haul!"

"No!" Terry shouted, and vainly lunged for the brace that had been set free. He was a second too late. However, somebody else grabbed it in time, and since the wind was light, we were able to haul the sail back around. Under Terry's instructions, we continued to fall off the wind and resorted to jibing.

Terry did not take over after my failure, as some captains might have, and the next time around I got it right. After I gave the order to let go, the sheet and brace were released from the afterdeck on what had been the windward side, and in the bow the bowline, which helps keep the leading edge of the sail stiff, was let go. The foredeck crew scrambled to set the beitiáss in a different socket and pulled the tack into place before the sail filled with too much wind, which would have made their task impossible. Simultaneously, on the afterdeck, Erik hauled in the sheet and brace.

"Good job!" I called out, signaling that everyone could take it easy for a bit.

Since we were sailing into the wind to reach the opposite side of the fjord, I had plenty of practice and actually felt comfortable in my role by the end of the day. Eventually we had to give up our futile tacking and sail downwind into an anchorage south of Maniitsoq, learning for the hundredth time that we could make no progress sailing windward.

The following day we practiced with the small rudder and waited for a southerly wind. We failed on a number of our tacks, unable to turn toward port adequately, a result of Rob's most recent changes to the rudder. Terry did not think these subtle changes should have had any effect on the rudder, and he appeared baffled. Rob felt it made sense and set about making new changes once we were safely anchored that evening. I worked on my mead, with Arctic foxes yelping at us from the hills above.

My amended recipe follows:

Boil three gallons of water, ten pounds of honey, the peel of two lemons, a tablespoon of lemon juice, a dash of cinnamon, a cut-up finger of ginger, and a teaspoon of rosemary for fifteen minutes, then simmer for twenty-five more minutes. Add six apples, cut into chunks, and a packet or two of carrageenan to clear it. Let sit for four hours, then add four teaspoons of yeast.

It turned out Erik had made various sorts of alcoholic beverages with his father back in Denmark and understood the process. He made helpful suggestions whenever I was in doubt. Under his guidance, I boiled some water to sort of sterilize the plastic jug we had bought for the mead. Then I cut a hole in the cap to slip a rubber hose through to let gases escape. I strained the broth through a sort of sterilized dish towel into a sort of sterilized pot and finally poured the brew into the plastic jug. It seemed a long shot that the mead would turn out right, and I was interpreting the term *sterilize* quite loosely. Also, the yeast I used was intended for baking, not brewing. The smell, however, was divine. The honey aroma was strongest, a scent of authenticity for our Viking voyage.

Meanwhile, the rudder issue was coming to a head. Terry's logical side could not handle all the mumbo jumbo that Rob was performing over his creations. As I was cleaning up my mead mess, he started measuring Gardner's rudder. Terry had decided that what was going to make the rudders actually work well was repositioning their turning points. After measuring the Cleopatra rudder, Rob's, and the small rudder, he believed that the distinguishing difference between them was that the Cleopatra rudder was not balanced—much more wood ran aft of the withy hole than forward. (If none of this is making any sense, as well it shouldn't, then please skip to the next paragraph where an engaging, emotional situation arises.) Initially, on both Rob's and the small rudder, an equal amount of wood ran fore and aft of the withy hole. In other words, they were almost perfectly balanced—a bad thing, because that would lead to oversteering, according to the *Development of the Rudder*. Rob had since taken some of the leading edge off these rudders, but in Terry's mind it was not enough. To end the clunking toward port and help the rudders stay in a neutral position—a feature that would make the helmsman's job much easier—the rudders needed to be unbalanced. He told me out loud that he wanted to cut up Gardner's rudder with this in mind.

Gardner overheard and grew understandably angry. He didn't say anything, but I noticed that he was not talking with anyone and had retreated to a corner of the boat by himself. I walked over and asked him if it was okay if Terry cut his rudder up.

"Sure, no problem," he responded with forced bravado. There was a little quiver in his voice. I asked again, not believing a word. He had worked on the rudder for weeks, carefully shaping it from a squared-off oak log.

"It doesn't matter," he lied. I said something to the effect that if I had built it, it would matter to me.

"Cut my rudder up even though we've never even tried it and, unlike Rob, I actually built it on time and stuck to the lines. Go ahead. It is the only real Viking rudder we have," he said, finally sounding hurt and terse. Then, deflated, he added, "I would just like to see it in the water once. Then you can do whatever you want with it."

We did not cut it up. The next afternoon the wind grew steadily out of the south, and we headed up the coast with Gardner's rudder in place.

His rudder was the best one yet.

For once, Terry did not feel so perplexed about the performance of one of our rudders. Back in Nuuk, more by accident than by design, he had cut the withy hole in John's rudder a fair bit forward of the center of the rudder. It was already unbalanced. It did not clunk. "I have to admit that I'll believe to my dying day that John's rudder works because I moved the withy hole forward," Terry later told me.

This made sense. The trial-and-error period—in other words, our entire voyage thus far—was teaching me about the importance of the center of axis, or pivot point, for a side rudder. What all this meant was now I could easily say to somebody at a dinner party, "Well, of course these perfectly balanced Viking rudders that the Scandinavians have turned up cannot work—except on a certain Viking boat that happened to pull to starboard so much that it needed a balanced, compensating rudder to drive it to port," or some such nonsense. It was quite confusing, but I liked the fact that it was practical experience deciding things in the end—not all that theoretical nonsense we'd discussed over the winter.

Rob believed that Gardner's rudder was working better because he had reshaped the collar that held the rudder against the boat, smoothing out the semicircle of wood the rudder turned in. He believed its irregular shape had been forcing it forward, causing the abrupt clunking to port.

When I reread a section in the Viking Ship Museum's *Sailing into the Past*, I was convinced Terry was right. The very last line in a chapter entitled "Steering Experience with Square-Rigged Vessels" explained that *Saga Siglar*'s second rudder was "constructed with a built-in understeering, which means that the larger part of the rudder blade is abaft the rudder axis." In other words, *Saga Siglar*'s working rudder had the same balance or more properly, imbalance, to it as Gardner's rudder. This information had been right in front of us all along, but we had not had the practical information to utilize it. And that detail was not in the plans for *Saga Siglar*'s rudder.

No matter who was right, Rob or Terry, we had finally solved our rudder problems, and we experienced what I believe must be one of the best days a human has ever had while sailing on the ocean. For starters, we were sailing north without any rain. The wind grew to above twenty knots, and during the evening we averaged ten knots for a few hours. *Snorri*'s hull speed—her theoretical top speed based on her dimensions—was slightly less than ten knots. Rob explained that Snorri was able to better her hull speed by planing across the water.

The lore was true. Knarrs were the goats of the seas, skipping across the ocean like nimble ungulates over mountains. *Snorri* strutted over the tops of waves and gracefully outsprinted mono-lithic walls of water as she sliced down their fronts. *I'm free! I'm free!* she seemed to be saying. *This is what I was meant to do, you big dummies, not flail headfirst into an impenetrable wind!*

The shoreline formed a wall of snow-covered jagged moun-tains, across which rolled waves of mellowed sunshine. When it came time to switch watches, most of us did not want to give up our posts. Terry later told me that it was his finest day of sailing too.

"God, who wants to go to bed now?" This from Rob, who had not puked all day.

In case the point was not made well enough, Doug added, "This is the balls."

The sun highlighted a city-sized glade of moss and lichen, and Rob and I, by far the most tone deaf of the crew, burst into a rousing rendition of "Oh Shenandoah"—my chantey from the Viking-Inuit Games. (I know, it isn't a real chantey, but it was all I could come up with back in West Virginia.) We sailed on and on, not even thinking about stopping until we reached the once seemingly unattainable Arctic Circle.

It was not until we slipped across 66°30'N, the latitude marking the Arctic Circle, the following morning that our wind died. It was a little eerie. Why had the wind died at that very moment? We had no time to ponder as we power-sailed, but mostly just rowed, into a small cove near the settlement of Itilleq, dropping the anchor around 5:30 A.M.

We hung out near the Arctic Circle's demarcation for a few days. Rain returned, but this time the wind blew from the north. Elias had told us that the wind always blows from the north in that area, but he had also said it never rained. Our usual pattern on bad wind days was to wake up as late as possible, huddling in our sleep-ing bags under the tarp that stretched from bow to mast, eating a sinful breakfast of granola *and* pancakes, playing kapaka while still in our bags, going for hikes and kayak tours, and also doing a little boat maintenance. We performed these difficult duties at our an-chorage beside Ugarniafik Island, but we also took quick dips in the water so we could say we had swum in the Arctic. As an added treat, the two Johns and Homer gathered a potful of tiny mussels that truly were the sweetest I have ever eaten.

We rowed south late one evening during a midnight sunset, figuring it would be easier to get out of the fjord when the wind turned. Terry and I had decided the following day, July 13, would be devoted to hiking, even if the wind rose from the south. Terry is a sucker for hiking, always trekking to the tallest peak wherever we anchored. We could not keep passing these incredible spots without at least devoting one entire day to exploring.

While everyone headed for the high peaks, Erik and I decided to try some freshwater fishing at a lake four miles distant. After joking a bit about hunting, we decided to take the 16-gauge shotgun that Poul Holm had given us. I had wanted to buy a 12-gauge with slugs to have on hand in case we were bothered by bears on Baffin Island or northern Labrador, but no one sold slugs in Greenland. At the last minute, Poul gave me the 16-gauge and some bird shot to scare away the bears by shooting over their heads. I believed that the puny shotgun would only make a self-respecting bear mad if we actually hit it, but I still wanted to have some kind of firearm on board.

At the last minute Dean decided to accompany us, not out of some bloodlust but because he had had some experience with guns in the army and wanted to make sure we did not shoot our heads off.

It was difficult to hike in a tunic and helmet while lugging a shotgun as well as an ax, a leather water bottle, and a makeshift shield. Well, all right, I didn't have the ax, the shield, or even the helmet. I had once tried wearing the helmet for a full day, however, and still suffered from a sore neck. But I *was* wearing my tunics, and they tripped me up horribly. Although the heavy tunic had an ample skirt that did not hinder my movements, it was the lighter tunic, the green one, that encumbered me, because its skirt was too narrow. I soon became too warm and shed the heavy one early on, cursing aloud as I stumbled along in my green tunic. Oh, the woes of being an authentic Viking!

Erik took impossible routes that only a fanatic European hiker would contemplate, and I eventually ripped the remaining tunic a good four inches, creating a sexy slit. On the spot, I hypothesized that the slit skirt had been born not in the name of aesthetic appeal but merely for convenience.

Trekking through a landscape in which muskeg, or boggy fields of moss, alternated with house-sized boulders is difficult, especially if you have been spending most of your time on a boat. It was only two weeks since the Viking-Inuit Games, but I felt swollen, constricted, and weak. I cursed every difficult step Erik caused me to take. We would hop from mushy mound to mushy mound and then scramble up scree-covered shale hillsides only to be confronted with more of the same after resting a bit behind a boulder. Every time we stopped to rest, hordes of blackflies and mosquitoes zoomed in.

During one of these pleasant respites, Erik motioned to me and whispered, "Hare!" pointing at an Arctic hare on the closest slope. Dean was resting beside me, and I tried to hand him the shotgun. *Who, me?* his look said, and he waved me off.

I scrambled forward on my belly, playing soldier. I took in an awful mouthful of moss, but as I rounded an imposing boulder my prey still stood tall about fifty yards ahead, facing the opposite direction. It looked as though it were on tiptoe, which is something that Arctic hares do. They also grow to be big; they can weigh well over ten pounds. Their fur is thick, soft, and silky.

I crawled closer behind a smaller boulder and watched. The hare hunched over. I stared. It looked just like my cat, Bob. True, Bob was often annoying, but I couldn't shoot Bob. And I couldn't shoot this hare. I thought about pulling the trigger, and the image of blood and splattered guts decimated my already shaking resolve. So much blood. Death. Yuck.

I didn't even raise the gun. Some Viking warrior I was. I had hunted when I was a teenager but had since developed a distaste for it. We had so much food on board, including enough meat for months, that I could not rationalize killing this animal. If we'd had no meat and were low on protein, I hypothesized, I would have had no problem.

If I were truly living in the Viking age, I would hunt, kill, and butcher all day long. With my bare hands. No problem. Well, maybe.

Later Homer would say to me, "I knew you wouldn't shoot anything. So I kept wondering why you took the gun." I had guessed the same ahead of time but had wanted to see what I would do. I like the taste of wild game. I have no problem eating meat that another hunter has killed. But could I kill if I really didn't have to? I guess not.

I looked back to see Erik and Dean laughing at me. Over our sorry lunch of kippers, pale liverwurst, and Wasa crispbread, I asked them if they could have shot the hare.

"Yeah," said Dean, "but I would have felt really bad. But boy, some roasted rabbit sure would taste good."

Erik too said he would have killed the hare, although he had never shot an animal in his life. "I like the attitude about hunting here," he added. "It's simple. You just go hunting—no thinking or agonizing about it. It's their way of life." I stared at him as he spoke, trying to see if there was any mockery in his eyes. Then again, I couldn't even see his face. His head net was covered so thickly with mosquitos that I wondered if he was getting enough oxygen. His back hosted an entire platoon of the suckers, who occasionally succeeded at biting through his sweater. When they did, it made me happy. It was his punishment for laughing at my equivocation.

Although Erik had improved his lure tossing, no longer hooking me with every toss the way he had on *Snorri* the day before, he caught no fish that day. Part of his problem was that we did not have a fishing pole. They had all been crushed when stowed beneath the oars. Erik had to swirl the line above his head as if it were a lasso and then release it so that it arced toward the water, not into the lichen behind him or perhaps into his sweater. He had seen Greenlandic fishermen successfully land Arctic char this way on many occasions back in Narsarsuaq, but he had never asked them how they did it. A Greenlander would twirl the line over his head and then cast the lure a good sixty feet out. On a particularly good toss, Erik managed to fling the lure about five feet.

We returned to *Snorri* empty-handed.

The following day we moved on, rowing and sailing to the town of Itilleq. Greenlandic is hard even for Greenlanders to speak, with some words requiring fifty letters. And the letters are not always pronounced the way you might think they should be.

Itilleq. Easy enough: "it-teel-lech." Right?

Wrong. It's "itchy-thshlook." Nothing else will do.

Alone among the crew, Doug could usually pronounce the towns' names, although most of us tried mightily.

The town looked perfect—fishing nets and sleds propped against colorful houses. No paved roads. No apartment complexes. No bars. The townspeople appeared to be living a life that their fellow Greenlanders had rejected. The nation's unemployment rate of 10 percent meant nothing here, where the people fished and hunted. They used fjords as their highways, by boat in the summer, by sled in the winter. A return-to-the-past Greenlander would be at ease in Itilleq. Whether or not I was right, this is how it looked.

Everyone was friendly, but our conversations did not stretch much beyond greetings on account of the language barrier, except for Erik, who found someone who spoke Danish, had a computer to send off e-mails, and let him watch the Danes play World Cup soccer. Every town we visited had satellite phone communication provided by the government-run phone company, and thus Internet access. So even tiny Itilleq with its steadfastly traditional lifestyle was a part of the modern world.

We performed our now ritualistic shore leave. We strolled around, separated, and then got together to check out what each had found or done. Some had made it to the cemetery—in Itilleq, like in most places in Greenland, an odd little place with short weathered fences around each plot. Others saw the huge dogsled, bought ice cream sniffed out by Rob or Homer, or grabbed some beers. We all returned to the boat for a late dinner and our usual duty of entertaining dozens of kids, who played with anything they could lay their hands on and laughed at our every move.

We left early the next day after an unprecedented onslaught of mosquitoes. Sisimiut, our last destination in Greenland, was only forty miles away, but we spent three days getting there. We were not in any particular hurry and the winds did not always oblige.

There were some superb moments in those three days: soaking up eighty-degree sunshine on sandy beaches, happening upon a seven-foot piece of driftwood that Rob surmised was American cedar, and generally feeling as a group that we had arrived at the perfect place. My favorite moment was happening upon some very odd bugs. We were anchored off an island with grass-topped two-hundred-foot peaks that was part of an archipelago creating an inner waterway leading to Sisimiut. I was stooping beside a freshwater pond to test its temperature for swimming when an ancient-looking, thumb-sized bug swam up to greet me. I got on all fours and saw dozens of these crustaceanlike creatures. They had armored backs like hermit crabs, with two thin tentacles trailing behind. I scooped one up and found it was surprisingly soft to the touch.

Best of all, the bugs appeared to be playing. Their hundreds of legs spasmodically kicked at a speed equaled only by some of John Abbott's dance moves. Again and again they performed rolling somersaults, as if rejoicing. Maybe they were simply eating dinner, but they reminded me that we should always stop and do the water bug.

Or if you don't like doing the water bug, at least stare at one for a while.

Chapter Sixteen

Every travel book should include a dream. Here's mine from this time:

The gang and I are sailing *Snorri* somewhere along the coast of Europe, a place called the European Highlands. It is a rough country but alluring. We are on a river leading to the Atlantic. Just as in real life, we are having a mighty fine time.

A local guide sonorously speaks about the Highland Games, which are held there every year. His hand sweeps across the view we are evidently meant to admire.

I look down at the beach before us. It is covered with fat Celts sunbathing in black swimsuits. Thrilled to have come across them, I call out in amazement, "Those are my people!"

We row on and come upon an outdoor arena. "This was built by the Celts in the fifteen hundreds to . . ." The guide drones on, but I am overwhelmed by the huge stone sculptures of elephants, lions, and clowns that form the stadium's perimeter.

"Wow, I didn't know they had clowns like that in the sixteenth century," someone marvels.

The guide disappears and we row out to the coast. We raise the sail. We have covered less than fifty yards when John Gardner calls out, "There's a rip in the sail!" The rip is at least two feet long. Terry inspects it.

"We have to go back," Terry declares. We row back and then fly home.

Suddenly I'm in Doug's room in Somerville, Massachusetts. I realize I have to do the voyage one more time—for the third summer. I feel an overwhelming dread and say as much out loud. Terry tells me to stop whining.

"You know, we didn't have to come back home just to fix our sail," I respond. "We could've had sail material sent or fixed it with what we had. What are we doing here?"

"I was just wondering the same thing," Doug adds.

At that moment a hungry mosquito buzzed in my ear and I awoke, grinning with the realization that it was still only the second summer.

Chapter Seventeen

Sisimiut is a town of grace. While some of the towns and settlements we had visited in Greenland lacked either pride or beauty, Sisimiut possessed them both.

I could not put my finger on it at the time. I asked everyone I met, to the point of their annoyance, what made Sisimiut so special. They all liked the question but invariably pointed out the same things I was noticing. It was clean. There were beautiful homes (in addition to a few depressing apartment blocks). The people were inquisitive. There were numerous cultural activities. It was a sort of upscale version of Itilleq, the previous town we had visited. But even that was not it. Something made it different from anywhere else we had been. Finally I met up with Pauline Knudsen, director of the Sisimiut Historical Museum. Pauline, a good-looking thirty-seven-year-old born in Upernavik, far to the north, believed the answer lay in Sisimiut's past. "If you read some of the older books, the Danes were clearly pleased at how well the Greenlanders were obeying the Danish rules and laws—but not in this town. The people here were bad, uncooperative.

"The people of Sisimiut are proud of being Greenlanders. The majority speak only Greenlandic, no Danish. Two of our three physicians are Greenlandic. Our dentist is Greenlandic. The difference between here and other places is that people are taking part in things. If they don't like the way something is being done, they do it themselves. In other towns, I think they are more passive. It's a tradition in this town to say, 'We can do it ourselves.' "

The residents of Sisimiut had taken what they needed from the Danes, such as modern boats, guns, and electricity, made these things a part of their life, and thrived. They were, as a community, even while under Danish rule, independent thinkers.

We thrived there as well, staying for an entire week. Besides hanging out at the Seaman's Home, carousing at night, marveling at the abundance of produce in the grocery stores, and getting our fill of ice cream, we visited the museum, housed in a building prefabricated in Norway in the mid-1700s. Sisimiut itself was settled in 1756 at a nearby location and then moved to its present site in 1764. Pauline gave us a tour of the museum. She told us about stones found in fireplaces at archeological digs. The rocks would be heated and then put inside skin pots with meat and broth. For decades archeologists assumed that the earliest Greenland cultures, including those that migrated here four thousand years ago from Asia via North America, did not use bowls, but only the bags in which they cooked and which they also ate from. A recent dig at an archeological site called Nipisat, however, had uncovered soapstone bowls as well as sharpened tools. It had also always been assumed that they did not know how to sharpen their tools. As Pauline related these details, I could hear her hurt pride over the archeologists' mistakes and her obvious joy in the recent findings.

Pauline also recited the sad history of Greenland's natural resources. European whalers decimated the Davis Strait's whale supply from the 1500s to the 1800s. Then in the 1920s the seal supply was diminished by overhunting. Greenlanders switched to cod fishing. The cod disappeared not too long ago because of pan-Atlantic overfishing. They took to shrimping, but now that the shrimp appeared to be thinning out, they had moved to crabbing. The local crab factory employs more than two hundred people, not including the fishermen themselves, but it had burned down the previous week.

We had to stoop to enter the museum's peat house. The space encompassed roughly two hundred square feet or so and was decorated with turn-of-the-century relics. There was an enormous amount of Christian decorations on the wall. Most Greenlanders are Christian today, with the island having been exposed to more than two hundred years of missionary zeal, but many young people assured me that churchgoing and big events such as confirmations were done only for social reasons.

An earthy odor pervaded the room, but it was subsequently overpowered by the sweet scent of the seal oil candle Pauline had lit. A shallow soapstone bowl, similar to the one John Gardner had found the previous summer, held the oil. She lit pieces of dried lichen floating in the oil and then moved them to the side of the dish. That way roughly twenty wicks could be ignited at once, giving off more than adequate lighting. These soapstone candles, as well as homes similar to the peat house in which we were sitting, had been widely used until World War II.

"The Danes had been very respectful of Greenlandic traditions," Pauline explained. "But during the war the Americans came and the Greenlanders learned their ways. Afterward the people decided they wanted to be like other people."

And so modern Greenland was born.

It was after World War II that the vast majority of traditional Greenland villages began to be deserted. Later, in the early 1960s, most were voted out of existence in a referendum that officialized the centralization of living that had already been occurring. From then on, the government helped subsidize and facilitate the urbanization of Greenland. There were once nearly three hundred settlements and towns along the coast, and now less than ninety remain. Everybody wants their MTV.

Thanks to Doug, we got to take an even closer peek into Greenland life than we had anywhere else in Greenland. Doug wandered by a house one day where a man asked him to come up and share some wine. While obliging the man, Doug met a young artist named Clara whom he befriended. She asked him to come to a *kaffemik* at her parents' home to celebrate her brother's confirmation a few days later, and she told him to invite any of us who wanted to come. Erik and I decided to go with him. Having no dress clothes, we donned my Viking gear. Doug was not as eager to wear the inner garments, since I had been sweating in them for three weeks, but gladly wore the less odoriferous outer ones. Erik went as a grungy modern-day Viking.

Though *kaffemik* is a Danish word, meaning "coffee thing," the event itself is a wholly Greenlandic tradition. I had attended my first in southern Greenland at the home of Elias' sister. It had been her birthday, and she threw a lavish party with literally dozens of desserts and even more hors d'oeuvres. No one was expected to bring presents. It was refreshing and bespoke of a proud and re-sourceful culture. Give, give, give. Spare no expense or labor when times are good or a celebration is at hand.

Clara's parents' home was an apartment in one of the bleak, long apartment blocks that I had dreaded entering since first spying one in Nuuk. Graffiti smeared the stairwell walls, almost a decora-tive touch that lent a little bit of personality to the monolithic structure, and I began to prepare myself for the worst. Once inside, however, we were greeted with smiles and offered savories, sweets, cigarettes, coffee, and liquor. Most people dress in casual Western clothes on a day-to-day basis, but for the confirmation party Clara and her family had on their Sunday best. On the actual confirma-tion day, Clara's brother and the other confirmees would wear the official national costume. The boys would have blue trousers, a white or black anorak with a hood, and sealskin *kamik*s (boots). The girls would wear a much more elaborate costume consisting of many layers, including a long-sleeved cotton anorak, a silk waist-band, a separate collar, and an intricately beaded jacketlike cape. The pants would be made of sealskin with appliquéed patterns on the thighs, and their boots would be tall, furless *kamik*s.

Lovely artwork and family photos covered nearly all the con-crete wall space in the apartment. This family, and probably many others, had found a way to defeat the oppressive surroundings of the block building. The parents spoke a little Danish, nearly no En-glish, yet we all felt welcomed and instantly at ease.

Malurie describes a similar reception while traveling in the far north in 1950: "Before me I saw the most wonderful igloo an Es-kimo Peter Pan could have imagined in his wildest dreams. The walls were studded with multicolored candles; the ceiling was hung with colored streamers. In the middle of the room, pans of milk gave off a fragrant steam that mingled with the steam from a kettle of coffee; heaps of seal meat and narwhal skin—mattak—and buns were in one corner; chocolate and tobacco everywhere. . . . People had come from thirty miles around; my host was blissful; his round face was creased with satisfaction.... He was now ruined for a whole month, but never had he been more sincerely happy."

Clara's parents appeared equally happy. I did not know how much their party had set them back, but they had clearly gone to great trouble to make this the perfect occasion.

The first thing we were asked to try was Greenlandic chewing gum. Clara had a mischievous look on her face. I was a little surprised to learn that Greenland was manufacturing chewing gum until I was shown the bowl in which it was marinating. Floating in a dark, vinegary liquid, surrounded by slices of wild angelica, the chewing gum was decidedly not manufactured. It was, in fact, not chewing gum at all but marinated whale intestines—tasty, definitely chewy, and better than a lot of chitlins I've had.

While Clara's mother offered us slice after slice of various tarts, cakes, and pies, we talked about the Greenlandic artist Hans Lynnge. He was one of Greenland's greatest canvas artists, and half a dozen of his paintings adorned the apartment. Clara had gone to school with Hans Lynnge's sister, but Erik had an even greater connection to Lynnge. Erik's grandmother had an affair with him when the artist lived in Denmark. Lynnge, leaving behind his wife in Greenland, had apparently been something of a rake while overseas. "She never even went to Greenland, but she loved to tell stories as if she had," Erik said of his grandmother, and as he spoke he seemed to drift back into his memories. The *kaffemik* took on a different feel. I don't know if it was the closeness of the room or a reaction to the strange chewing gum, but I felt as though we had stepped through time to Hans Lynnge's day.

It was a warm, seductive afternoon and I didn't want to leave the apartment.

Not willing to let this feeling slip away too quickly, the following evening I sneaked into the skin tent erected outside the Sisimiut Museum. Since skin tents were traditionally used for summer hunting, I was probably trying to capture something of the past. I also wanted to see what one smelled and felt like. It turned out there were no odors beyond packed straw, some of which I used for my sleeping pallet.

I tried my best to sleep and soak up this once-in-a-lifetime experience. The problem I faced was not comfort; the skins and straw were more comfortable than my sleeping pad. It was fear.

It is nearly impossible to sneak around Sisimiut on a summer night. There is too much damned light, and as a result, children and grown-ups stay up all hours, especially on a confirmation weekend. A footpath I had not noticed when executing my brilliant plan ran just a few feet from the tent's entrance. Every ten minutes, all night long, I woke with a start, positive it was the museum authorities coming to chase me out, only to discover that it was once again merely a band of schoolkids.

We were planning on leaving the next day, but the voltage converter for our satellite equipment broke. A local technician tried to fix it but failed. He tried again the following day and it worked. In the meantime, he ordered a new converter from Norway in case his fix broke. We decided to wait an extra day for it to show up.

By this point even I was ready to leave, but there was always the same bright side to our delay: more time for the ice along Baffin Island to clear up. The last report showed too much ice around Hall Peninsula, and Terry had drawn up about half a dozen alternative routes to Canada—one of which included sailing back down to Nuuk and then crossing directly to Nain, Labrador. This, of course, was intolerable to me.

So I willed the delays to continue a little longer.

We left Sisimiut on July 22 without the electronic part. Finn, the technician, said he would bring it to us at an anchorage south of Sisimiut in a day or so. Finn was about to cruise up to Thule on his Jet Ski with two other people, and the errand would serve as an excuse for him to tool around. The vision of him and his buddies jetting out to us was weird, and when it actually happened a few days later, it was a little depressing. They came screaming up at fifty miles per hour and joked how they could get to Newfoundland, following our route, in less than four days.

Apparently Rob and Homer were not ready to leave Sisimiut. No sooner had we anchored only about four miles from Sisimiut than Rob and Homer put together the two-man kayak and paddled back to town. Our latest weather report indicated it would be a few days before we could even think about crossing Davis Strait, and Finn had not brought out our computer part yet. So it did not matter if they were gone for a day. While they were in Sisimiut, fog settled in and they had a difficult time getting back to the boat. Rob, however, was in fine form, having eaten about a gallon of ice cream, and when they returned, he made everyone turn their backs while he sorted out goodies in the stern. "No peeking!" he exclaimed. "You know what happens when you see Santa, don't you? No treats!"

He and Homer had brought presents for everyone, to boost morale. We were all feeling a little glum about not being able to set off immediately. Rob made each of us approach him individually. He simultaneously snickered and cackled so much that it was a little scary. Then he stuck his head into his bag and handed an item to Homer, who then handed it to one of us.

Rob was quite the Santa. Gardner got a porno magazine; Terry, a package of Hob Nobs; Doug, Tabasco sauce and candy, perhaps a comment on his cooking; Dean, orange juice and hot chocolate, because Dean squirreled away juice for himself and had a thing for hot chocolate. Erik got ketchup because Rob was convinced he was not a real Dane, and Danes, according to Rob, don't like ketchup. Abbott was given a variety of snacks because he tended to get peevish when he was hungry. I was given chocolate.

I had been, um, a little greedy with my own chocolate earlier in the trip. I had developed a need to snack daily on a square or two of an exquisite German chocolate called Ritter. When I thought nobody was looking, I would slip a piece into my mouth. Not only was this bad karma, conjuring up images of the guy in prison camp who has a secret hoard that he does not share, but I had, unbeknownst to me, been caught doing so. Rob believed that the only thing that would keep me from being cranky was a daily hit of chocolate. Later he would resort to the occasional kiss.

After Rob gave me my new supply, I did my usual thing and nibbled away at some chocolate while reading in my sleeping bag. Suddenly, however, I didn't feel comfortable eating my chocolate secretly. I wanted to munch freely in the open or not at all. I also decided my chocolate fetish was tying me to civilization, making me miss Lisa and the girls and other creature comforts.

I was delirious.

I pulled out my remaining three bars of Ritter hazelnut chocolate and offered them to all. I told them I was doing it only because I could not handle the secrecy.

"How noble," Doug quipped, but he had no trouble making quick work of his share.

An hour later I almost started crying. What had I been thinking? Obviously I had been luxuriating in my warm sleeping bag for too long or had simply spent too much time in Sisimiut. It was a cold, harsh world. I lamented as much to Rob, knowing he had an understanding ear and suspecting he might have another bar or two stashed somewhere. He sorted through his cavernous green knapsack and pulled out a Ritter Sport Coconut Crisp. I hid it away, and all was better in the world once again.

Except maybe I should not have wished so hard for our delays to continue. We ended up waiting and waiting and waiting.

Rob took this opportunity to settle a few of his more pressing theories. He would stand behind Dean and in a loud voice say in succession, "Bill . . . John . . . Bob . . . Fred . . ." When asked what he was doing, although not by Dean, Rob explained, "Well, he never answers to Dean, so I have my suspicions that his real name isn't actually Dean. In fact, I am convinced that he is in the federal witness protection program. There's something a little off about him."

Rob also had his suspicions about Erik. Sometimes he was convinced that Erik was a spy for the Viking Ship Museum in Denmark and had been sent to sabotage our boat. Maybe that was why we had failed the first summer. At other times Rob simply thought Erik was an international spy and that he was not really Danish. "What would a real Dane be doing on a Viking ship built in America?" he asked, as if to prove his point. So every morning Rob would nudge me and ask that I add one more thing to the list he had me make. It was titled "Erik: Pro-Dane . . . Anti-Dane." To Rob's feigned chagrin there was much more in the pro-Dane column, including these items: "He appears to know the traditional Danish measurement system—must check to see (1) if he knows all European systems (2) negates his knowledge of the Danish system"; "He said, 'Folgers is not coffee!' "; "Very anal—knows too well how butter should be spread." However, this last item also made it into the anti-Dane column because Rob believed that Erik was such a good actor that he knew only a Dane would be unconsciously compulsive about spreading butter properly. Added later to the anti-Dane column was the fact that Erik did indeed know and understand inches, feet, and yards.

Despite Rob's antics, this was a tough time. Even after Finn brought us our part, we could not go. Herb Hilgenberg, who had helped us with weather the previous summer, was interpreting weather charts and advising us via e-mail and sometimes single-side-band radio, when we could get it to work, as to when we should cross the Davis Strait. Given our failed crossing the year before and just the normal pressures of making an open ocean crossing, we wanted the weather conditions to be ideal. As a result, Herb kept telling us not to go—day after day after day. Meanwhile, the unsolicited e-mails we received during this time were monumental. People were encouraging us to hang in there. Others asked specific questions about the flora, and yet others railed at us for not just taking off.

To pass the time, we began working on craft projects. Most of us made traditional sailing tools. Homer made a small ditty bag—a hand-stitched canvas bag used for holding tools. Erik made a needle case from reindeer antler. John Abbott made a knife handle. Terry worked on an *ulu*, an Inuit woman's knife used for scraping skins and cutting meat.

I also made an ulu. I had tried to buy Lisa a traditional ulu in Sisimiut, but most of the shops had only elaborate tourist ones that were not very utilitarian. I wanted her to have the real thing. One store that supposedly sold good ones was sold out. Why not just make new ones? I asked the clerk. The answer was a little surprising but, I guess, to be expected, even in Sisimiut. The store had had fifty made in Denmark for that year's tourist season and now it was too late to get any more. The clerk didn't think it odd that a traditional Greenlandic knife was being manufactured in Denmark and not Greenland.

I asked around some more and found that most people, if they are going to bother to have an ulu at all, make their own using scrap steel (not stainless, because stainless is too hard to work). Some guys at the Sisimiut shipyard gave me a sheet of steel big enough for many mistakes, and so while we waited for Herb to tell us we could go, I worked on Lisa's ulu.

There was not much wind and we mostly stayed put. When we grew too irritated, we would row to a different anchorage—once to an abandoned town invaded by summer campers. We loved roaming around this and other abandoned towns. There were usually one or two buildings that still had furniture, mechanical blocks used by fishermen, and even calendars from the 1960s. They were little museums with hidden clues to the past amongst the rubble.

Some days were harder than others. On the bad days I could not stop thinking about my family and feeling guilty that I was merely lazing about, waiting. I would argue more with Rob then, bringing up things from over a year earlier that had pissed me off. My gear was stored next to his, and I might "accidentally" knock over his stuff if it was crowding my space. On good days I worked on my knife or just let my surroundings overwhelm me.

One day I rowed Dean, Doug, and John Abbott to shore in our dinghy and then pushed off from the shore. Instead of rowing back to the boat, I let a current carry me along the same peninsula they were exploring. I turned onto my stomach and stared over the edge of the boat at the water. The ocean floor undulated between four and fifteen feet below me, carpeted with green urchins. Barnacles were everywhere. Then I began noticing starfish, green-gray, red, and white, then a forest of kelp, urchins eating algae, starfish eating urchins. An occasional stone crab darted out.

I continued to float along like that for twenty minutes until I neared a sandy beach. I looked up and saw an animal scurry down from the sorrel- and dandelion-covered hillside. It was no bigger than a dachshund, and as it picked at some beach debris, I decided it had to be an Arctic fox, even though it was still a little too far away to be sure. I had an especially difficult time identifying it because it looked nothing like any fox I had ever seen but more like a large weasel. Like most Arctic animals, the Arctic fox does not have very many projecting body parts, so that it may more easily retain body heat. It has a rounded head and very short ears, the extreme opposite of a red fox's pointy features.

The fox scampered off when I began rowing toward it. I climbed up the beach anyway, following its tiny tracks past an eight-foot-long whale jawbone. When I looked up, the fox was staring at me, not more than twenty feet distant. I moved forward, and it jumped to a safer spot five feet higher. I stood still as we looked inquisitively at each other. Close up it was as sorry-looking as I—all mottled brown and mangy. His tail was white but thinned out. In its summer coat the animal was certainly in no danger of being hunted for its fur, although at one time fox fur had been a major trade good for Greenlanders. I squatted and clicked at the fox to draw it closer. It nimbly ran farther away, into a maze of boulders. I dashed after it, challenged to a game of tag. I stopped where I had last seen the fox and waited. A minute later it popped up less than ten feet away, startled that I was still there. This time it scampered off for good.

Later, after I picked up the guys I had dropped off earlier, Doug pointed out that this might be the last time we would walk on solid ground in Greenland.

How wrong he was. A few days later we rowed to another anchorage. It was now July 28. Instead of sitting on our butts, moaning from boredom, the crew kept at their crafts, making more and more incredible items. Gardner even took to making usable rope from discarded scraps. Time took its toll, however. Gardner asked me more than once if I thought someone was going to lose it before we made it to Canada, obviously worrying that he was going to be the one. He looked like someone just trying to maintain his composure. At the same time Doug read aloud to us a letter he had e-mailed his mom, in which he wrote how he felt he did not fit in with the rest of us. Doug took a lot of hikes alone, but I felt he was as much a part of the group as anyone.

Personally, I was most irritated by this guy Herb. Our reliance on him was troubling me. We were going nowhere because of his warnings. Was he right? Suddenly I realized that we were being dictated to by him—not by our wits or our guts or even our whims. How had this come about? This was just the kind of thing I had never wanted to have happen. Finally, after one particularly long day, I told Dean and then Terry that once we got to Labrador, we would not be using Herb—that this was not what the trip was about. Dean thought speaking about a weather forecaster in this manner was blasphemy, but Terry was in agreement, although it was clear he wanted to be the one making that decision.

That night Herb told us we could not leave for several days—a low was building to the south and gale-force winds would interrupt our crossing.

The gale never materialized where we were and was not even evident on the weather charts. A few days later Herb told us we might be able to go in a day, but when the next day came and we were taking down the tarp and readying ourselves to begin the crossing, he advised us not to go. I could see every last one of the crew sink into despair.

When were we going to leave?

Suddenly a low hum grew louder and louder. A motorboat was headed for our anchorage. Everyone began to brighten at the thought of a visitor. The boat pulled alongside and it was . . . Elias! He was back from Maniitsoq and desperate to see us. He had booze and food. Did we want to take turns spending the night at his house, showering and eating a last good meal before crossing?

He received a unanimous yes, but only after he was dragged aboard and forced into a game of kapaka.

As the first wave prepared to head back to Sisimiut with Elias, I realized just how poorly some of us had been feeling. Gardner, standing in front of his dry bag, whipped off his shirt and then twirled it in the air like a stripper. He began singing, "Another one bites the dust!" while undulating his hips madly. He knew all the verses. With his grizzly beard and greasy hair, he looked truly crazed, and I worried for whomever he would run into at the bar that night.

Elias really wanted to show off his town and led us through areas that we already knew quite well. The night Rob, Terry, Dean, Erik, and I stayed at Elias' house he prepared a late-night snack of beluga whale, a deep-water fish called *skolæst* in Danish, and frozen salted minke fat. I didn't really want to eat the beluga, since it is one of my favorite whales, but Elias' pride and mood seemed to depend on how much we ate. The beluga, cut into small chunks of skin and blubber, was marinated in curry powder, onion, and salt. It was Elias' specialty and quite tasty, although a bit rubbery.

The minke blubber was my favorite dish. Elias' uncle, a great whale hunter, had taught him the trick of freezing and salting the minke. It melted on our tongues like butter.

Before serving the whale, Elias quizzed us, "Do you know what the Vikings ate so that they did not get scurvy?" Elias has a wonderful collection of European women's dress hats, and we were wearing them as we stood around his kitchen. It was hard to take him seriously.

He obviously wanted to be the one to inform us, but I could not help blurting out that they ate the skins of walrus and beluga, both rich in vitamin C. Arctic explorers in the nineteenth century had learned about scurvy the hard way, suffering and dying from the debilitating disease except when supplied with walrus by the Inuit.

"No!" he nearly shouted. "They ate onions. The sagas say they brought them from Iceland."

Erik and I had not heard this one, but it seemed likely to us that they would have brought onions with them, and onions do have scurvy-fighting powers. Elias went on to ask what his people ate to fight scurvy, and I gave my answer again.

"That's right," Elias said. "And that's why we like the skin so much."

"You like it because it tastes good," Terry quipped, slurping down some melting minke.

Scurvy usually sets in after roughly a three-month absence from fresh meat, vegetables, or vitamin C. It begins with a dull aching all over and stiffness in the joints. Then your gums begin to blacken and your teeth start falling out. It is very hard to chew dried salted meat in this condition, which is not of much consequence, since this is what helped bring on the condition in the first place. Nevertheless, you get hungrier and weaker. You chew on some of the leatherlike meat, which is almost gone anyway because your expedition leader had not counted on getting iced in, and five of your teeth drop to the frozen floor beneath your bunk. Your expedition leader decides, as did Kane and others before him, that you need exercise and forces you onto the deck for your daily round of torture. The exercise merely speeds up the disease. You die a few days later, toothless, at the ripe old age of twenty-nine.

Those Arctic explorers guessed that they needed to eat fresh meat and vegetables to fight off scurvy but refused to eat raw meat and blubber like a common savage. Instead, they suffered and died.

Elias took us back to *Snorri* the following afternoon. I stepped onto the catwalk where we stored our gear and began packing my overnight gear into my dry bag. The crew who had been on board told me how raucous their night had been, drinking and playing ka-paka with Elias' son Pilutaq, who was still sleeping in his bag. Homer was lounging in Rob's hammock, a fishnet scavenged from a beach. Doug was working on a patch shaped like a knarr, embroidering runic letters spelling *Snorri*. John Gardner was working on his ditty bag. John Abbott was still carving his knife handle. He asked me if I'd talked with Lisa when I was onshore. I said yes, and then he asked how I was doing.

"Really good," I answered slowly. I packed more of my gear away. A little time passed. I looked up at John and said, "Actually, I'm feeling bad. Really bad." Our wedding anniversary was the next day and so far, I had missed nearly a third of Helen's life.

"Oh, yeah?" Abbott asked, concerned. "What's up?"

"I miss 'em." That's when I started bawling. I couldn't have held back even if I'd wanted to.

"Wham!" Doug said, but not meanly.

"Group hug!" Gardner called out, and gave me a hug. I apologized a little later, but they all told me to shut up.

"Thank God you did that. Otherwise there's no telling what you would have unleashed on us," Abbott explained. He was right.

I felt good after that, much better than I had in quite a few days. Missing Lisa and the girls on top of all the waiting had gotten to be too much. As I sat around jawboning with the guys about Pilutaq's wish to go with us, I could not help but compare myself to Elisha Kent Kane. Of all the Arctic explorers, I felt most akin to him—for both good and bad reasons.* "He was not a captain, knew little of navigating, and wasn't used to leading men," writes Pierre Berton in *The Arctic Grail*. Yet he wanted to explore and also find the lost British explorer Sir John Franklin. During his epic attempt to find Franklin, his ship was frozen-in for two winters in the northern end of Greenland. I tried to imagine him crying during his predicament: "September 2, 1854. The men are lying about our makeshift home, still praying the ice will set us free. As I laboriously boiled our last deerskin jacket, secretly passing tiny bites to my pet rat when no one was looking, I began to cry. Soon I was wailing louder than all of our sled dogs combined. The men, sailors and scientists all, gathered around and began to slap me across the face. 'Straighten up, mister!' they shouted. 'There's no time for such silly stuff! There's heroic work to be done! Get a move on.' "

Did Kane ever cry? Did he do it in front of his men?

* For the bad reasons, read Berton's *The Arctic Grail*. Berton does not let Kane or virtually any of the Arctic explorers off very easily. For the good, read Kane's own *Arctic Explorations*.

When Elias showed up with the last of our group, he and his wife, Karen, put an end to Pilutaq's fantasizing about going with us, reminding him that he had a job waiting in Denmark. As a result, their leavetaking was a little awkward, and within an hour we found ourselves alone again, waiting for the right weather. That night Terry, with a newly shaved head, kept bringing up all sorts of little things that were driving him crazy about each of the guys. I couldn't help but wonder if a cry might do him some good as well. Sometimes when a person gets a new hairstyle or change of clothes even, his or her emotional outlook changes as well. Terry's haircut, however refreshing—"My head feels like my mouth after eating a peppermint patty"—had not made this waiting game any easier for him.

On August 3 we decided to row out of our anchorage with no real destination in mind except maybe to get a little closer to the ocean. We rowed eight miles in six hours having delightful conversations about when each person lost his virginity. Homer was fourteen, Rob fifteen, Gardner fourteen. I was nineteen. Abbott couldn't remember. That one was on a par with most conversations between rowers on the foredeck. On the afterdeck, where Terry and Dean usually rowed, conversations were a bit more staid and at times even intellectual, especially if Erik was around. Sometimes I rowed in the bow, sometimes in the stern, merely to get a well-balanced conversation.

A humpback whale breached within a hundred yards of us and then fished for an hour within sight. Talk turned from loss of virginity to bathroom habits, specifically to how much toilet paper should be used. We had neglected to purchase any more paper in Sisimiut, and given the present rate of usage, we would run out very soon.

"I believe that the proper amount is four squares," Doug announced. Terry quickly concurred.

"Folded properly, it should definitely do the trick," Terry said. "Anything else is just a waste."

"Folded?" Abbott exclaimed. "You gotta be joking. Who folds his toilet paper? I only use four squares, but I bunch. Bunching is much better."

Guys like me, who had obviously been using more than the average four squares, kept their mouths shut, so we never learned

TERRY MOORE

Minke whale

what the majority of the boat preferred. However, Terry suggested that people try using other things beyond toilet paper—rockweed, for example, when we were onshore. Abbott retorted, "Rockweed? That's for wimps. For me, there's nothing better than a blunt wet rock."

We rowed on, finally reaching an atoll of rock islands that evening. There was a gathering of motorboats near where we wanted to anchor; sure that they were tourists, we cheered because we believed they'd want to have a cookout with us Vikings.

We rowed a little closer and came upon massive yellow-pink floating blobs that were clearly some kind of guts. Finally someone was able to see through the binoculars that the speedboats were gathered around a whale carcass. We had happened upon a hunt. We rowed between a maze of rocks, trying to get to the carcass, but were stymied by the narrow waterway about two hundred yards out. As we anchored at the closest point, the other boats zoomed off, loaded down with clear plastic sacks of whale.

Reconnaissance missions revealed that the whale was a minke and only scraps of meat remained along the thirty-foot spine, plus a little blubber and meat on the head. Very little, actually, and once the tide and ravens found it, it would be gone within a day or two.

Rob stuck his hand in the blowhole, and it was still warm inside. Erik sliced off a piece as he squatted over the ribs, tasted, and pronounced it delicious. Doug quickly followed suit. They eventually carved up enough scraps to fill a four-gallon pot. Rob filled another with blubber that he planned to render to make tallow for some boatbuilding purpose. He never followed through, though, and about a week later, when it began to stink, Gardner made him throw it away. The carcass itself was a disturbing site, especially since we had spent the afternoon marveling at another whale's beauty, but it would have been ludicrous to pass up so much fresh meat. I liked the idea of us grubbing along, picking at others' leavings.

Whale scavengers. How much we had changed.

Chapter Eighteen

That evening Herb told us once again we could not go. He was also mad that we had not stayed in constant radio or e-mail contact. Herb had a history of taking things personally with us, but what did he expect? We were, after all, on a Viking ship. This time, though, he suggested we should consult the services of a professional weather adviser, saying that he was too frustrated with us. Either way, it appeared that we had even more waiting to do. Whale Carcass Anchorage was the last group of islands before the Davis Strait, so we would have to row or sail back to the mainland in the morning. It was too exposed, and the scattering of small rock islands did not afford much hiking opportunity, which was our main method of taking a break from each other. Terry and I formed plans to keep the crew happy that mostly consisted of setting aside time for all-day hikes. We went to sleep, sad that we had to wait yet again.

The next morning Michael Carr, a professional weather adviser, sent us an unsolicited e-mail, essentially asking what the hell we were doing sitting on our butts when we had great crossing conditions right in front of us.

"Huh?" we responded.

He explained that we might get slightly hammered in about a week but even that looked doubtful.

I instantly wanted to go with Michael's advice. Terry was a little more hesitant but seemed to be leaning that way as well. It was August 4, and we had been waiting for thirteen days since leaving Sisimiut. We had more than twelve hundred miles to go.

We held a *thing.* Most of the guys, except Doug and Rob, were for following the new advice.

"Maybe I'm playing devil's advocate, but aren't you just reacting emotionally to Herb?" Doug asked Terry and me.

Then for some reason Rob suggested that there was no skill involved with what we had done so far, pissing Terry off to no end. But Rob was definitely concerned. "We're just like the English explorers, ignoring the local advice," he added—a bit inexplicably, considering that Herb was based in Toronto. I tried not to get mad, sensing that he was speaking mostly out of fear. We talked about his concerns for a while and then, as a group, decided to follow Michael's advice.

We took off at three-twenty that afternoon, rowing in a soupy fog. It was a liberating feeling to shed restraint and go simply because we were willing to take a chance. We had been in danger of losing all spirit of adventure in favor of conducting a safe and mature expedition. We all knew that Michael's report could easily be as incorrect as Herb's, but Carr's query shook us from our fear-induced torpor.

There was a dreamlike quality to our departure, with the breaking waves, the rowing, and the resounding rounds of chanteys. It could have been any time—now, a thousand years ago, the future. We breathed deeply and rowed hard.

The fog lifted soon enough and we power-sailed for the next few hours. By seven that evening we were only two miles off the Greenland coast. We lowered the sail and just drifted along.

Again we made ritual offerings to the ocean gods, just as we had done the summer before. Doug toasted Neptune, Poseidon, and Thor with a hefty shot of Jack Daniel's. Erik offered a clay pipe he'd made as well as a bit of homegrown weed he'd stashed away. When they saw what he tossed over, a few of the crew cursed him beneath their breaths. Homer, who had been frantically looking for his "thinking stone" over the last few days, threw that in. His mother had given it to him to help clear his thoughts in troubling times. The stone had looked pretty well rubbed. I offered some tobacco,

DOUG CABOT

Abbott's sacrifice

as I had done the year before. But Abbott made the contribution that I believe sealed our fate. With a bit of fanfare, he stretched his braided ponytail on a crossbeam. Homer grabbed its bitter end, a nautical term that I now liked bandying about, and after a few warm-up strokes, I swung my Viking ax clear through his beloved tail: *whunk!* Off it came. Then Abbott the Short-haired rose to his feet, albeit a bit shakily, and tossed his offering to the sea. "This hair on my head has gotten me through many travails and travels of safe journey," he intoned heroically. "I'm hoping an offering will ensure our luck."

Luckily for Homer, Abbott did not pull a Svein the Jomsviking move. Of all the Viking sagas, the *Saga of the Jomsvikings* best captures the heroic, macho image of the Vikings. It is a work of historical fiction, recounting the battles and political turmoil of the late tenth century in a fantastic manner, with lots of slashing off of arms and hands, heartfelt vows, and creepy double-crossings. Near the end of the saga, the foolhardy although undeniably brave Jomsvikings are captured by a Norwegian earl and are being executed one by one by a man named Thorkel Leira, who chops off each of their heads. The eleventh victim, Svein, is brought forward. His long hair is a silken golden blond. Thorkel asks him what he thinks of dying. "I have lived the best part of my life," Svein replies. "I do not care to live after those who have died here. But I want to be led to slaughter not by slaves but rather by a man not lower than you; nor will such a one be hard to find—and let him hold my hair away from my head so that my hair will not become bloodstained." This is done and then Thorkel brings down his ax. Svein jerks his head forward at the last second, however, and the man holding his hair has his arms cut off. Svein quips, "Whose hands are in my hair?" Svein is allowed to live because of his trickery, and eventually so are the remaining Jomsvikings.

I could not help wishing we could pull a trick of our own to ensure our escape across the Davis Strait, but I also felt that our bravado, our daring to go in the face of conflicting advice, was just the thing we needed to make it all work.

That evening Doug prepared minke stew, one of the best meals of the voyage. The whale tasted like a superb cut of beef and it felt like the right thing to be eating. Maybe Leif Eriksson had a similar meal before finally setting off into the unknown, but I doubt his was as richly prepared.

Doug's Minke Whale Stew

9 pounds cubed minke whale
6 onions
2 heads garlic
3 small cans mushrooms
9 bouillon cubes, dissolved
 in a little water
1 quart cream

1 cup Jack Daniel's
¼ cup brown sugar
1 teaspoon each of cayenne,
 oregano, salt, and pepper
Marinade:
 oil, lemon juice, soy sauce,
 and garlic

Marinate whale meat at least six hours. Brown over medium heat. In separate pan, sauté onions in ¼ cup oil with brown sugar, until onions are brown. Add cream, dissolved bouillon, and chopped garlic. Add whale. Heat, but don't boil, for ½ hour. Add booze and seasonings and mushrooms. Cook another ½ hour and serve with reconstituted mashed potato flakes to nine hungry pseudo-Vikings.

The next night we had whale again, however, and it was probably the last time for most of us. Rob had noticed that huge steaks remained around the minke's skull, so he had sliced off some slabs and stored them in a pot in the bilge. He did not stop to wonder why the Greenlanders, who know whales so well, left such copious amounts of meat in this one section of the carcass. Abbott, trying to duplicate Doug's success, prepared an elaborate whale-and-gravy meal with Rob's steaks. He served it up, bragging about how good it would be, and we commenced to eat. On *Snorri*, we loved nothing better than eating; it was one of our passions. However, almost to a man, we each took only a few bites and then no more. It was not that it tasted bad. It simply was wholly unappealing, as if it flashed gastronomic message saying *Eat me and you'll be sorry.* It was not meant to be eaten by humans. No one got sick after that meal, but I also noticed that no one ever expressed a desire for whale again.

Doug's stew and Abbott's ponytail sacrifice worked their powers, and the first twenty-four hours of the crossing were bliss—for Rob. The wind, when it blew at all, dribbled lightly from the northwest. We poked along on a relatively flat sea, and Rob began to believe that he might finally have his sea legs. He no longer seemed upset that we had ignored Herb's advice. He felt so good, in fact, that he gave a long farewell address to a flock of fulmars swimming in our wake. Over the past two years we had become attached to these fearless gulls. Even in the worst of wind and waves, they could always be found circling *Snorri* and skimming the foaming whitecaps like some winged messengers intent on getting through. Their determination was reassuring. Rob, of course, felt an even greater attachment to them, since he had fed so many as a result of his frequent seasickness. And so he bid this particular flock adieu, wishing them a safe and fruitful year.

After completing his address, he cupped his right ear, listening to what sounded to me like heckling from a member of his audience. "Really?" he responded. "Okay. If I find some, I'll get it for you." It seemed like they were about to engage in a rather lengthy conversation when Homer began to relieve himself and scared them off.

That night, however, Rob learned he had not finished acquiring his sea legs. The wind rose above twenty knots, accompanied by sharp, cresting waves. Port watch—Dean, Rob, Abbott, and I—went on night shift from midnight to six in the morning. Since the wind was from the south and we did not want to go north, we had to head slightly into the wind. Bow watch was murder. Walls of crashing water would tumble over you and then the wind finished you off. I stayed just warm enough in my wool clothes—just shy of hypothermia, really—but I was soaked to the bone. Dean took a hit that even Mike Tyson could not equal. He reeled around gasping for air.

Rob became incapacitated and puked mightily, piercing the wind and waves with his death gags. The only time he was able to do anything was when he rose to vomit. We were going to have to fight our way to Baffin.

At six-thirty, after spending fifteen minutes peeling off my four layers of wet Viking garments, I began wiggling into my sleeping bag. In an hour or so, if I was lucky, the feeling would return to my hands and feet. They would be bruised and painful from being bloodless for so long, but I was luxuriating in the thought of all that soon-to-be warmth. I chuckled to myself how a year earlier I would have been crying to go home. Suddenly Rob dove from the far end of the underway tent, barely missing me as he vomited onto the deck just inches beyond. Outside the tent, Rob's fulmars were still there, although he was no longer addressing them.

In time the fulmars were accompanied by a herd of pilot whales. Two to three dozen of the beluga-sized whales began escorting us, swimming beside *Snorri* for hours. They peered at us closely as they rose between the swells, and the young were the most curious. One rose many times only a few feet away, performing excited half twists to get a better view.

"I don't really eat whale meat!" Abbott called out as he tried to take their picture.

When I decided to leave my sleeping bag and dress for my midday watch, I felt like a tough guy for the very first time in my life. My sleeping bag had been warm and toasty. As a result, my feet had indeed gone from numb to bruised, as predicted. My hands were swollen but also warm. However, I now had to get into my heavy, nearly frozen wet woolens, which I had been using as a soggy pillow, and step out into the cold, windy world. I clenched my teeth and did it, feeling like a true Viking . . . or an utter fool. Back in Sisimiut, I had sent home nearly all my modern clothes. Even if I wanted to back down and not wear my Viking garb to the end, it would be nearly impossible.

Admittedly, I was no longer invincible Viking Man, reveling in his Viking clothes and I was constantly on the verge of hypothermia. But I was determined to stay in those clothes. If Leif could do it, so could I, no matter how useless my hands were becoming.

All of Michael Carr's predictions were coming true. With the appearance of the pilot whales, the wind shifted again and steadily grew out of the north-northwest. By late evening the wind blew a constant twenty-five knots with an occasional gust above thirty. The swells rose to twelve feet. We had to put two reefs in the sail and replace a wooden block on the rudder that broke apart from all the strain. This necessitated lowering the sail, and the ensuing rocking brought on an even greater bout of nausea for Rob. He quite literally wanted to die.

As Terry and I stood on the afterdeck, watching Rob lose his intestines and knocking into each other now and again, Terry shared an epiphany with me. He no longer thought Erik the Red had accidentally fallen off his horse and injured himself riding down to the boat, thus excusing him from Leif's voyage to the west.

"Now I know what Erik the Red did," Terry said, sporadically glancing at Rob to see if he was still alive. "He didn't fall off that horse. He threw himself off. He wasn't a dummy—no way was he gonna do this!"

He was not just speaking of what the conditions were doing to us, although it was a rough experience. For once, even I was worrying not just about my cursed toes or some hurt feelings or about any of the other guys, except maybe Rob, but about the boat. Was the withy getting too much slop in it? The forward shrouds chafing from the reefed sail? The rudder pulling too hard on the framing? Terry had rubbed off on me, making me aware of how fragile *Snorri* was. I was finally realizing that *Snorri* was not like a Toyota Corolla. It was not as simple as Rob makes a boat, Rob repairs the boat, we add chafe gear, and then the boat's good to go forever. No, all those things are done and then maybe, just maybe, the boat will hold up for, say, crossing the strait. Once across, new chafe gear would have to be added. The shrouds would need hardening, the rudder mending, the bilge cleaning out. Some other crucial thing would have to be fixed.

One of the obvious differences between the Viking world and

ours had been staring me in the face all along but had still been difficult to comprehend. Life for them, and for us on *Snorri*, took patience, attention to details and surroundings, and skills honed through experience. If something broke, you were too late. You had to foresee it all so it would not happen.

This way of living had been as foreign to me as eating whale stew.

Regardless of my newfound understanding, we were moving steadily across the strait, and the north wind had chased off the rain that had been dropping on us for the last day or so. On the fourth day of the crossing, the wind shifted to the south again. A few hours later it shifted to the west. We were going to miss Baffin. Then it shifted again. It went on and on like this for a day and a half. It was taxing physically, mentally, and emotionally and I was glad that a couple of us had improved adequately as sailors so that Terry felt comfortable enough turning the boat over to us. He had privately made Erik and me watch captains back at Whale Carcass Anchorage, not wanting to offend some of the others, and unlike the year before, he was getting as much sleep as most of the crew.

During this time I was making a lot of the calls during my watch, double-checking with Terry, who would be sleeping or resting in the underway tent. I would change our course, call out orders, and trim the sail to take best advantage of the wind. One time, while I was busily doing so, I stumbled and simultaneously a brace snapped into my face. Rob, on the helm because it helped to ease his nausea, laughed out loud. "I was just about to tell you how good you're getting at this," Rob said, not completely without compassion. "Really. But I'm also glad to see you're still your normal self."

Doug, besides also showing an increased skill in handling the boat, was getting virtually no sleep. After four nights out he had slept only six hours. I asked him why, a little concerned.

"I don't know. I guess what's going on outside the tent is much more exciting. The pictures in my mind are too vivid," he tried to explain. "Also, it's easier to get nervous in there. Every shudder of the boat is so much louder. I keep having these images of the rivets working themselves out of the planks every time there's a *boom*!"

I understood what he meant about the images. The crossing was this seemingly endless, edgy experience that would never be duplicated for any of us. Period. As one or the other of us crawled out of the tent a few minutes before midnight watch, the moon and

Jupiter might be rising off to port while over on starboard the sun would be lazily disappearing for the night. In the morning, the sun would rise above a distant fog bank, creating a theater of colors and shapes on the clouds looming above us. It was all so stunning. We had beauty. We had pain. And we had a good chance of making it.

It looked as though we were going to end up somewhere near Lady Franklin's Bank and Franklin Island off the Baffin Island coast. Sir John Franklin was the British naval officer whom Kane went in search of in 1853. Franklin led two expeditions in the 1820s in the North American Arctic in search of the Northwest Passage. His first expedition ended up with eleven dead expedition members, but the second was much more fruitful, mapping huge sections of the Arctic coastline. Made a knight presumably for his work on the second trip and not the first, Franklin developed an insufferable Arctic itch. Twenty-five years later, in 1849, he set out again to find the Northwest Passage after an awful stint as a colonial governor in Tasmania. Perhaps he felt as if he needed to clear his name and prove to the world and the enemy who had driven him out of his governorship that he was a great man. All 129 men on board Franklin's final expedition perished. They died of scurvy, starvation, and lead poisoning from tin cans poorly soldered with lead. Somehow, finding him and his men became the holy grail of Arctic exploration, and more than fifty expeditions went in search of them between 1848 and 1859. As a result, the, or actually a, Northwest Passage was finally found by Robert McClure between 1850 and 1854.

Getting back to our little voyage, on August 8 our wind disappeared. We were totally becalmed some three hundred miles from Greenland, just fifty miles from Baffin Island. We decided to row during our watches, only two or three oars at a time, not in hopes of actually getting anywhere but simply to keep ourselves busy. The meals over the past few days had been fairly meager because of the pressures of cooking in rough seas, so now we splurged, whipping up feasts of canned pork, tomatoes, garlic, curry, and olives over rice. And even better, we created bannock stuffed with savory olives or with sugar, nuts, and cinnamon. Bannock is a simple pan bread introduced to Europeans by Native Americans. We adopted and adapted a basic recipe consisting of the following ingredients and proportions: 4 cups flour, 2 tablespoons baking powder, 2 teaspoons salt, ½ cup powdered milk, and roughly a quarter cup of oil. We simply beat all the ingredients together and poured the batter into our twelve-inch frying pan. Ideally, the pan should not get too hot and since the burners worked best on the highest setting, a somewhat elaborate series of steps were taken to make sure the bread cooked through without burning. Homer, who had never been much for cooking, became our master bannock chef, and his creations helped greatly during this idle time. Homer's bannocks were such a wholesome treat and morale booster that even Rob, who claimed he was trying to commit suicide by consuming nothing, not even water, for three days, ended his hunger strike to devour a few slices.

After a day and night of leisurely, surreal rowing, the wind returned from the north and we putted along at two to three knots. Early on the ninth Dean claimed he spotted land when we were still more than forty-five miles out, but Rob scoffed that it was merely a wave. Terry thought it was a line of clouds. No one was convinced, but from that point on most eyes were glued to the horizon. At four o'clock Abbott, through a scattering fog bank, saw a land mass that was inarguably Baffin Island. The crossing had taken five days. Except we still had not made landfall.

Our handheld GPS device placed us due east of Cape Murchison, but I took bearings on the cape and what I thought to be Lady Franklin Island in case the GPS was malfunctioning. This was not inconceivable, since nearly everything electrical on *Snorri* messed up at some point, but we were where we thought we were. We had never given Viking navigational tools much of a chance on *Snorri*, mainly because they are all so hypothetical. I went to great pains to track down and take along some "sunstones"—andalusite, tourmaline, and Icelandic feldspar—because there is mention of such stones finding the sun on a cloudy day in a Viking saga. While they never worked for us, others have told me they found that the stone operated just like polarized sunglasses, and they could locate the sun with theirs if there was some blue sky overhead. We also had a wooden dial that when held out in the sun supposedly showed us if we were staying on the correct latitude. Some of the guys—Rob, Dean, and Terry—said they understood it and it probably worked. However, according to many historians, this sun dial, unearthed at an archeological dig, might have been only a kid's notched toy and not a navigational instrument at all.

Yet, in truth, we were constantly navigating like Vikings, especially Terry, by eyeballing the shoreline, watching the waves, smelling the air, and using a weighted line, in our case a lead line, to check the ocean's depth.

Cape Murchison slowly materialized through an ever-present light fog, and the next day, when we were still twelve miles off the coast, the first thing we were able to make out on land was a DEW (distant early warning) line station. DEW stations were built in Iceland, Canada, the United States, and Greenland during the cold war to detect attacking bombers from the former Soviet Union. Most of the stations are no longer operational, but they have not been dismantled. The Canadian government took possession of the ones located on their soil and hired private companies to maintain them. Would this eerie guardian be the site of our historic landfall—the first Viking ship on Baffin Island in hundreds of years?

"Aw, just my luck," Rob complained. "I've puked my way across the Davis Strait to be one with nature and we run into a DEW station!"

The wind died yet again and we remained mostly becalmed. Thanks to general fatigue, rowing was not as amusing as it had seemed a few days earlier. We drifted with the current.

Being a new convert, Dean suggested we play kapaka, and so Abbott, Dean, Rob, and I sat down on the afterdeck, nibbling on potato chips and orange-flavored chocolate chip cookies that Dean had squirreled away. Dean had droplets of clear snot hanging off the end of his nose. Abbott, growing scruffier and wilder-looking by the day, had transformed into Festus from *Gunsmoke*, sporting the same facial hair. And Rob, reeking of vomit and wearing his once-white-but-now-grayish-brown long johns, bore a striking resemblance to dozens of drunken bums I've stumbled over in New York subways. He announced in his lisp, which increased dramatically in his weakened state, "I have to say the one thing I've gotten from this trip is I want guns. I want to move up here and become a hunter-gatherer." We shrugged our shoulders, fearing the worst for his mind.

Dean had been on to something with his suggestion that we

play cards. Kapaka always seems to please the northern gods. The winds returned a little after two in the morning.

We sailed southwest the next day, past Cape Murchison, ever so slowly toward Blunt Peninsula, a small offshoot of Hall Peninsula. It was excruciating to sail past so much shoreline and not stop to touch the ground but we needed to use the wind when we had it, even after what was now a six-day crossing. Terry and I studied the charts and decided to head for Chapell Inlet on the northern side of Hall Peninsula. This was a few hundred miles south of where the Vikings might have landed but at least it was Baffin Island. There looked to be a vast number of good anchorages, and if the wind held, we could probably be there by early evening. It was a cold, foggy, drizzly day, but all our spirits were too high to complain. We were headed for land.

Icebergs loomed around us, most of which had hatched off Greenland and then blown and drifted west to Baffin. Soon we were dodging bergy bits and growlers, even smacking into a few because there were too many to negotiate. Excitement was welling up in all of us, and we did not bother to contain it. We did jigs, sang, and slapped each other on the back. Sailing an open boat in such varying conditions across the strait had been exhausting, but the excitement of having accomplished the crossing was too much to keep us down.

We were moving along pretty steadily by this point and at seven-thirty that evening we were just two miles from our intended anchorage. It was hard to tell in the fog and rain, but what we could see looked like Scott's Fortress, a coastal mountain marked on our chart.

Then things grew a little spooky.

We got a little closer, and Terry and I realized we didn't really know where we were. The ridges weren't visible and the shore we were headed toward was a lee shore, meaning the waves and wind were blowing right onto shore, making it a dangerous approach. Added to this was our hard-earned knowledge that all charts detailing Arctic and subarctic waters are more than suspect.

We got even closer, and the coastline was not adding up to what we were looking at on the chart. We could not see the inlet.

We were less than a mile from a very rough-looking shore. Rob yelled out, "Hey, I really understand Bjarni now. Why would any sensible fellow even think about landing here?" All we could see was barren, lifeless rock with relentless waves crashing against it. This, not the ocean's edge in Greenland, was surely the end of the world. Leif had derided Baffin as worthless, and given our present view of it, I completely understood.

Terry headed us into the wind so that we could creep northwest along the shore. We hurriedly dismantled the underway tent. The oars were out. All hands were ready and more than a little tense. We were being forced ever closer to the hostile shore. We could not find Chapell Inlet.

At this point we began power-sailing—six oars—away from the shore, back out for another look. Everyone was completely quiet, a good indicator that we were intimidated. We couldn't make any headway against the wind, and even if we could, we were too worn out from the crossing to keep it up, despite the adrenaline ricocheting through our shaky limbs. Terry and I conferred on the afterdeck and decided to head back to shore, to what looked like a protected anchorage behind a rocky peninsula. From there, one of us could run up a hill and try to spot Chapell. Terry believed we had overshot it at the outset. We tacked and then dropped the sail. It was nearly ten o'clock and getting dark.

We were about a hundred yards from our anchorage. I could not have imagined a narrower and more uninviting spot, but it might just do for the night. It was the kind of place where you say to yourself, *I could easily die here.*

The surf thundered around us.

"Hey, what's that up there?" John Abbott yelled, motioning to a rocky hillside about a hundred yards to port. "That yellowy white spot?" He pointed like a retriever straight at a boulder-sized object halfway up the rock. The boulder thing moved its head, and we all gasped, "Polar bear!"

The bear lifted its head, glanced down at us, readjusted its muscled mass, and then plopped back down.

Snorri coasted forward into shallower water. Someone on the lead line called out, "Two fathoms." Actually, I was on the lead line, but I was feeling rather disembodied.

"Drop the anchor!" Terry called.

We hurriedly gathered together on the port side, and I suggested we get the hell out of there.

We debated our options. Someone remarked that the bear was exhibiting no interest in us and pointed out that even if we went somewhere else, polar bears were supposed to be able to swim nearly as well as seals and could get us wherever we were. I switched positions. Terry, though, became convinced that Chapell Inlet was only two miles south of us and that our present anchorage was too precarious. I switched back to favoring leaving.

We raised the anchor and crept by the bear, who didn't even bother to raise its head this time. Dean summed up the moment: "This is the first time in the trip we ain't been on top of the food chain." It was a spine-tingling feeling, equal parts fear and excitement. We rowed for more than two hours at a snail's pace in what eventually became pitch darkness, gabbing nonstop about polar bears and, as usual, arguing about the best rowing position. A little after midnight we attempted to slip through an uncharted gap leading to Chapell Inlet that was so narrow it seemed unnavigable. We flipped on our somewhat useless handheld spotlight and shakily began to slide through, water breaking on all sides on rocks that we could not even see. We all held our breath, for it appeared we were surely about to die. Luck and some stellar guidance from Terry got us by, however. We rowed into a tiny cove just inside the inlet and dropped our anchor for the second time that night.

Cove is too kind a word for that spot, evoking serenity and maybe warmth. This was a boulder-lined harbor whose hard shoreline could not even support rockweed because of the pack ice that scraped its surface nearly year-round.

As I prepared canned pork and beans and we munched on fresh apples, the guys debated whether we needed a bear watch. More out of regard for our collective exhaustion than reality, Terry had determined that our anchorage was secure enough to bypass anchor watch. I, however, could not even believe we were debating the issue of polar bear watch. Polar bears enjoy traveling great distances in a day. They can climb over the side of a three-foot-high boat faster and better than we could burp, something we were all quite proficient at. And, lest anyone forget, polar bears love meat. Although I had no hard stats to back me up, I assumed one would be happy to eat me. (In reality, polar bears do attack and kill people, although infrequently since contact with humans is generally infrequent.) I interrupted the discussion and tersely announced that bear watch would start at two A.M.

Bear-shaped bergy bits floated by all night. A boulder beach sloped down to the water directly off our bow—a lovely spot for bears to loll about after snacking on nine tasty men. There were sturdy, bold shores, excellent launch pads for bear attacks, off both port and starboard. "Not a very hospitable place, is it?" Erik said as we nestled into our bags.

Chapter Nineteen

Not many descriptions of Baffin Island's southeastern outer coast exist, and there is a simple reason for this: Not very many outsiders have visited it.

It would be easy to blame it on Leif calling the place "slab land" and labeling it worthless. But only Vikingphiles even know about this.

No, I think that Baffin, which is the fifth largest island in the world and is named after one of the few British Arctic explorers who did not die in the Arctic, has not had many visitors outside of whalers, fishermen, and explorers in past centuries and intrepid tourists and climbers in the twentieth century because it is cold, desolate, and devoid of any of the glamour of the Antarctic.

There are cruises to Baffin, but those people who have been on them have stayed mum. I wish I could do the same. Keep my big mouth shut. Pretend we made like Leif and got the hell out of there. Baffin is an unspoiled land and I do not want to be its Christopher Columbus. But although its ten thousand inhabitants will surely despise my name for all eternity, I have to tell the truth.

Baffin Island is sublime. Yet even that word falls short because it does not adequately capture the frightening aspect of this seemingly desolate land. It is the most heavenly hellish place I have ever been.

When we finally walked onshore at the head of Chapell Inlet later on August 11, I wanted to say something pertinent to fit the occasion of our arrival on land and the beauty of our surroundings, but unlike Leif Eriksson or Neil Armstrong, I was flummoxed. The other guys in my shore party—John Abbott, Dean, and Homer— were making comments: "It looks like the moon." "This is scary." "You could shoot a great sci-fi movie here." I did not know what to add. Toting handheld flares that would only enrage a polar bear as it rushed in to devour us, or perhaps attract other bears to the feeding frenzy, we walked to the highest point of land and sat down. Homer, John, and I shared some tobacco. We mumbled a few platitudes. Mostly, though, we sat there in silence, staring across the barren landscape, mesmerized by the extent of rock, rock, and more rock and the silence that engulfed us.

Remembering the bear, we did not stare for too long.

We would spend four days working our way south along the Baffin coast so that we could begin crossing Hudson Strait. Besides admiring the starkly gorgeous hillsides and endless rock ranges, we would be consumed by our fear of bears. One afternoon Rob, who had fully recovered from his week of seasickness, laboriously tied a flare to the end of a six-foot pole. "I'm making a bang stick," he explained. "If we get visited by a polar bear tonight, I'll probably burn the boat down trying to get it to work. And it will be another one of those *Marie Celeste* mysteries; 'Whatever happened to those nine goombahs who went off on a Viking ship?' "

In fact, Rob was not as worried about bear attack as the rest of us and, rising early at our Chapell Inlet anchorage the next morning, he went ashore to explore by himself. He was determined to find an outlet to the inlet because Erik had pronounced the outlet nonexistent. While ashore, the dinghy floated away and Rob had to wade chest high to retrieve it. When he returned to *Snorri*, he hurried to scribble "Private" on the chart for Chapell Inlet, for some reason thinking that he was being quite clever. At about that point I woke up to Terry loudly saying, "Huh!" The dinghy was floating away. I didn't look up for a few minutes, but when I did I wish I hadn't. Rob was standing on *Snorri*'s railing completely nude except

DOUG CABOT

Rob goes ashore.

for his red life jacket. His whole body was quivering. Although he'd never told me, Rob was not much of a swimmer, and the Viking Games swimming test had petrified him. Terry, having some mercy, asked what Rob would give him to swim after it for Rob. Rob tried bribing him with Hob Nobs, the oatmeal cookies that Terry had grown to love above all else, but Terry evidently remembered from an earlier swim that the water around Baffin was even colder than in Greenland. They were a team now, though, and they frantically let the anchor line run free and began rowing *Snorri* toward the dinghy. At the last minute Abbott rose from his sleeping bag and snagged the dinghy.

Nothing quite so exciting happened the rest of that day, and on our third night we sailed back to the mouth of Chapell Inlet, since there had been no outlet. As we neared the exit ferocious gusts began whipping down the steep hillside to our starboard. Terry called every crew member to be ready, and for the first time a gust heeled *Snorri* over. It must have been well over forty knots. Just as suddenly the wind shifted again. Dean stood on the afterdeck holding both braces, as though he were reining in a runaway stagecoach.

Whoosh! The sail filled from behind. It was a moment directly from every kid's sailing dream—a big square sail filled to bursting, held in with all one's might by two straining ropes. The next second the wind shifted again, and we rounded the corner still within the inlet to a slightly protected harbor, where we dropped the sail and then the anchor. Abruptly, someone pointed out a yellowish lump a couple hundred yards away. It was a bear, of course, but there was nothing we could do since we were now pinned in by a southerly wind.

That night as I stood on bear watch with the shotgun, Rob's perilous bang stick, my Viking ax, and John Gardner's eight-inch knife close at hand, I took little comfort in Barry Lopez's suggestions in *Arctic Dreams* that polar bears do not eat much in the summertime. Lopez had made a series of visits in motorboats and airplanes, as well as extensive interviews and scholarly research, to write his moving, lyrical account of the Far North. From him, we learned that a polar bear can travel up to a hundred miles in a day. They can flip a seal with a swat of a massive paw. They are not the murderous, ferocious creatures that lore has made them out to be. In the summer, they do not eat much because the hunting is too difficult. Lopez reported this useful information from a position of safety, not an open, motorless Viking boat.

Fetching water the next morning at a nearby stream was harrowing, but Rob, John Abbott, and I brought back more than a hundred gallons. We were dangerously low on water, down to about two days' worth. We were mocked endlessly for taking nearly all the boat's armaments with us, but we returned with the purest water yet. No one else went ashore, and no crew member would do so for the remainder of our time on Baffin Island.

We spent two nights with this bear, who never moved much more than a hundred feet or so. Then we sailed back out the mouth of the inlet. We reached Kane Channel, presumably named after Elisha Kent Kane, after more than six hours of rowing, past a slew of icebergs and bergy bits. We needed to go through the one-and-a-half-mile-long Kane Channel to find an anchorage for the night, but when we arrived the tidal current was streaming toward us at roughly three knots. There was no way we could row against it, so we dropped anchor. Needing a rest, we were about to slump to the deck to wait the hour or so it would take for the current to slacken and then begin running in the opposite direction. Naturally, someone looked down the channel and spotted what looked like two bears sitting together. We pulled out the binoculars. Whoever had spotted the bears had been wrong. It was not two polar bears but one massive bear the size of an elephant.

"What's that right there?" Erik said a little shrilly, pointing down the channel but a little closer to us. It was a second bear. Then Terry spotted another bear directly across from us.

We stared across the channel, willing them not to move.

"If there are three on that side, what makes you think there are not three on this side?" Rob asked. I whipped my head around fast enough to pinch a nerve.

"Here it comes! Here it comes!" Homer yelled suddenly. The big bear had lumbered to its feet and was ambling into the water.

"Are we gonna pick a number between one and nine to see who gets eaten?"

"That fucker is coming here by water!"

"We should climb the shrouds."

"We should pull up the anchor and get the hell out of here."

"It's going in the water!"

"Oh, shit!"

We switched to a stern anchor and readied the sail for a last-minute effort to sail back the way we had come.

The bear, with just a bump of its head and rump visible, was swimming steadily down the channel toward us. It looked like a chunk of ice.

One of the smaller bears moved down to the water, staring straight our way. All three bears were looking at us, including the swimming bear. "Now I know how food feels in the supermarket," Rob remarked. The little one at the edge of the water, who was still bigger than any of us, looked as if it were about to head across, maybe waiting for the current to go completely slack.

Meanwhile, the elephant bear was getting closer to the little bear but still angling toward us. Suddenly the little bear saw the big bear and ran fast up the hillside, obviously scared of the much larger creature.

If it was scared, then we were nearly pooping in our pants.

The large bear kept coming. The tide went slack and a fog began rolling in. We were finding it hard to track the bear, which was unbelievable given its size. The animal blended in nicely with the bits of ice floating throughout the channel.

"This gives him the upper hand now, doesn't it?" Homer quipped.

The second little bear, also bigger than any of us, got scared off too. The big bear swam past the boat, clear on the other side of the channel. We were sure it had some plan to get us from behind.

Oddly, it kept going. After a half hour the bear was well past a group of icebergs that were miles out to sea. The tide began to run in the opposite direction. We raised anchor and began rowing down the channel against a light wind. We were making two knots at best.

Once we were well into the channel, we spotted a fourth bear on our side of the waterway. This one trotted down to the water and looked ready for action, bouncing on all four legs like an excited toddler. The first scared bear returned and began running along the shore, keeping pace with *Snorri*.

Then the fourth bear started swimming after us. Manning the tiller while everyone else was rowing—we had all eight oars in even though we had long since concluded that the two forwardmost rowing stations were useless—I studied the charts and determined that, given the headwind, our only hope of anchorage for the evening was about a mile down the channel on the same side as the three original bears.

For once no one complained about rowing or argued about the best position.

As we turned the corner, gingerly poking along in the light fog and unmarked waters, one of the rowers screamed at me, "What are you doing?" He could not believe that I was heading us so close to where the bears had been. Terry took a break from rowing, looked at the chart, and agreed with my decision. Luckily, the bears seemed to have been outwitted by our route and were finally nowhere in sight. We found a three-fathom spot and dropped the anchor.

No one could stop talking about the bears.

Suddenly one appeared on the shoreline not more than 150 feet away. It seemed reticent, more curious than bloodthirsty. Even so, it slowly approached the water's edge. We were waiting to see what the bear was going to do, but Terry suddenly decided we had to scare this bear off—that moment. We grabbed pots and pans, Terry's conch-shell horn, and a whistle or two. On the count of three, just as the bear dipped a paw in the water, we started screaming and making noise with our instruments. The bear looked confused, and then Dean blasted the shotgun over its head. It ran a good fifty yards up the hill.

Then another bear appeared over the same hill and trotted down to the water. The new arrival clearly had not read the bear section in Lopez's book. There was nothing reticent about this one, and it looked hungry. We stared slack-jawed. Its front legs were in the water before we could react. Then we jumped back into our noisemaking routine. "Yahhhhh!" *Bang! Clang!* Dean fired the shotgun again. If the spreading shot cleared the bear's head, it was only by inches.

Both bears tore out of sight. We cheered at our success. A little later, however, they returned, as well as a third one, but did no more than stare at us with puzzled looks. They appeared to settle in for the duration.

We performed two-person watches that night, more than a little intimidated. It was, of course, hard to tell the bears' intentions, but we were in the middle of nowhere and had not seen any other humans for ten days. Even if the bear was only able to get at one of us and even if we were able to beat it off, that person would surely die.

Doug and I were on watch together from one to two-thirty that morning. Earlier I had asked Dean to ask Doug not to walk around with the gun. Having been in Vietnam, Dean was our expert. The gun was loaded and Doug was being careless with it. I had noticed that he had gotten a little offended by Dean's reprimand, so we talked about this during our bear watch. The talk turned to the topic of having to squelch one's pride while on board. I was surprised but also pleased to learn that Doug had been dealing with the same issues I had. It often made me chafe when Terry or Rob corrected me on something or totally ignored my advice, and I had thought that I alone was so touchy. "I decided I could either get offended at every turn or approach this as a learning experience," Doug explained. "It's been pretty great once I decided to do that. I realized I had to do that after last year." He did, however, think that Dean and I had overreacted to the way he was handling the gun, but I explained to him about my ever-pressing and growing concern that they all return home alive. There would be nothing amusing in an accident. The guys had become my family. Something happening to any of them would be about as awful as something happening to Lisa, Anabel, Eliza, or Helen. It was unthinkable.

Chapter Twenty

We left Baffin Island the next morning on a blustery north wind. We would try to ride it across the mouth of Frobisher Bay and the Hudson Strait—a combined distance of nearly a hundred miles. If the wind looked to be abating, we could always duck behind Resolution Island on the northern edge of the strait. With this in mind, we started a course that would take us just above the island.

The bears had disappeared during the night, but we saw one more a mile away from our anchorage on a small island. We were unconcerned. We had a strong wind accompanied by rain and light fog and had nothing to fear from the bear.

The water was another matter. It was choppy and hard to read. Ledges appeared from nowhere, and since we were moving along at seven to eight knots, we had to keep a good lookout for random rocks as well as ice debris. The boat buzzed with our collective energy, brought on by days of bear watches, poor charts, and exhilarating weather. And we were about to face one of the biggest challenges of the voyage. If there was one thing Terry had always seemed to dread, it was crossing the Hudson Strait. It is a forty-mile-wide waterway with tidal currents that can wreak havoc on motorized ships. I believe Terry had hoped we could bypass Baffin

Island simply to avoid this crossing. In missing Baffin, we could have sailed down to Labrador farther out to sea and not have had to worry about crosscurrents that could drag us all the way to Ungava Bay. Of course, some people have a theory that that is where the Vikings really ended up, so it might have been serendipitous to get tugged in there.

Anyway, there we were, finally facing this dreaded crossing, and the conditions were ideal. Would they hold, though, and how would we fare in these difficult waters and worsened climate? Thanks to the cold Canadian current traveling south from the Arctic, the air temperature hovered just above freezing. It was very wet with the fog and drizzle, and although we were somewhat inured to hardship by this point, our reserves were not as deep as they had once been.

This was one of those times when I knew we felt the same way the Vikings once had. We had all our modern equipment and could even e-mail someone halfway around the world, but none of this helped us get from point A to point B any faster or more comfortably. We knew what it was like to be at nature's mercy just as the Vikings had always been. We knew what it was like to get bashed around on an open boat with only our luck, our wits, and fine craftsmanship to help us. It was exhilarating and it was, I believe, why the Vikings sailed where other Europeans had never dared. Most scholars will say I am wrong. They will say that Vikings sailed to North America or traveled down European waterways all the way to Constantinople to plunder, find better land, or trade goods. They will say that the Vikings had no time or energy for adventure for adventure's sake. They are wrong. They do not know. They have not been on a Viking knarr sailing at eight knots in the fog, flanked by polar bears and only guessing at what the fates have in store for them. There are few finer moments, and the Vikings surely craved these times and rejoiced in them, just as we did as we said good-bye to Baffin Island.

First, however, we had to miss the ship-crushing rock that Doug suddenly saw looming five feet in front of *Snorri*. He was way too late but still managed to scream out, *"Rock!"* and then turn around to brace himself for the impact. He glanced down from the bow to see this fateful ledge one more time. What was this? Our prow had landed on a massive rock, yet nothing happened. And the rock was staring at him, maybe even blinking and then swimming off to the side of the boat. Other rocks began to swim off as fast as they could too, bulldozing waves of water as they fled from *Snorri*.

"Walruses!" he called out in great relief. They were everywhere, swimming just inches from *Snorri's* side, rising to the surface in groups of five or six off to starboard and port, and far off on nearby rocks. In western Greenland walruses long ago learned not to rest on solid earth, perhaps because of efficient Greenland hunters. Not so in southeastern Baffin, which, it turns out, is a breeding ground for the fabled creatures. It was not difficult to imagine them smashing a small wooden boat, as Elias had once warned us and Barry Lopez confirms, in a fit of rage and panic. They are powerful, weighing over three thousand pounds and stretching to ten feet long. They used to live as far south as Massachusetts, but today the Atlantic walrus is an endangered species, hiding out in select spots in the far north.

With our speed and their fright it was a regrettably brief encounter.

It took only a day and a half to reach our next anchorage—False Bay, Labrador—but it felt like a week. The wind and opposing currents created the choppiest seas yet. It remained bitterly cold, and at times, when the wind would shift unexpectedly or we had to change course as a result of miscalculating the effects of the tide, we had to sail slightly windward. *Snorri* and the crew took a beating. Halfway across, between bouts of puking, Rob started singing an indecipherable song, except for the refrain. That part was loud and clear: "Damned Hodding Carter!" I believe we all felt that way, including me.

I tried to cook dinner for my watch. The seas were impossibly rough and it took me a long time to get the stove going. Looking down into the boat was horrible enough, making even me nearly seasick, but then a seven-foot-high wall of water slammed over the port beam and continued across the deck until it dumped all its mass on top of me and the stove. I just stood there in shock for over a minute, staring toward the afterdeck as if some answer might be revealed. I noticed that Terry was trying his best not to laugh, but otherwise no answer came.

The meal was ruined and I had to start over. I was soaked to the bone but once again found occasion to praise my Viking woolens. Just minutes later, although I was sopping wet and weighted down,

I was already warm—except for my feet, encased in modern boots, but still plaguing me.

We ended up zigzagging, first going too far west and then too far east, because we miscalculated the currents. Terry felt embarrassed, but it did not matter. We made it across without getting sucked to God knows where and arrived just ten miles off the Labrador coast by the morning of August 16. It took us another fourteen hours to get to an anchorage, however, because of faltering winds. As usual, we ended up rowing the last few hours—an effort somewhat similar to going off on a ten-mile run after a butt-smoking, coffee-swilling all-nighter. It just isn't something anyone should have to do, unless, of course, like a fool, you are trying to see the world the Viking way. In that case you should be eternally damned to repeat such a feat again and again until your toes fall off and what flesh you have left is pecked away by starving ravens.

When we dropped the anchor at False Bay that night, Rob began opening cans of ground beef and tomatoes and a jar of capers, and I started chopping onions, garlic, and olives for a pasta dinner. The rest of the gang worked at *kaje*ing the yard (*kaje* is an old Norse word; it is the action of swinging the yard inside the shrouds as it is lowered so it can be stored lengthwise within the boat, or swinging the yard outside the shrouds when the sail is going up), raising the tarp, stowing lines, and so on. We were all heavily engrossed in our projects.

"Uh . . . um, a bear," Erik called out, not too strongly.

So what, we all thought. *There's a bear onshore. Who cares? We'll deal with it later.* The closest shore was a good two hundred yards away. Some of us did look up eventually, but the bear was not on the shore.

It was fifty feet from the boat and rapidly approaching.

"Where's the gun?"

"Get the gun, Dean!"

"Whoa!"

Suddenly we were all screaming at the bear and banging on the side of the boat, hitting dry bags, the mast, nothing that could make enough noise. The bear kept coming. We got to some noisier items—pots, the conch shell—and our voices rose a few octaves. The bear faltered a bit. *Aw, come on, guys*, its face seemed to say, but the animal kept coming. We couldn't find the gun. We screamed louder. It finally turned around. We continued screaming as it swam away.

Just twenty minutes earlier, as we rowed into False Bay past a towering shoreline rising straight above the ocean, Erik had said aloud, "This doesn't look like bear country to me." Most of us had agreed.

So much for learning from experience.

The following day we went on brief hikes. No one was too keen on coming upon the bear, although Terry and John Abbott did and had to abruptly change course. The vegetation was nearly identical to Greenland's: roseroot, crowberry, blueberry, and harebells. It smelled more familiar, though, more like home, than anywhere we had been thus far, thanks to an abundance of actual mud and goose shit. The landscape was similar to Baffin's: no trees, endless hills and mountains.

With everyone safely back on board, we had a *thing* to study the charts. We had sailed nearly twelve hundred miles since leaving Brattahlid in Erik's Fjord, Greenland, and we had roughly six hundred miles to go. That distance could take a week. After all, we had just sailed a hundred miles in twenty-four hours. Or, on the other hand, averaging our first twelve hundred miles, it could take us more than a month. Terry explained he felt we needed to hurry south. We could linger down there if we wanted. Otherwise we might find ourselves stuck hundreds of miles from L'Anse aux Meadows, Newfoundland, in the beginning of the fall storm season. Weeks could turn into months, and then we could get frozen in, and then . . .

Part of me agreed with him wholeheartedly. Besides worrying about our safety, I wanted to see my family—to kiss Lisa endlessly and squeeze my children until they popped. But after all the struggle and time, I could not believe it might be over soon. It had never seemed possible.

I knew that Doug was itching to be finished because his brother was getting married the first week in September. He might still have a chance of making the wedding. Abbott needed to be back at the University of Vermont to run the outdoor program. His students were already returning.

Gardner wanted to get going for more urgent reasons: "I want to sail down the coast. I don't really have the desire to hike anymore after seeing all those bears." He had become obsessed with bears. Before turning in, he would say, "Night-night, don't let the big bears bite." Or if somebody was heading off on a hike, he might say, "See ya . . . unless the bear sees you first." He did not want to linger in an area where we might be prey. "I might like to see an old whaling station, but that's about it."

Rob chimed in, "Not me. I want to see it all." He wanted to poke down the coast, maybe arriving by October. None of the other guys really expressed an opinion, except Erik, who said he did not care at all when we arrived.

None of our opinions really mattered, of course. We were at nature's mercy. Meanwhile, we went about our business. Onshore that second night, Terry and Homer built a fire from driftwood. Most of us were too tired to take part, but we went along to make Terry and Homer feel their efforts were appreciated.

I was glad I did. The fire smelled cozy, and receiving warmth from something outside my body was a luxurious, inebriating feeling.

Being guys, though, we had to make comments about the fire, especially since it began with a whimper. If we had not made comments, then it would have been too embarrassing—as if we really thought that Homer and Terry could not build a proper fire. By ribbing them and ceaselessly putting in our two cents, we were assuring them that we had confidence in them.

Yeah, right.

After laying the wood, Terry and Homer bent down before the fire and took turns blowing it to life.

"Before long, Terry and Homer were alternating blow jobs . . . and then the night really got under way," Abbott began.

"It's got sustainability now," Dean tossed in.

"It's good if you've got wet wood to build a square outside your teepee," Abbott added.

"You should've put those chips under it," Gardner helped.

"Maybe you need some smaller pieces first."

"How about digging a channel to funnel the air toward . . ."

"Men, men, men, men . . . men," Doug muttered aloud.

Chapter Twenty-One

No hyperbole can capture the beauty of where we sailed on August 18. We were puttering down the coast in a dying wind that had never amounted to more than a breeze when Gardner decided he wanted to go fishing at Helge River. It was late in the afternoon and there did not appear to be much of an anchorage at the river's mouth, but it was the first actual river we had come to on the voyage. It also did not appear that a front of any kind was on its way. We headed in.

The Helge River begins a short section of the Labrador coast called the Iron Strands. This was not a location about which any of us had read. The Vikings did not speak of it in their sagas, and our cruising guide was equally quiet on the subject.

Pity them all.

We anchored. After witnessing Erik's vain attempts at fishing in Greenland, I had bought a new fishing pole in Sisimiut. Gardner began readying it but dropped the reel overboard. Our only reason for going to this spot had been for him to fish, but now a rosy and iron-colored shoreline stretched for hundreds of yards before us, beseeching us to stay.

I went ashore with the first party. We landed above the beach on a hard, boulder-strewn point. A grassy plain spread out to the base of three-thousand-foot mountains, a mile or so distant. Tent rings, some old, some very recent, were evident on the moss- and lichen-covered ground. An animal trail cut through to the river. We walked along the trail, and moss and lichen gave way to soft grass and blueberries.

I turned down to the red beach. Bear prints. Caribou. Then wolf. I slipped off my boots. The sand was cool and comforting. I walked toward the river. The surf fluttered onto the soft shore. It was late and the mountains had transformed into jagged purple silhouettes. I spun around in a circle.

I watched the others walk off in all directions. Were they feeling as I was? I felt I had to get Rob, Terry, and Abbott off the boat. It would be fine for *Snorri* to be empty in these calm conditions. They had to see, feel, and smell this land. Now.

I began trotting back to the dinghy, wishing Lisa could see this too. I spun around again. Chills ran through me. My hair stood on end. Suddenly someone screamed out, "Yes!"

I was the one screaming. I rushed to the rocks overlooking the point and screamed, "Yes, yes, yes!" until I was hoarse. Tears were running down my face.

The beauty had sucked me in. I had sucked it in.

I got everyone off the boat, and a little later, groups of us huddled together. Nearly all seemed equally moved by this place. We hugged and smiled at each other in a way that men hardly ever do.

Doug wrote of this same setting, "I joined the first crew ashore, and was quickly struck with the fact that here is one of the most beautiful places I shall see. . . . I reflected on my place in the amazing scene, and its place in me. I recognized that I am more able than I was, say, in Europe, to apprehend the magnificence and quiet meaning without overlaying or just plain obscuring it with doubts about its meaning or any access to it. Yet, I also saw that there remains a tension, a balance, a silent struggle almost between me and It, when it comes to a place that I would wish to take right inside me. The tension is still there—I imagine it is there for everyone who thinks about it, who seeks to escape himself and invite the outside inside. But I saw the tension as a fine challenge too, so I spread my arms, palms up, to the whole grand scene, as a sign to myself and to It that I would like to see more. And just in those few minutes of willing receptiveness, and of believing in my receptiveness, I think I got a little somewhere. I walked downhill feeling chastened and happy about it."

We needed that day. The sixteen miles that we sailed and rowed to the Iron Strands would be our greatest single-day mileage for the next two weeks. Rob joked during these weeks that we discovered a new climatic feature—the dreaded southeast Labrador trade wind. If the wind blew at all during this time, it was invariably from the southeast. In fact, we were not discovering anything new; we had simply ignored history. For the last few centuries, Newfoundlanders have always talked about going "down north" to Labrador, just as people in Boston used to say they were going down east to go up to Maine. The reason for this is that boats coming from the south went *downwind* to go up to Labrador.

We tried everything we could think of to go up south. We would row all day. We would tack twenty miles out to sea, then tack back, covering only six miles southward. Some days were so agonizing and difficult, even the icebergs made more progress than we did in the Labrador current, which runs south at a knot or so along the coast. We tried spending a night off the coast with our sea anchor set, thinking the same current would help us. It didn't, but at least we did not go backward.

We rowed so much that I had to threaten to medevac Homer out by helicopter if he did not stop complaining. At my insistence, we kept forcing our way south rowing. It simply sucked to have come so far and get stuck. Morale on board dipped to an unexpected low.

We should have seen this coming. After all, until the latter part of the twentieth century Labrador was always called "the Labrador," and you are not supposed to trifle with anything beginning with "the." Think of the Matterhorn, the Sudan, the Bowery. A person does not expect to waltz through those places unscathed, and the same certainly goes for the Labrador.

We all took turns acting childish and churlish. Terry's day stands out more than others because he was usually so guarded and reserved. Rowing along, we came upon a bay with a warm western wind. It was late in the day and we were just a half mile from a good anchorage, but Terry thought we should seize the opportunity. We raised the sail. Immediately we were making six or seven knots. We were going to make up for lost time. We switched to a watch schedule in case we ended up sailing through the night.

Suddenly the wind shifted and backed the sail. Terry slammed something hard to the deck. I figured we would now lower the sail and head back to Whale Island, the closest anchorage. That is what we started to do, but then the wind rose from the west again. To my amazement, Terry ordered the sail raised, and we turned around, heading southeast again.

All too soon the wind shifted, and Terry cursed loud and hard. He slammed something else onto the deck.

Seeing that not everyone was quite as involved as he, he ordered all hands to be on duty. There was nothing for most of us to do but watch him flail about, which annoyed him even more. He said something sarcastic to Doug, who was being a little testy himself, but pretty much left everyone else alone.

We flopped around some more and then finally reversed direction and headed back to Whale Island. By this time, gale-force gusts were ripping around the channels near the island and we had to fight for a good two hours to get back.

Later Terry apologized to me, "I know it was mostly me," he said when we were alone. "I got too frustrated when all those things were happening, but I couldn't help but feel that nobody else— well, almost nobody else—understood what was happening. . . . All I could see was everyone's worst qualities."

I, of course, was equally or even more wacko at times. I have always been irritated by other people's noises: jaws making a popping sound while chewing, burps, farts, joints cracking, even scratching. Dean was the gravest offender on *Snorri*. Every time he burped he elongated it into the word *whoa*, sometimes dragging it out for seconds. I've already mentioned his loud farts. The combination was driving me crazy, and I yearned to smack him silly.

If Rob spouted one of his ridiculous theories, I grew insanely irritated, although everyone else intelligently ignored him. When lowering the sail, I might "accidentally" elbow him if he was on the other side. This, however, turned into a joke, and from then on we pummeled each other whenever the sail covered us.

When some of the guys started working on crafts like the ones back in Greenland—Erik on another reindeer antler needle case and Abbott on another knife handle—I would mutter about people messing up the boat and start scrubbing the deck right beneath their feet.

Worst of all, I was reading *Lure of the Labrador Wild*, the true account of an ill-conceived, boneheaded voyage up the Susan River in southern Labrador at the turn of the century. Two members of the three-man expedition were from New York City. The third man, George Elson, was a guide from Labrador who knew nothing about the area in which they were traveling. Hubbard, the "leader" of the voyage, was a writer. The other, Wallace, was a lawyer and wrote the book. There were enough parallels between Hubbard and me to make me uncomfortable. He was emotional, open about his feelings, hotheaded, and driven. But what really got to me was the crux of the story. Through Hubbard's bad planning and poor luck—they went up the wrong river—all three men began to starve two months into the trip.

As each day on *Snorri* passed with little progress, I began to curse the other cooks under my breath. Couldn't they see that we just might starve to death too? That if they continued to use our rations so carelessly, we would end up like the *Lure* boys, splitting up in a last-ditch effort to save ourselves, and attempting to sustain ourselves on such delights as green lumps of moldy flour:

> It was time for George and me to go. But I could not say good-bye just yet. I turned my back to Hubbard and faced the fire. The tears were welling up into my eyes and I struggled for self-control. George sat silent too and his face was strangely drawn. For a full ten minutes we sat silently gazing into the fire. Finally George arose.
>
> "Well, Wallace, we'd better start now."
>
> "Yes," I said; "we'd better start."
>
> I collected myself as best I could, and, turning to Hubbard, held out my hand.
>
> "Good-bye, b'y; I'll be back soon." And then, as I looked into his poor, wistful eyes, I broke down and sobbed.
>
> I crawled over to him and put my arm about him. I kissed his cheek, and he kissed my cheek. We embraced each other, and for a moment held our faces together. Then I drew away.

George was crying, too. The dear fellow went over to Hubbard, stooped and kissed his cheek.

"With God's help, I'll save you, Hubbard!"

George Elson made it back to civilization and got help, and a rescue party saved Wallace. Hubbard, the emotional writer, died of starvation alone in his tent.

I held a cook's meeting for a third time, suggesting strongly that we use less food. We counted our cans and other staples. There was enough food for forty-five days. I was not comforted and sniped at each cook when he prepared a meal. We might easily be out there for another sixty days or more.

We cooks were pretty competitive with each other, and it grew worse during this time. Eating was our most anticipated event of the day, and food was our muse. Erik, seeing that good meals made everyone happier, created extraordinary dish after extraordinary dish: Danish pancakes, homemade fried enchiladas, and chicken with West African peanut sauce. This last was the kicker. It tasted so good I wanted to kill him. How could I ever equal it? The sauce was perfect: creamy, enveloping, and powered with just the right amount of cayenne. Damn him for being so well-rounded.

Others were not immune to this trying time, either. Homer picked on every single thing Abbott said. If Abbott asked him a simple question, Homer would pretend he did not understand, forcing John to repeat himself again and again. Homer even stopped telling his long-winded, unbelievable tales.

Doug argued or disagreed with nearly every decision Terry made. He did not like the anchorages Terry chose, the sail position, or most decisions that did not entail sailing out to sea and waiting for something better to happen. Also, Terry's habit of waking everybody when he was finished with early morning anchor watch was driving Doug crazy.

Gardner snapped at everyone a couple of times each day. He was, in his own words, close to losing it. When he was an assistant cook and the cook would not let him do more than chop onions and open cans, he would pout and insult that person for the rest of the day. He virtually lost the smile that had always been so charming.

Abbott, who had been cursing an inordinate amount compared

TERRY MOORE

Gardner takes over

to the previous year, now took to cursing every single thing that went wrong for him. If he bumped his knee, he would let loose a torrent of words more suited to a swarm of mosquitoes than a tiny boo-boo.

Erik, Dean, and Rob became more introverted. Rob, who had taken to planting sloppy kisses on me whenever he thought I was missing my family too much and acting ornery, stopped kissing me. His quips virtually dried up, but not because he was as despondent as the rest of us. He was enjoying the slow pace. For once he was not sick, and it allowed him more chances to hike. But, noticing his shipmates' moods, he was too afraid to joke as much as usual. Erik was about the only person who stayed upbeat. Out of nowhere, he would shout, "Why, I'll row all by myself, boys! Let's do six oars!" We all wanted to kill him.

Equally telling of our mind-set was an all-encompassing superstitiousness that took over.

On Whale Island I picked up a skull that I thought to be from a walrus. I was going to bring it home to figure out what it was. After a few days of rowing and very little mileage, I offered it back to the

ocean with a small prayer for forgiveness. It grew worse. One evening, after I had been reading a little more about Norse mythology,
I decided that we had been invoking the wrong Norse god. We had
often referred jokingly to Thor. For instance, Doug's offering of
Jack Daniel's before our crossing was made to Thor. None of this
had been serious, which I decided was bad enough, but when I
realized we should have been praying to Frey, the god of fertility, I
realized how grave our error had been. Frey statues with little erec-
tions have been found throughout Scandinavia. He was probably
the most popular god after Thor. I had always thought this was for
obvious reasons: Who doesn't need a little help now and then? A
closer reading revealed to me that Frey had something even more
enviable than a perpetual boner, however. He had a ship named
Skidbladnir. She was big enough to hold all the gods, and when not
being used, she could be kept folded into a purse. I found that pretty
cool but, reading on, learned the best thing about _Skidbladnir_: She
always had a favorable wind.

Why hadn't I seen this before? I had narcissistically remembered that there was a god named Hod who was tricked by the
evil Loki into killing the beloved Balder with mistletoe. But I had
not read a thing about Frey or his _Skidbladnir_. Oh, misguided
not-quite-so-young man!

The evening of my discovery, I hopped out of my sleeping bag
in the buff and stood on the crossbeam just before the mast. It was a
little rainy and foggy, so I stayed as close to the tarp as I could. Being naked, I figured I already had Frey on my side, so I lifted up my
arms and called out, "O mighty Frey, forgive us! I beseech you:
Lend us your following wind!"

Terry took a different tack. He truly believed that we had
pissed off the Inuit god Torngat, who oversaw all the weather in
the local region. The mountain range that towered directly above
us along the coast was called the Torngat Mountains. "Somebody
has done something to make Torngat mad," he said on more than
one occasion. As if in confirmation, one day when Terry announced that a light north wind that had just filled us with hope
should last for a few days, the wind shifted to the south in less than
half an hour.

Dean no longer would comment on the weather because I had
told him his pronouncements usually brought bad winds. He also

started making a box for his wife, showing the gods that he believed the voyage would not be ending for a very long time.

Even when we were busy being sour or superstitious, we could not help but notice the grandeur of the northern Labrador coast. While no other single spot equaled the Iron Strands, the place as a whole surpassed anything we had seen.

The very act of seeing was a trip all by itself. Icebergs and islands seemed to float in the sky. The horizon was dotted with fabulous castles. Waves danced far above the water's surface. Points of land shape-shifted: cliffs that were merely ten feet high seemed to tower hundreds of feet above the ocean. All were the result of an Arctic mirage caused by the very cold temperature of the air just above the surface of the water, with a layer of warmer air above it. Since whaling days this has been called looming or *fata morgana*, Fairy Morgan, of the Arthurian legend. There is a nonwhimsical, scientific explanation for this phenomenon. Rays of light traveling through air are curved by the atmosphere. Since light travels slightly faster through warm air than cold air, light rays (say, coming off an iceberg) that would normally pass over an observer's line of sight curve back toward the cooler air, visually elongating the iceberg vertically. Because *fata morgana* raises objects higher than they are, one can see them from much farther away than normal because the curvature of the light rays compensates for the curvature of the earth. Uh-huh. And now I will explain the theory of relativity . . .*

No matter the reason or its name, the effect was dramatic and went a long way in overcoming our doldrums. We would sit on a crossbeam and poke each other in the ribs, making such witty remarks as, "Hey, that one looks like your face after an all-night sail." The mirages were like gazing into a campfire, mesmerizing and entertaining.

The views onshore were just as soothing.

We had stopped seeing polar bears, and the bear scat we occasionally happened upon was weeks or months old. So we began walking again, when we were not rowing, and realized that even we could live off this land in the summertime. When walking over lush

---

* You might want to look at E. C. Pielou's *A Naturalist's Guide to the Arctic* for a more intelligible explanation, as my mottled attempt has been derived from this very useful and informative guidebook.

green hills, we could go no more than two or three yards before we had to stop and eat more blueberries. They were more common than even the ever-present moss and lichen. One day when I was off on a hike and watching a minke whale feed along the steep bank directly beneath me, I plopped on my stomach to eat some berries, then rolled on my side to eat some more; when my elbows started to give out, I sat up, still eating. Fog rolled across Ramah Bay, but it was hot and sunny on my hill.

Then I began collecting blueberries in my water jug to make a pie.

Hod, you're the tops! What a guy! You're one selfless trip leader, that's for sure! I heard it all in my head as I spent nearly an hour and a half gathering the succulent pea-sized morsels. I felt quite good about myself. The great provider.

Before heading back to the boat, I glanced in my jar, and it just did not look like enough berries. It was too late to continue picking, so I decided I might as well eat a handful. I'd give the rest to the guys to sprinkle on their cereal. Once I'd eaten the first handful, though, it seemed that the remaining berries would only torment them, so I reached in and ate handful after handful. When I was done and felt slightly bloated, I had eaten nine handfuls, enough for all on board and at least one pie, if not two.

To make matters worse, Abbott and Erik showed up with ample blueberries to fill two bannocks and more for pancakes the following morning. I confessed my transgression, and Doug thought it fitting to read aloud a situation reported by Peter Freuchen in *Arctic Adventures*. Freuchen founded Thule, Greenland, setting up a trade mission there in 1910 with Knud Rasmussen, and led several expeditions in the Far North. In the scene from which Doug quoted, Freuchen and two men were on an excursion in eastern Greenland and supposedly had not eaten for five days. Freuchen set off with a rifle and successfully killed a hare. Walking back to where his mates were passed out, he debated eating the hare on his own. They were all sick of each other's faces, as he put it, and he was sorely tempted to devour the hare. "Half singing, half crying, fighting the temptation to steal the food from the two men in camp, I walked on, hardly able to put one foot before the other." Suffice it to say that Freuchen did not eat the hare and Doug laughed heartily at the comparison.

This just confirmed my belief that Freuchen was a big fat liar.*

We did not see a single soul besides each other from August 3, when we saw the whale hunters in Greenland, until August 28. The isolation only added to the mystery and beauty of the Labrador Torngats. Small Inuit communities had once flourished in this region, and we passed many a tent ring from more nomadic days. Now the towns were all gone, including those run by Moravian missionaries. The Moravians were an evangelical sect founded in the 1400s in Bohemia. Over the years they set up missions throughout the world, including the United States and Canada. Their work spread to Labrador, and in the 1800s they established missions along the coast that provided Christian teachings, of course, but also much-needed medical care and education.

When whaling along the coast ceased and fishing began to slow down, the Canadian government forcibly moved residents to Nain on Labrador's midcoast and to a few sites even farther south. The Inuit were soon faced with overcrowded housing and, for many, a loss of livelihood. They are still looking for a way out of their cultural destruction.

On August 25 I decided to paddle our one-man kayak to Ramah, one of the abandoned Moravian missions, six miles up a bay from our anchorage at North Head. Terry had gone there the day before and had accidentally left one of our two-way radios behind, giving me the excuse to take a solitary break before we continued rowing south.

Just before shoving off, I glanced up to see all the guys staring down at me, mouths agape. What had I done this time?

"You look so . . . weird," Abbott explained.

"You're not a Viking," Erik added. I had taken off my Viking clothes and was wearing someone's yellow rain suit over long underwear. The change made me uncomfortable, too. My temporary clothes were too light, falling far short of the security blanket of my Viking outfit, but I could fit into the kayak.

I had made about half a mile from *Snorri* when my trip nearly

* Actually, Freuchen is wonderful, if full of a bit of hyperbole. How could one not like a person who writes, "I was disappointed in people who . . . advised me to stay home, take a job, and behave myself. Which meant to me, stay at home and be dull and never do a thing you have not seen thousands of others do in exactly the same way."

ended abruptly. Waves reverberating off the granite walls of North Head made the paddling tricky. I had to constantly shift my weight and quickly got a painful crick in my neck from fear of capsizing. The confusion of eddies, currents, and breaking waves was even worse. Just as I thought I was getting a grip on these terrors, a minke whale rose twenty-five feet off my starboard bow, bearing straight down to smash me beneath the surface in punishment for eating one of its cousins a few weeks earlier. I screamed.

The whale dove and did not reappear, and the rest of my trip was insignificant, except for the awe I felt paddling beneath thousand-foot granite walls. I reached Ramah about two hours later, a waterfall pouring off the northern shore indicating that I was at the right spot. Although I was hot from my paddle, I chose not to bathe under the fall, inviting as it was. It would have taken a good hour for my body to reheat itself and I wanted to do some exploring before I had to leave. The rest of the guys were rowing *Snorri* out of the anchorage and I was to meet them at the mouth of the bay as soon as possible.

I pulled the kayak onshore next to a rock perfectly placed to luxuriate beside the falls. There, sitting on the rock, as Terry had said it would be, was our radio. I followed a fading path up the embankment and within a few steps I found what turned out to be Doug's camera case. He had also explored the area the previous day.

I strolled up to the plain that had once held the town of Ramah, pretending calm but feeling more than a little spooked. Not a single building remained. It was quiet and I felt exposed and vulnerable, the guilty intruder. I came upon a graveyard, bordered by embedded stones. A woman who had died in the 1800s had a fresh headstone, apparently placed within the last few years.

The town had been segregated. Stone foundations marked the white people's homes and buildings; overgrown vegetation marked the mounds that had been the peat homes of the Inuit. Fox dens riddled the mounds.

There was hardly any debris on the vast plain except some rusting barrels and broken bits of pottery near the peat houses. I squatted to get a better look; maybe I would even find a piece of the past, say, a pottery shard, that I could hold in my hand.

Suddenly a minke whale surfaced just yards off the town beach, and its spouting echoed across the still landscape. Then a caribou snorted. They seemed to be telling me to leave. I wasn't in the mood to be chased off, but I had to leave anyway to meet up with the boat.

When I caught *Snorri* in the middle of the bay a few hours later, Terry and I fought in front of the crew like never before. The conditions were as miserable as ever: rising and falling wind, mostly out of the southeast. We argued about luffing the sail, drift, pointing too high, what degrees off the wind we were making. He was pissy. I had my back up. We both were wrong, except for some of the technical points, which he had right. The crew watched us, growing more silent.

We accomplished about eight miles south that day and anchored in a short channel between a bold rock island and Blow Me Down Mountain. A strong current tried to pull *Snorri* off both our anchors all night and bash us into the greedy rocks.

Chapter Twenty-Two

The guys sang "Happy Birthday" to me the following morning and then we were rowing before six-thirty, to ride the dying current through the channel—but not before John Abbott served a delicious batch of blueberry pancakes. It was my thirty-sixth birthday.

It was a tough day but a good one, in which we showed our resolve and reclaimed some of the spirit that had slowly been ebbing from our worn, tried bodies.

In the beginning we rowed. Within an hour or so, we were all shirtless. The only blessing to our windless days had been the resulting heat. Although cold at night, it probably reached seventy degrees during the day and half of us were sunburned, even.

Off to starboard a whitewashed, sheer shoreline stood six hundred feet tall. Wide black-and-red stripes ran its entire face. It took forever to pass those stripes, maybe three hours of rowing on a glassy surface.

Then Rob's southeast trade wind rose as the day warmed up. Instead of tucking into the closest anchorage, we decided to tack out to sea. We were going to sail windward, although we had proven again and again that a Viking knarr does not excel in such conditions. We decided it didn't matter. Moving along at five knots would be fun all by itself. So what if we were going northeast on the outward tack and not much better than west on the return? It felt good. The sun shone hard and everyone gabbed as if we were on a summer day-cruise in Maine's Penobscot Bay.

We sailed nine miles out. On the return leg, the wind died when we were three miles from Kangalasiorvik Island at the mouth of Saglek Bay. We rowed with renewed vigor and were anchored on the island's western shore by six that evening. We had covered more than twenty miles all told to make seven miles southwestward. Homer could not help pointing out that if it had stayed calm or if we had just waited a few hours, we could have rowed to our anchorage much faster than our combined sailing-rowing effort.

No matter. Being frivolous had helped our moods. After we had our at-anchor tarp rigged, Homer shared some of his dwindling tobacco with me, and Erik read aloud a birthday poem he had composed:

> *Hodding Carter once a Barter*
> *For Coin and Stamps*
> *Today Away from USA*
> *Sailing with a Bunch of Tramps*
>
> *How did he get there?*
> *To that place of nowhere*
> *And how will he ever*
> *Find his way home?*
> *(Ya know he ain't that clever)*
>
> *Today he completes a year*
> *But not even his kids are here*
> *Just this furry lot*
> *The knights of Camelot*
>
> *How will he feel, that woolen son*
> *Far from home, but near the Fall*
> *Will he crumble and be gone*
> *Or will he say "I stand tall."*
>
> *Will odd-named Hodding*
> *Ever rhyme with something?*
> *Will he ever meet the glory*
> *When he finishes his story?*

Did he leave to escape suburban life
The comfort of house and wife
Or, is burrowed in his soul
The Nomad Seeking out his goal?

I don't know much about this lad
But when he leaves, we'll all be sad
And if for nothing else we will recall
His mean bean and the way he smells.

Erik's quaking voice as he read aloud grew to an endearingly rich baritone. I would put him, or Doug, up against the best Viking skald any day. To row and sweat and worry and still compose verse is an extraordinary feat.

The crew's collective spirit was pulling the voyage back from despair. To be immobilized for so many weeks simply because of weather is an anathema in our times. It is unheard of and seldom experienced by any Americans or Europeans. Yet we were experiencing it. And we had waded through the various stages of optimism, disbelief, despair, and finally acceptance. Elizabeth Kubler-Ross would have been proud. We would get there when we got there. It became that simple. Somehow we arrived at this conclusion nearly simultaneously. A great beastly ballast had been lifted from *Snorri*, and that evening we seemed to float a tad higher.

We spent the following day drying gear, cleaning the boat, serving more hemp twine around the top of the foremost shrouds where the yard threatened to wear away the standing rigging, and retrieving water. We were down to two thirty-gallon containers— about four days' worth of water. Rob, as usual, was heading up the water party. Abbott, Doug, and I went along, and when I asked Rob why he always fetched our drinking supply, he responded, "I just like getting the water. It feels good."

I felt the same way. It was a pure thing. In collecting it, we were not harming anything. Toiling beside the fast-moving water was refreshing. The streams bashed along the rocks, meandered through sand beds, pooled up with small fish darting in and out of shadows. That day we rowed the dinghy to a stream that was one and a half miles away. We made it in half an hour, dragging a dozen of our containers behind us, the rest crammed between our legs. Doug came along a little later in the kayak.

It took roughly an hour to fill all the plastic jugs. The large ones were too big to be submerged in the stream and had to be filled piecemeal.

Afterward Abbott and I bathed in ice-cold pools. Rob was not much of a bather, by which I mean that compared to the once-a-week ablutions I performed, he would go at least twice as long without a bath.

Initially we lashed two of the thirty-gallon jugs to the back of Doug's kayak. Having read that Inuit once hauled walruses or large seals this way, we figured Doug should be able to do the same with the water. However, since fresh water is heavier than salt water, the containers rode with all but their tops beneath the surface. Even in our loaded-down dinghy, we were making better headway than Doug toward *Snorri*. So we added Doug's containers to our load and then ran a line from his kayak to us. Our idea was that together we might be able to row and paddle against the mounting head-wind. It took more than an hour to get back, making a three-hour project out of merely collecting water.

Our second night at Kangalasiorvik Island brought guests—not bears, which we had not seen for eleven days. It appeared that all the bears had migrated north for the summer. Our visitors that night were even more frightening to us—other humans. David Conover, the documentary filmmaker, and Russell Kaye, my photographer friend who had decided not to join the voyage the previous summer, had been following us through our Web site journal entries and corresponding by e-mail. They had traveled for three days to meet up with us for forty-eight hours.

Any discomfort I or the rest of the crew might have felt on arranging a meeting and then actually having it come to pass was dispelled the instant David and Russell climbed on board with cigarettes and booze in hand. For me they had new pictures of Lisa and the girls, as well as ones of the house Lisa had bought in my absence. We were moving to Maine.

We all felt thrilled to be talking with someone besides each other, and we competed for their attention. David and Russell must have felt like movie stars, and they appeared as pleased with the occasion as we were. Bottles of rum and other distilled refreshments were passed around, and cigarettes were smoked as if cancer were a thing of the past. We stayed up past midnight—a good three hours past our regular bedtime.

David and Russell traveled with us for two days, filming such ig-noble moments as our grounding in an attempt to sneak through a shortcut to the southern end of the mouth of Saglek Bay. There was not much wind, and they had to settle for shooting us rowing or puttering along under a limp sail. We felt bad for them, that it was too uninspiring to be recorded, but they felt just the contrary. They could not stop raving about the dramatic setting, and David said to me, "You guys are really out there. I've never been so removed." We, on the other hand, felt that since they had been able to find us, we were in a nearly metropolitan setting, especially since there was a radar station that we could see at the southern end of Saglek Bay and that Nain, where David and Russell had chartered their boat, was only 120 miles away. Hell, we could row there in ten days.

The next morning Russell toted over a bag of Essa bagels from New York's Lower East Side, tubs of cream cheese, and the *New York Times*. While I had made a blueberry bannock, it seemed a meager treat before these riches, and only our guests ate the home-made bread. Eating the bagels was a near-divine experience, but the mere presence of the newspaper was unsettling. I didn't want news from the outside world, except about my family. Part of the appeal of a journey like ours was leaving all that behind. At the same time, however, I read many of the articles. It was like junk food, almost irresistible.

We also saw our first woman since Sisimiut. The charter cap-tain, Henry Webb, had two crew members along, and one was fe-male. She smartly kept her distance, shyly bantering from the charter boat's deck.

Henry Webb gave us a caribou haunch from a fresh kill. He fed an extended family of dozens but seemed pleased to have some-thing to offer us. His crew also cooked up a caribou-and-noodle stew rich with fat. It was too rich for some of my choosy shipmates in fact, and I wondered if they had been treated a little too well gas-tronomically. One should never pass up food when living in the outdoors, especially with a copy of *The Lure of the Labrador Wild* ly-ing around.

When we grounded behind Big Island the first afternoon with

Russell and David, a Zodiac gingerly worked its way up the shallow channel we had failed to get through. More visitors! Three graduate-student scientists from the radar station wanted to see our Viking boat. The guys went gaga over the young, blond female scientist who came on board. She might have been daring but she was no dummy. She did not take off her nearly bulletproof storm suit. At some point she asked just how long it had been since we had seen a woman, and a couple of the guys were embarrassed enough to be able to pull their tongues in.

The scientists were part of a cleanup crew attempting to contain PCB (polychlorinated biphenyl, used for its insulating and heat-transfer capabilities, is highly toxic) contamination from insulators and transformers degrading at the radar station.

Of all places for contamination, this seemed the most egregious. I can almost understand the PCB contamination where we lived in West Virginia; we had used the electricity and deserved to have to deal with the fallout from that usage. But up here? What had the Inuit benefited from the advanced early warning radar sites? What about the bears, caribou, wolves, and every other creature that would suffer from the contamination? It was an ugly situation, and we felt embarrassed that it was left up to the Canadians to deal with it. According to the scientists, the United States was not contributing anything to the cleanup, although the toxins had come from a U.S. military installation.

While we were talking with the scientists, a helicopter buzzed us for a few minutes. All of a sudden we were being inundated by the modern world. That night over a dinner of pasta puttanesca, I noticed that some of the guys were shying away from David and Russell. We were not ready to take on civilization for so long. We had more than five hundred miles to go in who knew how many weeks. Yet the following morning when the charter boat disappeared in the fog off Cape Uivuk, headed back to Nain, most of us felt a little deflated. I think I had wanted more from them, not necessarily a longer visit but something precious that would see me through to the end of the voyage. I wanted them to hand over my wife and kids. Seeing these friends from my other life was a hard hit and dragged up emotions I had been trying to push aside since Greenland. As Doug would say, *wham!*

After they had motored out of view, we tacked back and forth beside an iceberg that seemed more a crystal city than a mere shelf of ice. Staring at its monstrous beauty, I decided that I had to reimmerse myself in the moment. I could not let myself, the crew, or Lisa down by sulking about our separation.

So we pressed on and miraculously, after a lazy Sunday of lying in our sleeping bags, eating fried eggs and blueberry pancakes past noon, the wind turned more favorable.

The first day of this new wind wasn't much, but we did sail and row twenty-three miles southward in fog, anchoring on the southeast coast of Harp Peninsula in yet another narrow channel near dusk. We were fully protected, separated from the ocean by what appeared in the fog to be a labyrinth of islands and channels. Our long summer days had come to an end, and it was already dark when we dropped the anchor at eight-thirty.

In the complete darkness, phosphorescent microorganisms and glowing jellyfish were a nightly entertainment, lighting up *Snorri*'s sides. If I shook the anchor line in the water, it shone like a light saber swishing through the murk from the thousands of clinging luminescents. Equally impressive was the dancing curtain of northern lights. We stood on deck, oohing and ahhing as if at a fireworks display.

That night we put one-dollar bets on three topics. Gardner, ever anxious, both thought of the idea and played bookie. He asked when we would get our first ice in a water bottle; when we would see our first snowfall; and, most crucially, when we would arrive at L'Anse aux Meadows. Terry thought we would not see snow or ice and Rob thought we would see both very soon. Doug had us arriving in early September, and Homer thought we might make it before Halloween. I bet we'd be finished in three weeks.

Doug, holding out for a miracle, urged Gardner to wake us all at five-thirty the next morning. It was September 1. Back in Nuuk, Greenland, we had nearly all believed or hoped we would be home by then. We were under way a little less than an hour later, the earliest start of the voyage. We had to row three and a half miles east behind a slew of islands to get in position to head farther south—a painful time, because we knew the wind was blowing from the north beyond the islands. By ten o'clock, though, the sail was full and we were making steady headway.

As the day wore on and we continued sailing, we even dared to raise the underway tent. It was raining and foggy, but that was not really why we raised the tent. It hadn't been up for weeks, and we hoped raising it might send the right signal. As I've mentioned, we were uncontrollably superstitious, so we had consulted each other for quite a while about what to do. In the end, we reasoned that if we didn't raise it, we might be insulting whoever or whatever was helping us out. Yes, we raised the tent because we had some hope and because we didn't think the off-watch people should suffer in the cold and wet. But we also raised it because we were mortal and knew our destiny was controlled by something or someone outside ourselves. Or at least we wanted them/it to think we thought that.

So, despite the visit from our friends, we were as wacky or even wackier than we'd been a few days back. Or perhaps we were on to something. Maybe there were all sorts of little gods running around out there, with more than enough time to toy with a group of hubris-filled wanderers who had dared them.

No matter what it was, it worked. We sailed on and on. Never faster than five knots, averaging only three, but what mattered was movement. Nearly everyone started talking about what they were going to do when they got home. Dean talked about his cats and, for the first time in a while, his wife, Barclay. Rob, while I was steering, gave me a crushing bear hug, saying, "I love being up here."

Thirty hours later we had sailed ninety miles through fog and drizzle. At the end of that time we found ourselves once again becalmed. We remained that way through a second night but we sat ten miles offshore as if we were lazing about in a shallow pond, chatting about gas-powered blenders and the best method to flavor ramen noodles, while munching troughs of apple-laced granola. The sun had finally come out and the boat was crisscrossed with drying nylon and an occasional stinky Viking woolen. We reasoned that even if a southeast wind rose, we could beat toward shore, only losing a few miles.

While waiting for something to happen, we also performed upkeep. Everyone pitched in, but Erik outperformed us all. He shortened the lines attached to the rakki, the wooden collar that holds the yard against the mast, which had been made too long back in Sisimiut. The extra length had caused excess chafing on the shrouds. He re-served the halyard. He even rigged the sun shower and made himself presentable.

Egged on by these heroic efforts, I managed to perform a few awe-inspiring feats myself. When Doug cooked a most delicious turkey chili with brown rice, I out-ate everyone else by at least half a portion, downing two troughfuls. The plastic troughs we ate from held more than four cups of food, and usually just one made me stuffed. Then I had my ration of three Hob Nobs. Not a few of the crew looked at me in awe . . . or maybe disgust.

Since we appeared to be drifting southeast, we threw out the sea anchor to take better advantage of the current. By the morning of September 3, however, we had drifted only an additional two miles.

The wind returned, but from the southeast, somewhat dampening our spirits. We would not be going any farther south for the time being.

We had reached the outer islands that barricade the entrance to Nain, coastal Labrador's northernmost community, with a thriving population of 1,250 citizens, and we sailed southwest between some of these islands to consider going there. Terry had looked at some weather charts and determined we might not get good winds for another week. Maybe we would sail all the way to Nain or hole up on one of the outer islands. We were a little low on kerosene and would try to get someone to bring us some fuel from Nain if we did not sail there.

Were we seeing trees on some of the islands? It was hard to tell even with the binoculars, and the islands closest to us were barren and torn by the ocean. We anchored at North Carey Island around 1:30 P.M. in a cove protected from everything except a nonexistent northwest wind. By anchoring in such a setting, maybe we would anger some god into sending a rousing northerly.

The bottom was sandy, and a long beach partially curved around us. The hillsides were green. We dropped two anchors and the whole crew went ashore to investigate.

In a tiny nook, halfway up a small hillside, a spindly, gnarled three-foot spruce was straining to live. It was our first real tree in months—since we had left the United States—and I yearned to claim it beautiful. It was not, but at least it was a tree. A Viking could maybe have whittled a toothpick out of it, certainly not a plank for a knarr, but with this tree we knew we would soon be reaching Markland, the name Leif gave to the woodlands of mid-coast Labrador. We were out of the north.

Somehow we knew this meant we were going to make it. A spontaneous party arose. After all, we had just covered more than ninety miles. Everyone began gathering firewood. We intended to build a towering bonfire, and luckily the beach was strewn with driftwood, even whole logs, which we gladly chopped at with our many axes.

Then Abbott began talking about sweat lodges and their cleansing effect. He and Gardner decided we needed to build one at that very moment. For the next few hours he oversaw the construction of a sweat lodge that looked as if it might withstand a tornado or at least a marauding polar bear.

Meanwhile, I wanted to roast our caribou leg, which had been hanging from the stem since Henry Webb gave it to us four days earlier. Someone mentioned that it might be fun to cook it buried in the ground. Terry had cooked meals this way while serving in the Peace Corps in Micronesia, and under his guidance we began to load our fire with rocks—as many as could fit in without smothering the flames.

Erik and I rowed around the cove, hunting for kelp, screaming and trilling in some mad pantomime of hunting live game. Somehow we managed to gather a few ten-foot pieces, plenty enough to make a protective covering for the caribou.

Erik gathered Labrador tea and we bathed the caribou haunch in olive oil, salt, pepper, and the wild herb, then wrapped it in the kelp. Three-inch-thick squares of peat were lifted off rocks with the help of drift plywood and set beside the fire.

All was ready. We removed the burning wood and started another fire to heat rocks for the sweat lodge, stamping out any smoldering pieces that were too small to move. The rocks were molten. It was like staring into the bowels of a volcano.

We set the caribou on the rocks and then quickly piled the peat on top of it. Soon we had a mound as high as a dog house and with only a trickle of steam escaping. You could leave your hand on the peat for minutes without it getting too hot.

I could not help but think we were closer to the Vikings than we had ever been. Anchor, build a fire, and eat. Later, I learned that we'd been more akin to them than I knew. When celebrating, the Vikings would build a fire, heat stones, and then cover their meat and stones with earth—exactly as we had.

Sweat lodge

A bottle of Scotch was passed around. Doug and Gardner smelled each other's armpits and also asked my assistance to determine who had the foulest odor. Doug smelled sort of sweet, but John stank badly. Neither would smell mine.

We ate the caribou a little before dark along with some canned potatoes that Abbott cooked up. He had cooked similar potatoes two days before with brown sugar and butter, and nobody had had the heart to tell him how awful they were. He had liked them, however, and so we had to eat them again. No matter; the caribou was succulent, a little smoky with an ever-so-slight hint of the ocean from the kelp.

Soon afterward we undressed. It was less than forty degrees out. We were about to enter a space barely large enough to hold all nine of us. We would be naked, sweaty, and probably quite stinky. We had spent over two months together. "I highly recommend that anyone who fears being in hot, closed, dark quarters sit near the exit," John Abbott intoned before we entered. "Anyone with homo-claustrophobia should be very careful."

Quickly, under Abbott's orders, rocks were transferred in cooking pots to the middle of the canvas-topped sweat lodge and laid out in a reserved spot in the middle. Abbott seemed happy again, ordering people about in a joking manner. He had recovered not only from the malaise we had all been suffering but perhaps also from his broken heart.

We sat around the rocks, shrieking a bit and bumping into each other. Someone closed the entrance flap. We had one flashlight and could just make out each other's faces. Then the light was turned off. Silence. A cup of water was poured on. Sizzle. Hiss. A wave of moist heat tumbled over and into us all. We grew hot and steamy, and we began to sweat.

Then, as if we had not seen each other in months, years even, we began to talk. I cannot remember the conversations, only bits and pieces, but a bond was cemented between us that will never be broken.

When the first batch of rocks lost their power, we took a dip in the ocean. Many of us plunged in whooping and hollering, but the older men carried out their rinsing in their own special way. Dean strode waist deep, as if into inescapable battle, silently, measuredly. He lowered himself slowly beneath the surface and then casually returned to the lodge. Rob, on the other hand, gingerly tiptoed about, shin deep, and then flailed handfuls of water over his roasting body.

We repeated the process two or three times—huddle, sweat, talk, dip, yelp. We did not return to *Snorri* until eleven o'clock. More than just sweat washed off us that night.

The wind continued from the southeast for the next few days, as predicted, and most of the crew took advantage of our downtime to take a boat ride into Nain. Their boat taxi, run by one of Henry Webb's brothers, brought out additional kerosene and some flour. I volunteered to stay with the boat—not necessarily out of martyrdom, but because I did not want to go to town without *Snorri*. It did not feel right. Terry and Doug decided to stay behind too.

We mostly lazed about the boat the night they were gone and the following day. Having learned that cooking meat the way we had done was usually part of a sacrificial meal, I tossed the remaining earth-cooked caribou into the sea for Frey. We also spent some therapeutic time letting off steam about each of the others who had left. Doug confessed to something that showed how desperate he had been feeling in northern Labrador. He had sent an e-mail to his mother asking her to see how he could get from northern Labrador to the United States in time for the wedding. Apparently she had not much luck, although she had contacted several travel agents. "It was such a lesson," he told us. "In this world, where I'm used to being able to go anywhere or do anything, to not be able to . . ."

The guys who went to Nain spent a little less time sitting around talking than we did. When they arrived in town they did not have a place to stay. Unwilling and for the most part (except for Rob and Dean) unable to pay the steep hotel price, they went to the hotel bar and hung around forlornly until someone offered them the conference room above the bar as a bunk room for the night. After that, they reveled at the bar with a wedding party. As things heated up, both men and women started paying $2 to bite off Life Savers strung around the bride's dress. The crew joined in. Dean, bleary-eyed by this point, evidently did not see the Life Savers. "For the life of me, I couldn't figure out why these guys were paying two bucks to bite her ass, but I said what the hell and did it anyway," he told me on their return.

They convinced a hairdresser to open her shop at two in the morning and got haircuts. Gardner was also shaved, and he returned looking all of sixteen years old.

All who had gone ashore talked about how friendly and kind everyone was, dispelling the rumors we had heard that the Inuit and Native Americans living along the Labrador coast all hated whites and were violent (though Abbott, when not biting Life Savers, spent much of his time trying to convince one woman that not all white people were evil). They reported that there were only twelve fishing boats in the harbor, certainly not enough for the community to make a living off the sea, although Erik did return with a sack of scallops, having heard me yearn for some. But to them, the most amazing sight they had seen in town were twenty-foot spruce trees. They had gawked and poked each other at the sight, like a bunch of Arctic natives in their first boreal forest.

Nain was not in a forest, just far enough inland to protect a smattering of trees, but on September 7, after another overnight sail more than fifty miles down the coast, we did reach the beginning of Markland. Where Leif and his crew first alighted was flat, forested, and bordered by a gentle white-sand beach. " 'This land,' said Leif in the Greenlanders Saga, 'shall be given a name in accordance with its nature, and be called Markland.' " After which they got back down to the ship as fast as they could.

Leif's Markland is generally believed to be what is now referred to as the Wonder Strands—a stretch of sandy beach north of Cape Porcupine, about 150 miles south of Nain. Our Markland began at Shoal Tickle Bay, where we arrived at 7:30 A.M. on September 7 and dropped anchor off a hillside covered with thirty-foot spruces.

Homer had an itch. He immediately went ashore to smell the woods and scratch his back against a tree. "It's something I've been looking forward to for a long time," he told me. He had also done it in the middle of Nain. We all took turns at the novel experience of hiking in the woods.

Luckily, the wind drifted out of the south for two days and we were able to wallow in our new surroundings. I say luckily because a new sensation was taking over me. Although I missed Lisa and the girls horribly and could not even fathom the time I had spent away from my young family, I was clinging to the experience of our voyage. I was beginning to get e-mails about our arrival, asking me when it would be and informing me of all the planned events. It sounded like a logistical nightmare, and nobody seemed to understand that we could not plan anything. Many of the planners knew nothing about boats, and those that did knew nothing about boats without motors. Other Viking boats had come to L'Anse aux Meadows, but they had had either motors on board or chase boats. They were able to appear when the press and politicians expected them. How were we going to pull this off to anybody's satisfaction? Only with a very unlikely set of circumstances could we arrive in a grand manner.

I also wanted to relish the moment for other reasons. When would I ever be sailing a Viking boat along the Labrador coast again? How often does one get to shove a two-thousand-pound block of ice away from an anchored wooden boat while swallowing the last morsel of a blueberry pancake? Or better yet, would I ever get to play dentist and make a temporary filling for Rob again?

Rob's teeth are every mother's worst nightmare and a dentist's treasure chest. His mouth is overflowing with silver. One of the fillings had recently fallen out. Knowing how much stomach bile had passed through that mouth just the night before and over the past two months, I was a little hesitant to help him, but his pleading eyes won me over. In fact, the most agreeable thing about the episode, even beyond the artistic experience of molding a good shape with a cotton-tipped stick, was the warmth of his mouth. My fingers had been feeling numb that day and they heated up nicely in there. Of course, like a good dentist, once my hands were firmly ensconced within, I began asking him such questions as "How is your life?" "Do you like sailing on *Snorri*?" "What is it like?"

The whole experience was over in ten minutes, all too quickly for my cold fingers. A lot of our hands were swollen and aching from the constant exposure and cold. Homer's were literally twice their normal size and had turned a raging purple. He winced every time he used them. For others, including me, our fingernails were starting to peel away from our fingers. It hurt and made tasks that required anything dexterous of our fingers—such as tucking in a reef on the sail, pulling in a sheet, or, for the guys with modern clothes, unzipping their trousers—quite difficult. Working in Rob's mouth had been a welcome but short-lived respite.

When the wind veered to the north on September 9, we headed south again. We were finding that things were just the opposite in Labrador than in Greenland. In Greenland we had to wait for the rain if we wanted to go north. In Labrador we had to wait for the rain if we wanted to go south. So for the next few days, as we made well over a hundred miles south, we were thoroughly drenched. At one anchorage the wind and rain whipped through the tarp, soaking all our sleeping bags. The wind blew so long and hard during this time that the ocean swell climbed to twenty feet. We went out anyway, and the wind lines that whistled over the waves' tops and the foaming breakers that threatened our safety were like something out of a mythical tempest. It was surely intimidating but also exhilarating. I found that I loved its strength and the thrill it gave me to be alive in it.

Normally we had to pump the bilge every hour for about fifteen minutes, using a pump that supposedly worked at thirty gallons per minute. On this day, the eleventh of September, we had to use two pumps at a time nearly nonstop. If I had been plopped on board *Snorri* straight from dry land, I would have been terrified. This was the stuff I used to have nightmares about when I first thought of this voyage. It was what made the thought of sailing an open-decked Viking boat appear insane to an outsider. Yet the only thing we were scared about, except for Rob, who was only scared of having to live, was whether the rigging would hold up. We knew *Snorri* could handle the seas. This was what she was made to do. And as if to prove this point, we came upon a modern sloop running before the wind on this harshest of days. Not only did we come upon her but we passed her. She was swinging from side to side like the hand of a metronome while *Snorri* glissaded across the water like a hippo on ice skates: steady and fast. Nothing was going to mess with her.

Rob had bought hardtack in Nain, having read about it in so many sea adventure books that he had to give it a try. He pulled it out during these stormy days and let us all try it. I hadn't known it was possible to make something so hard out of flour and water. I was worried that Rob might break one of his few remaining healthy teeth on it. Erik hated it but had seconds. Dean could not even bite through his. Terry spat his out. Doug and I sort of liked it but only after letting it soften in our mouths. Rob claimed he found it comforting, but no amount of hardtack was going to calm his stomach. When not puking, he spent most of his time lying on his back in the underway tarp mouthing the hard tack. Crumbs lay sprinkled throughout his beard and scattered over his chest. Abbott had to leave the tent at one point just to keep from laughing. Later Rob was able to joke that he was thinking about starting a fat camp. "All my fellow fatsos have to do is come sail on board *Snorri* for two weeks up here and they'll lose all the weight they ever wanted."

I thought about pointing out that the local way to eat hardtack would have been to soak it in water overnight and then steam it, making a dish called brewis. You were supposed to serve this up with a plate of salt cod and potatoes cooked with scrunchins (fried fatback) and onions. That is how it has been eaten in Labrador and Newfoundland for centuries. You could also steam the hardtack and serve it with a few slices of bacon for breakfast, or with molasses for a snack. Even without the molasses, each hardtack, the descendant of the sea biscuit, packed 289 calories into Twinkie-shaped rolls. It is made only from flour, water, and salt, and in a pinch it could certainly be used to chase off a polar bear. I thought about telling all of this to Rob until I too looked in the underway tent. People were not meant to be so miserable and remain alive.

We stayed out at sea probably longer than we should have that evening and had to find an anchorage in the dark on account of the wind dying out. It was harrowing to cruise into a narrow channel at five knots when we were unable to make out more than an outline of rocks and breakers against the blue-black sky. Waves broke on shoals all around us, and I bent over the chart with a small flashlight in my mouth and a pencil and dividers in my hands, calling out position changes every other minute. Three or four guys stood bow watch, seeing imaginary icebergs and calling out additional course changes because of noises or mere shadows. We slid past it all unharmed, however, rematerializing in a silent, shallow cove called Emily's Harbor.

We hung out in our sleeping bags eating tuna melts (Gardner and Erik had bought two loaves of bread in Nain) and tomato soup the day after our big sail and then rowed for an hour to an anchorage that would allow us to sail south more easily when a north wind returned.

Afterward we hiked the surrounding islands. This was Cod's land. (Read *Cod* by Mark Kurlansky if you want to know what we did to this species.) Shacks and houses abandoned with the disappearance of the cod stood hopelessly waiting for their owners' return. Inside, though, up-to-date calendars revealed that the buildings were periodically being used by someone, if not cod fishermen.

Erik and I walked together. By this time I had long since decided that if we had had no charts, compass, or GPS device, Erik could have gotten us to Newfoundland. He had turned out to be the kind of person you'd call first when contemplating an insane adventure, knowing not only that he would go but that your trip would be much the better for it. He was always seeing things that the rest of us missed. "Hey, Hod, look at this," he would call. I'd trudge over and there would be an unusual plant, artifact, or animal dropping that nobody else had noticed. During our walk he may have even cleared up the grapes-in-Vinland mystery. We came upon some cloudy pink berries. The berries themselves seemed grapelike in that they were clustered together and tasted sweet. "These are the grapes of Vinland. These leaves look just like grape leaves in the autumn, like in someone's backyard," Erik said. "We don't have to go any farther." He was joking, but it was as good an explanation of the "grapes" that Leif found in Vinland as any that I have heard of. They were, in fact, cloudberries or baked apple—a southern Labrador and Newfoundland staple. All in all, there are six different wild berries that thrive in this area. Any of these could have been the so-called grapes to some sea-tossed Scandinavians. With such an abundance of berries, any fool could have made wine. Also, as others have pointed out, Leif knew a bit about real estate development. His father had called the iciest island in the world Greenland. The claim of wild, alcohol-making berries would lure a Viking to anywhere in the world.

Over the course of our voyage, we had casually been studying and trying to answer many questions about the Vikings. What had happened to them in Greenland? What did they eat? How did they feel? What did they fear? I felt that we had happened upon a lot of possible answers but that most of all our voyage was showing how they might have gotten to Vinland. Questions such as "Where is Vinland?" and "Did it really have grapes?" did not interest me. I had come to realize that it was like trying to find exactly where Moses crossed the Red Sea, Hercules made off with Hippolyte's girdle, or Brer Rabbit fled through the briar patch. It really did not matter exactly where Leif went ashore to try and settle a new land. What mattered was that Leif and the men and women who both preceded and followed him bothered to do something.

Chapter Twenty-Three

On September 13 we left Emily Harbor on a strong north wind; of course it was raining. Contrary to our past experience, however, as the day wore on, the rain stopped but the wind didn't. By late afternoon we came upon the Wonder Strands. I had often imagined walking on those fabled beaches, staring at the woods stretching nearly to the water and rejoicing that we had reached Leif's Markland. But the wind did not abate. We were averaging seven knots and so, having learned our lessons well, we did not stop to celebrate, only looking at the trees and beaches through binoculars. I had been told that Allied forces had used the Wonder Strands to practice amphibious assaults during World War II and that the debris from war games still littered the sand. All I saw through my binoculars, though, was an adequate spot to practice beaching our knarr. According to historians, the Vikings would often beach cargo boats because of their shallow draft. While theoretically possible, it was definitely not something they would have done on Baffin Island or Labrador. We had seen a total of three beaches and none of them had been protected, including the Wonder Strands. Maybe that is why Leif and his crew hastily returned to their vessel after viewing these abundant trees.

Breezing by the Wonder Strands, we knew we were going to make it all the way to Newfoundland—maybe not by the next day, but soon. The buzz on board was nearly deafening. No one was huddled against a frame sulking or staring off to the far horizon—poses understandable when our end had seemed unattainable. Now a new conversation arose when an old one faded. Each of us wanted to stay on bow watch for hours on end or hold the tiller as we screamed along.

I even stopped worrying about our supplies and told Erik he could use as many cans as he wanted for dinner. He marched over to the barrels and started yanking them out, "A ten-can meal! Yippeee!" a couple of the guys shouted. "Yahoo! Whoa, eleven! Yeah!" I hadn't meant for him to go that crazy but kept myself from objecting.

We decided to sail through the night. It was surely going to be our last all-nighter, and I could not sleep during my off watch, so I stayed on deck. Doug did the same. By this time I was in a mental state different from any I had ever been in. It was probably exhaustion, exhilaration, or exposure, or some combination. But I felt as though *Snorri* and the wind were in collusion. They had hatched some plan to get us south, where our presence was required. Blackened silver clouds streaked overhead, barely outpacing us, I talked to Frey, thanking and imploring him. I also got horribly cold. My feet were numb throughout the night. My hands tingled and could barely be trusted to hold the tiller with any strength. It did not matter, though, because I knew this was *Snorri*'s finest moment. She was covering more ground in twenty-four hours than she ever had or ever would. By midmorning we had gone 130 miles. With only a bit of last-minute rowing we anchored in Cape Bluff Harbor.

It was a place of mesmerizing beauty. Gentle hills surrounded us on nearly all sides, except for the small opening through which we had rowed to reach the anchorage. Soft pines and deciduous trees clung to the hillsides. Squishy muskeg filled in the gaps. There had been permanent man-made navigational aids stationed on ledges and along the shore when we approached the harbor—an unheard-of treat for us—and these features, combined with our natural surroundings, put us firmly back in our old world.

Tears rose to my eyes as I watched my friends rustle through their bags, fix breakfast, or prepare to hike onshore. I was proud of what they had done and how they had accomplished it—with respect for each other, integrity, and dignity, but also wonder, wide-eyed enthusiasm, and a bit of goofiness. Pride in them rolled within me like an irrepressible wave. *Don't hold back*, I wanted to tell them. *Cry, stomp your feet. It will be too late when you get home. Rejoice now.*

Homer and Gardner served up three bannocks that morning, and then I knew I had nothing to worry about. They were already finding a way to celebrate.

Later I floated to the far shore in the dinghy, letting my own emotions run free, thinking about my family. I was daydreaming about Lisa's beautiful eyes when I happened to look up and catch Abbott's bare ass hiking over a boulder—a very rough contrast to my daydream. Just before I went ashore I passed a tiny dolphin—no bigger than Anabel or Eliza—feeding at the mouth of a small stream.

Onshore I took off my boots, and the soft muskeg was a delight to my battered feet. I walked a hundred yards, stopping to eat the sweetest blueberries I had yet found. Pushing aside some small birches, I saw Erik bathing in the stream. It was cold but I joined him. Then Abbott showed up. We told him it was incredibly warm and he should simply dive right in. His yelps were very satisfying.

Once clean, we squatted by the stream and watched hundreds of brook trout darting in and out of the deep pools. We listened to leaves rustling in the wind. There are not many things that can soothe the soul as readily as rustling leaves, and you do not really know this until you have spent a summer or two without them. It was a sumptuous moment.

This was a much-needed calm. We were afraid of reentry and the big bash that awaited our arrival. The guys kept asking me questions: "What's going to happen? What do we have to do? Where will we sleep? What about our meals?" We were so used to crawling out of our bags, ducking from under the tarp, peeing, and then scurrying back to our bags until we all had to tackle the day. Then, together, we stuffed our sleeping bags into our dry bags, put away the tarp, ate, and headed out for the day or night. That was our life. It was that simple.

We were holed up in our retreat for another day because of unfavorable winds. With Gardner in the lead, a couple of the crew caught more than thirty trout—a wonderful treat when dredged in spiced-up flour and pan-fried in olive oil. In *Lure of the Labrador Wild*, Wallace kept mentioning their huge catches of trout—up to a hundred sometimes. The three members of their expedition would eat all of them but still feel famished. The notion had seemed absurd to me, but now I understood. The trout were delicious but all too slim.

I rowed Terry to shore at one point and took the opportunity to thank him for getting us to our goal, although we still had about eighty miles to go. He felt nearly offended by the attention we were about to receive at L'Anse aux Meadows. We were receiving constant queries from the Lands' End folks and an organization called the Viking Trail Tourism Association, based out of St. Anthony, Newfoundland, which was overseeing our grand entrance. They were trying their best to get us to agree to an arrival date and time. Since we never knew where we might be an hour into the future, it was an amusing request. There was going to be a marching band. Hundreds of schoolkids. Dignitaries. Speeches. A buffet dinner loaded with cod tongues and as much fresh meat as one could ever desire.

"What have we done? We haven't saved the world, found a cure, or discovered anything new. I guess it's the puritan in me, but I'm leery of all this attention," he said. "I wish we could just arrive like we do anywhere. Celebrate amongst ourselves. Laugh. Cry. But I guess after the big event, we will make time for that."

At one time I would have agreed with him, but not anymore. Everybody deserves a little party now and then, and the crew had gone through a lot. Terry had accomplished a Sisyphean task—captaining a green crew nearly two thousand miles across hazardous waters. I wanted him and the others to revel in our deed.

We nearly blew it all the next day. We poked out of our safe little harbor and found ourselves in thirty-knot winds and snarling twenty-foot seas that were breaking every which way and threatening to swamp us. After we had suffered a few hours of this, Terry opted to duck into St. Michael's Bay, only ten miles south. That night Terry and I stood side by side on the crossbeam, naked, and simultaneously called out, "O Frey, hear us one more time! Deliver us to L'Anse aux Meadows! . . . You're the greatest!"

It nearly worked. The following day we began sailing in a strong north wind over roller-coaster seas. Midday we came across a Coast Guard Canada cutter that had been assigned to escort us. Outside of Battle Harbour, a fishing boat dropped off a few visitors: David Conover and Russell Kaye again, and Allison Hepler, who was Bob Miller's widow and Rob's close friend. Having been promised hot showers and a multicourse meal, we had been planning on docking at Battle Harbour, but now we had to sail right past it, taking our wind when we had it. Battle Harbour is an old settlement that has been turned into a historical museum by Parks Canada. Besides demonstrating how an old Labrador fishing community operated, it was also the site where Peary claimed to the world that he had set foot on the North Pole (although he really didn't).

The Coast Guard captain urged us to keep going farther, that they would safely see us across the Strait of Belle Isle, but even as they predicted that the wind would not die, it began to peter out. We covered fifty miles that day. All that was left was the twenty-six miles across the strait. We just could not risk it. Braving crashing seas, the narrowest channel yet, and eventually a headwind, we rowed behind Henley Island, directly across the strait from L'Anse aux Meadows. To reach a safe anchorage, we had to kedge—row an extended anchor line a few hundred yards forward in the dinghy and then haul the boat to the anchor. The wind was too strong to row against. We did this three times for more than an hour and then finally dropped anchor as close as possible to the protected shore.

We tried making the crossing the next day, rowing past Henley, but the prevailing wind would have blown us out to sea, well to the east of L'Anse aux Meadows. We tucked back into our harbor, where the world found us, ending the voyage on one level for most of us. Rob's mother, Michael Kreutzfeldt, who was Erik's friend and coworker in Greenland, Ryan Alexander, a friend of Lisa's and mine, and, most important to me, Lisa and Helen all came aboard. They had grown tired of waiting for us at L'Anse aux Meadows and had hired a fishing boat, the *Caribou Run*, to bring them across the channel. I don't have the words to describe the happiness I felt when I held my wife and daughter again. Lisa had not been able to bring Anabel and Eliza, but I would be seeing them very soon. My overwhelming feeling was relief. Our life together would soon be moving forward. Helen, though, seemed confused by my mere presence and would sooner go to Homer than me. She cried whenever I tried to hold her. I hoped time and a no-longer-absent dad would change all that.

We began the crossing again the next morning. It was a good thing, I was told over the radio, that we had failed in our attempt to cross the day before, because the organizers had not been ready for us. They were currently hurrying everything into place, and although we were now being "permitted" to cross, we were told not to arrive at the visitor center. If we made it, we had to find someplace to hide until the following morning, when the festivities were planned for ten o'clock.

It was all so surreal, but we had known it was coming. The overwrought planning even threatened to make our arrival anticlimactic, but the Norse gods would not have it that way. We would get to pay our dues one more time.

We embarked under a squally north wind. We even had two reefs tucked in, since this was the tail end of the gale that had battered our anchorage the night before. Rob's mom, Allison, Michael, and Ryan had stayed on board, although Lisa had gotten off because of Helen. Everyone was silly at the thought of sailing so quickly downwind to Newfoundland. Then the wind began to die. We let the reefs out. It died some more. We got the oars out and power-sailed. By one o'clock it had died completely. We dropped the sail and just rowed.

We rowed for nine long hours, until ten-thirty that night. By this time we were bucking a flood tide and were getting swept westward, then northward, then southward—depending on our angle to the current. I began to worry, and my stomach turned in knots. How could we have come all this way and then fail so publicly? *It's got to get better,* I kept thinking. *The tide will go slack. It will turn at any moment.*

The boat had grown silent. Our guests were horrified or at least completely dismayed. We rowed and rowed. We could not keep *Snorri* angled properly. Soon enough we were going backward.

There was no way we were going to make it to L'Anse aux Meadows that night. We dropped our anchor in seventeen fathoms of water.

Around midnight, a skiff with a Lands' End representative and a man named Morgan Anderson, who was in charge of the waterfront for the L'Anse aux Meadows site, came out to greet us. After a few instructions about the following day were delivered, they ferried our guests back to shore.

We had five miles to go. We decided to keep rowing but first take a one-hour nap. At one-thirty, after our rest, the tide still had not gone slack and the wind had started to build out of the southeast—our intended direction. It was forecasted to blow more than twenty knots by the morning. If we were going to arrive at the site by ten the following morning, then it appeared we must use the dinghy with the motor to push the boat. We could not row in the current wind conditions. We had used the dinghy the morning before to push us a hundred yards against the tide, the first time we had ever used it to aid our progress, and so it now seemed stupid not to use it again. Our private trip, the one that allowed us to go when and where we pleased, dictated only by nature and our individual whims, had been over back at Henley Harbor. Still, I debated not using the motor and disappointing all those people who were showing up for our arrival, but it just didn't seem worth it. So I climbed into the dinghy with John Abbott. We pushed *Snorri* against rain, wind, and current into the twentieth century—a quarter mile shy of the spot that had been marked off for our arrival. We would try to make a grand arrival for everyone in the daylight hours, probably by rowing or kedging against the wind.

We fell asleep around five-thirty.

We were awakened two hours later by the hum of a long-liner fishing boat circling us. Then we saw the flash of camera lights. Dean farted and peed for them. They asked if it was okay to pull alongside, and a few minutes later we were tidying *Snorri* and talking to three reporters.

We began kedging our way to the appointed anchorage at eight-thirty. It was a tough day—winds gusting at twenty-five to thirty knots in a steady rain. When we started, not a single person could be seen near the replica sod houses and huts that mark the boundary of the Viking site. An hour later, when we still had more than two hundred yards to go, the marching band and what looked to be a thousand people had arrived.

Those in our group who had been reticent about the big celebration seemed cheered by the audience and the festive mood that swelled from shore. We sang our chanteys as we pulled ourselves closer and closer.

When we got to "Bound for L'Anse aux Meadows" goose bumps rose all over my body, and every one of us could not stop smiling. For once, my eyes were not the only ones watering. We were even able to row the last hundred yards because we were in the lee of the shore and kedging was no longer necessary.

We set our anchors and a mild cheer went up. They were all waiting for us. We had decided to wade ashore, not wanting to arrive in front of such a large audience in our inflatable boat or be carried ashore by local skiffs. Real Vikings would have done the

The crew arrives at L'Anse aux Meadows

same, we surmised. But it was awfully cold out. The rain might have been letting up, but not the wind. The water was deadly in northern Newfoundland, just like everywhere else we had sailed. We had about three hundred feet of water to cross.

I checked the depth because a couple of the guys worried about it being over their heads. We would be going in with our clothes on. It was seven feet deep, but I fudged a bit, saying it was less than six. We couldn't back out now.

Spontaneously we hugged each other, a final tender moment. Then we stood about, hesitating. Was it because we did not want to get hypothermia, or was it something else? I saw all the guys looking across *Snorri*'s deck longingly, possessively. I had decided to donate the boat to Parks Canada so that they could keep *Snorri* on display at the L'Anse aux Meadows visitor center, but after all this time, we did not want to let go. It was our boat. *Wait* . . .

Suddenly Dean pulled off the top of his long underwear, and a deafening roar rose from the crowd.

The rest of us hastily stripped down to lighter clothing and stood on *Snorri's* prow. On the count of seven—Rob's idea, because three seemed too short, I guess—we jumped in. I had left my boots on, fretting about my damaged toes, and could barely keep my head above water. But once I reached shallower water, I spun around to check on my buddies. That view has frozen in my mind forever: Strong arms caught in midair. Legs rising to the surface. Faces set and determined.

These guys were no longer my crew and captain. They were not even just friends. They were my family. *Snorri* had been our community—our home. As I struggled to shore I mentally urged them on. *This celebration is for you. You did this. Go.*

I fell into Lisa's arms. We hugged hard. Friends, family, and strangers rushed to embrace us.

From there we were led into the main sod house. It was smoky and rumpled, like every child's fantasy of a Viking's home. Two nurturing fires blazed. They had towels for us and a change of clothes. The people working in the houses wore clothes similar to mine, and they had prepared traditional Viking coastal fare: flatbread, smoked and grilled fish, roasted moose, smoked mussels, and squid. We gorged ourselves. We had eaten no breakfast that morning because our kerosene stove had finally broken down and we were out of propane for our emergency stove.

Before we emerged for the arrival speeches, the Viking encampment workers gave us each a wool cap, traditionally hand-knit on a single needle. We felt both welcomed and appreciated. We were, in fact, overwhelmed, and we were probably unable to convey to them how good their gifts and warmth made us feel.

We attended the public ceremony, where the local mayor, a member of Parliament, the Parks Canada superintendent for the area, and a Lands' End officer gave speeches. Afterward, each of the crew recounted a week of the voyage for the audience. And suddenly we were done. The children asked us for our autographs, and then they and all the adults started to trickle away. We talked to reporters, milled around the Parks Canada site, and felt more than a little unsettled.

I half expected the magic of our accomplishment to start slipping away like all moments do, but this one had a life of its own. It carried us into that evening, into the days that followed, and remains with us still.

Lands' End threw us a party that night at a local restaurant called Leifsbudir (the name means "Leif's booths" or "Leif's buildings"). This was dinner theater, Viking style, and the actors, most of whom also work at the sod huts, made us perform with them. It was goofy and good fun. Then Abbott took to the stage and said the crew wanted to thank me for everything. Sometime during the voyage Gardner had decided they should each give me a gift: the tools of a real sailor. Those items—some of which I had been so annoyed by while stuck in northern Labrador—had been laboriously shaped, sewn, and carved for me by each member of the crew. I was taken by surprise, but I probably shouldn't have been.

Gardner's gift figuratively bound them all together and literally gave the tools a place for safekeeping. It was a ditty bag, sewn together from spare sailcloth, bordered with rope he had woven together, and highlighted with reindeer antler grommets. Doug had embroidered a patch shaped with the runic letters for *Snorri*. His rendering managed to capture both the boat's lines and its spirit. Homer had made a smaller ditty bag that I could use as a dop kit. Terry had carved, planed, and sanded a fid for untying knots and splicing. Dean's present was a seam rubber—a lot of cold-weather-induced nose droplets went into that piece of wood. Rob had bent an old nail into a hook and fashioned a Danish penny into a base, creating a sail hook, which is used to hold canvas tight while sewing. Erik had hollowed out a reindeer horn, wrapping it in leather, for a needle case. And one of the knives that Abbott had forever appeared to be working on was for me.

Before the voyage, out of all these gifts, I would have known only what the knife was for, but now I not only possessed them all but knew how to use each, thanks to their makers. I will be forever grateful.

Chapter Twenty-Four

Our days at L'Anse aux Meadows, readying *Snorri* for her new life and eventually dragging her onto a skid for the winter, were bittersweet. We had a true heroes' welcome. Everyone in the community knew who we were and went to great lengths to take care of us, throwing parties and cooking us meals. All establishments in the area had names like Viking Nest, Valhalla, Norseman Café, and the like, and we tried them all on for size. Even more astounding to us, people actually listened to our stories, and we felt kinship with these individuals who lived daily lives in a rough, nature-ravaged land.

It didn't really look like the place described in the *Greenlanders' Saga*: ". . . as soon as the tide rose under their ship, they took their boat . . . and brought her up into the river. . . . There was no lack of salmon. . . . The nature of the land was so choice . . . the grass was hardly withered. . . . Leif gave the land a name in accordance with the good things they found in it, calling it Vinland." There was no river, no lake, no salmon, no choice land and certainly no grapes. Yet, we felt at home.

We spent a lot of time in the Parks Canada visitor center looking at the items recovered during the various archeological digs. I think we were all amazed at the paucity of items; a spindle whorl for turning raw wool into thread, a cloak pin, some rivets, some nuts, and a handful of other items were all that had been found. The most important discovery, beyond the remains of the buildings themselves, had been the evidence of smelting of iron from bog ore, presumably to make replacement rivets. This alone is probably what convinced most authorities that L'Anse aux Meadows was a real Viking site, not just another Kensington Stone.

So we stood around gazing at these objects and spoke about our trip with whoever wanted to share in our excitement. It was over for us, however. We had found our Vinland, and we slowly split apart. After a final party at our motel, where we drank my barely alcoholic mead, some of the crew flew directly home, while others meandered back—Erik was still traveling in the United States six months later.

We keep in touch. I hear the least from Homer, but even he miraculously manages to track down a phone while on one of his wild escapades. Last I heard, he was jumping mountains on snowboards somewhere out West. All of us seem to miss each other and worry how *Snorri* is faring in her new home.

I have an uncontrollable urge—like I've never felt before—to go out again and discover something else. For that is what we did. To the scholars, we showed that the journey was not a simple jaunt to be undertaken in a mere nine days. Even taking into account our poor abilities and faulty approach, the historians now know that the Vikings were not zipping back and forth between Greenland and North America all summer long. In fact, what seemed preposterous before may now be true: The scant recorded voyages to Vinland may be all there ever were. Perhaps, based on our experience, they traveled a half dozen times and then gave up. Although Norway had attempted to control all trade to its northern colonies, of which Greenland was considered one, they could not. There is ample evidence of trade between Greenland and Iceland and between Greenland and England. In other words, Greenlanders were getting what they needed from Europe, either legally or illegally, and they did not need North America.

So although the Vikings might have been the first Europeans to the New World, they did not stay for very long. It was simply too far out there.

That is not really what we discovered, though. Like nearly all our understanding of history, it is conjecture. In retracing their voyages, we did not find a new continent, a new passageway, or even a new way to use the bathroom in an open boat, but we did discover what it felt like to sail into the wind, heading straight for an iceberg, albeit unknowingly. How many rocks it takes to ballast a knarr (2,978, roughly). What it feels like when you are no longer on top of the food chain.

We discovered what happens when you wait beyond your own ability to wait. And we discovered something the Vikings knew all along. Those travelers, whom history has relegated to raping, pillaging, and frothing at the mouth, created a guide called the *Havamal*, a poem about how to lead one's life. Besides warning its readers to watch for enemies lurking in corners and exhorting them to treat a guest with fine towels and friendliness, it also speaks of family and a friendship we had come to understand:

> *When I was young*
> *and walked alone,*
> *alone I lost my way.*
> *I felt rich*
> *when I found company.*
> *Man delights in man.*

You never know what you might find when you step outdoors. You look out. You look in. And you almost always find something new—like eight remarkable strangers who become as close as family.

I have a discarded coil of pine-tarred hemp from *Snorri*. Sometimes it's in my office, sometimes in my car. I fiddle with it, practice a bowline behind my back, or occasionally see how fast I can coil it. Always I breathe in the rich scent, and I am back on board *Snorri*, surrounded by my friends, and bound for Vinland.

RUSSELL KAYE

2nd year crew
left to right: Erik Larsen, John Gardner, John Abbott, Hodding Carter,
Terry Moore, Doug Cabot, Dean Plager, Homer Williams, Rob Stevens

ABOUT THE AUTHOR

W. Hodding Carter likes going on adventures. He spent two years in Kenya with the Peace Corps. His highly acclaimed pieces for *Esquire*, *M* magazine, *Outside*, and other national publications have taken him to Burma, to Wales, and into the thick of the Louisiana Oyster Eating Contest (in which he placed second). He is also the author of the book *Westward Whoa: In the Wake of Lewis and Clark*. He currently lives in Maine with his wife and three daughters.